W9-CKM-155

Truth, Memory, Justice:
One Hundred Years
After the Bolshevik Revolution

Marion Smith and Murray Bessette,
Editors

Truth, Memory, Justice:
One Hundred Years
After the Bolshevik Revolution

Marion Smith and Murray Bessette,
Editors

VICTIMS OF COMMUNISM
MEMORIAL FOUNDATION

Academica Press
Washington – London

Names: Smith, Marion- editor; Bessette, Murray- editor
Title: Truth, memory, justice : One hundred years after the bolshevik
revolution / Marion Smith and Murray Bessette.
Description: Washington : Academica Press, [2019]
Identifiers: LCCN 2019936767 | ISBN 9781680530735

Copyright 2019 by The Victims of Communism Memorial Foundation

Table of Contents

Preface

On a cold night in Petrograd, one hundred years ago, a small group of Red Guards seized the Winter Palace and installed the world's first communist government. The Bolshevik Revolution marked the beginning of a century in which adherents to communist ideology committed some of the worst and most widespread atrocities known to history. The founding of the Soviet Union inaugurated a century of political turmoil around the globe by pioneering, in spectacular fashion, a new model of political, economic, cultural, and institutional revolution. It was a model that, for decades, exercised considerable fascination and influence over the minds of elites and common people around the world—both through attraction and revulsion. The Soviet Union's influence was not restricted to the world of ideas. Through revolution, war, and conquest, the Soviet model was exported to the USSR's imperial sphere in Europe and found imitators in Asia, Africa, and Latin America, some of which still hold power.

Today, while the Soviet state created by the Bolsheviks has collapsed, the Revolution's aftereffects are still visible in Russia and the other former states of the Soviet Union that grapple with the political, social, economic, and geopolitical realities of incomplete transitions to democracy and free enterprise within a rule of law system. Beyond the former USSR, one-fifth of the world's population lives under a single-party communist regime in the People's Republic of China, Cuba, Laos, Vietnam, and North Korea. The enduring importance of the communist experience means the study of the Bolshevik Revolution continues to be necessary—and makes the observance of the centenary of the Bolshevik Revolution a particularly appropriate time to take stock.

On November 7–9, 2017, the Victims of Communism Memorial Foundation convened a major conference, "Reflections on a Ravaged Century" (named in honor of the late Robert Conquest), in the halls of the Library of Congress as part of the Victims of Communism Centennial Commemoration. In seven panel discussions, an impressive array of academics, practitioners, and public officials discussed topics including the history of the Bolshevik Revolution; the Marxist ideology that drove it; the Soviet Union's economy, politics, and foreign policy; Soviet influence around the world; and Russia's struggle to reckon with the past through historical and public memory.

This volume is a record of the remarks delivered at the conference, as well as a window into the rich intellectual exchange occasioned by this meeting of minds. Nearly all the original panelists' remarks are reproduced here. The editors have also included a selection of moderators' remarks and discussion session comments that are especially pertinent. The chapters derived from remarks delivered orally at the conference have been edited for style in collaboration with the conference participants. These contributions remain grouped according to the panels on which they were delivered, providing a sense of the flow of conversation and exchange of opinion at the event. The papers of two additional authors who were unable to attend in person — Paul Goble and Sir Roger Scruton — are also included.

The editors would like to thank the scholars whose words are found in these pages. Without Truth, there can be neither Memory nor Justice. Establishing a true record is fundamental. Through their lifelong work, our contributors have enabled us to learn from the past and to define a better future, provided we learn the lessons of the last century.

The editors would also like to give a special word of thanks to the members of the conference's host committee, including HE Anna Maria Anders; HE Sali Berisha; Prince and Princess Bryan Chingiz; Professor Stéphane Courtois; The Honorable Robert Dole; Dr. and Mrs. Lee Edwards; Dr. and Mrs. Edwin J. Feulner; Mr. Nicholas Gage; The Honorable Dr. and Mrs. János Horváth; HE Dr. Václav Klaus; HE Dr. Vytautas Landsbergis; Mrs. Annette Lantos; The Honorable Mr. and Mrs. Edwin Meese III; The Very Reverend Charles Nalls, CH (COL) (Ret.); Prince and Princess Nicholas Obolensky; Mr. Thomas Peterffy; Dr. Richard Pipes; Professor and Mrs. Paul du Quenoy; Lieutenant General Edward L. Rowny, US Army (Ret.); Sir Roger Scruton; Their Imperial Highnesses Prince and Princess Ermias Sahle Selassie; Dr. Robert Service; Mr. and Mrs. John Thomas Taft; Count and Countess Vladimir Tolstoy-Miloslavsky; The Honorable Armando Valladares; Colonel William E. Weber, US Army (Ret.); Ambassador Aldona Z. Wos, MD and Mr. Louis DeJoy; and HE Emanuelis Zingeris.

We would also like to recognize the members of our diplomatic host committee, including HE Floreta Faber, Ambassador of the Republic of Albania; HE Tihomir Stoytchev, Ambassador of the Republic of Bulgaria; HE Pjer Šimunović, Ambassador of the Republic of Croatia; HE

Hynek Kmoníček, Ambassador of the Czech Republic; HE David Bakradze, Ambassador of Georgia; HE Dr. László Szabó, Ambassador of Hungary; HE Andris Teikmanis, Ambassador of the Republic of Latvia; HE Rolandas Kriščiūnas, Ambassador of the Republic of Lithuania; HE Vasko Naumovski, Ambassador of the Former Yugoslav Republic of Macedonia; HE Pierre Clive Agius, Ambassador of the Republic of Malta; HE Piotr Wilczek, Ambassador of the Republic of Poland; HE Stanislav Vidovič, Ambassador of the Republic of Slovenia; HE George Maior, Ambassador of Romania; HE Peter Kmec, Ambassador of the Slovak Republic; HE Karin Olofsdotter, Ambassador of the Kingdom of Sweden; and HE Valeriy Chaly, Ambassador of Ukraine.

Our Congressional Host Committee included Senator Richard Burr (R-NC), Senator Tom Cotton (R-AR), Senator Ted Cruz (R-TX), Senator Marco Rubio (R-FL), Senator Thom Tillis (R-NC), Senator Roger Wicker (R-MS), Representative Ami Bera (D-CA), Representative Gerald Connolly (D-VA), Representative Trent Franks (R-AZ), Representative Mike Gallagher (R-WI), Representative Sam Johnson (R-TX), Representative Marcy Kaptur (D-OH), Representative Doug Lamborn (R-CO), Representative Dan Lipinski (D-IL), Representative Ted Poe (R-TX), Representative Dennis Ross (R-FL), Representative Adam Schiff (D-CA), Representative John Shimkus (R-IL), Representative Albio Sires (D-NJ), Representative Chris Smith (R-NJ), Representative Jackie Walorski (R-IN), and Representative Joe Wilson (R-SC).

Finally, we would like to thank the staff and interns of the Victims of Communism Memorial Foundation who helped make this conference and the Centennial Commemoration a success, with particular appreciation to Joshua Dill and Briggs Burton, who assisted in preparing the conference proceedings for this volume.

On the Centenary of the Bolshevik Revolution

Dr. Niall Ferguson

On November 9, 1989, the Berlin Wall was opened. On the night of November 7, 1917, the Winter Palace in Petrograd was occupied by the Bolsheviks. In the intervening period of 72 years, according to the estimates in *The Black Book of Communism*, the "grand total of victims of Communism was between eighty-five and one hundred million." Mao Zedong alone, as Frank Dikötter has shown, accounted for tens of millions: two million between 1949 and 1951, another three million in the course of the 1950s, a staggering forty-five million in the man-made famine known as the "Great Leap Forward," yet more in the mayhem of the Cultural Revolution. According to the lowest estimate, the total number of Soviet citizens who lost their lives as a direct result of Stalin's policies was more than twenty million, a quarter of them in the years after World War II.

All communist regimes everywhere, without exception, were merciless in their treatment of "class enemies," from the North Korea of the Kims to the Vietnam of Ho Chi Minh, from the Ethiopia of Mengistu Haile Mariam to the Angola of Agostinho Neto. Pol Pot was the worst of them all, but the differences were of degree, not of quality. Communist regimes were aggressive, too, overtly invading country after country during the Cold War. Moreover, we now know, thanks to the work of historians such as Chris Andrew, just how extensive and ruthless the KGB's system of international espionage and subversion was.

I am a historian, and I want not only to mourn the tens of millions of victims of communism but also to salute all those historians, as well as journalists, who during the so-called "short twentieth century" and thereafter bore witness to the crimes that were committed in the names of Marx, Lenin, Stalin, Mao, and the rest. I think, for example, of Robert Conquest, who seemed a lone voice when I was an undergraduate at Oxford in the early 1980s, but who has a worthy heir today in my friend Anne Applebaum. I think also of organizations such as Russia's Memorial Society, on whose work in preserving records and testimony we historians depend.

The "short twentieth century" is a phrase coined by a different kind of historian: Eric Hobsbawm, a lifelong communist who—even after Khrushchev's secret speech had begun the never complete process of official revelation—could never bring himself to accept that whatever had propelled him to join the Party as a young man, it had been a horrible mistake. How I wish that short century of his had been even shorter. Could it have been? Could more have been done to halt the communist pandemic after it broke out in Russia in 1917? And, if so, have we learned anything from the mistakes of those who failed to stamp it out when they might have? Those are the questions I want to ask here.

They are not questions we historians pose nearly often enough. That awful apologist for Soviet power, E. H. Carr, wrote in his wretched but all-too-widely-read tract *What Is History?* that to ponder the "might-have-beens" of 1917 was pointless. Those who did so, he argued, were just losers indulging in wishful thinking. I have always rejected that deterministic reasoning. It smacks too much of those inexorable historical forces the Marxists were always on about.

No, the Bolsheviks could have been stopped. After all, the only reason Lenin was able to get from Zurich to Petrograd in 1917 was that the imperial German government paid for his ticket—and more. According to Sean McMeekin's excellent new book on the Revolution, around 50 million gold marks ($12 million) were channeled from the Kaiser to Lenin and his associates. Adjusted for inflation, that's equivalent to around $800 million today.

The provisional government had every right to arrest Lenin and his nineteen associates on arrival. They were German agents, after all. And Alexander Kerensky, the Socialist Revolutionary minister of justice who took control of the provisional government on July 7, had even better grounds to round up the Bolsheviks: they had attempted a coup and failed.

The problem was that people underestimated Lenin, Trotsky, and company. They seemed an unruly bunch of intellectuals: writers of pamphlets, makers of speeches. No contemporary Western observer thought for a moment that their crackpot coup would last. As Hassan Malik has shown, American bankers completely failed to appreciate that the Bolsheviks meant exactly what they said about defaulting on the entire Tsarist debt. No one foresaw that hereditary nobleman Ulyanov, to give Lenin his original name, was equally capable of ordering mass murder.

On August 10, 1918, as the Bolsheviks waged the first of many campaigns of grain confiscation against the peasantry, Lenin sent a telegram to Bolshevik leaders in Penza that I have always thought speaks in the authentic voice of communism:

The kulak uprising in [your] five districts must be crushed without pity.... An example must be made. 1) Hang (and I mean hang so that the people can see) not less than 100 known kulaks, rich men, bloodsuckers. 2) Publish their names. 3) Take all their grain. 4) Identify hostages.... Do this so that for hundreds of miles around the people see, tremble, know and cry: they are killing and will go on killing the bloodsucking kulaks.... P.S. Find tougher people.

Between 1918 and 1920, as many as 300,000 political executions were carried out by the Bolsheviks. By 1920 there were already more than a hundred icy "concentration camps" for the "rehabilitation" of "unreliable elements."

So, please: no more of all those fairy tales—which we still sometimes hear today—of an idealistic revolution that only wicked Stalin betrayed. Communism was always a bloodthirsty monster. Its leaders invariably combined those strange qualities that Lenin, Trotsky, and Stalin had in common: a talent for warped, paradoxical reasoning—"democratic centralism," "the dictatorship of the proletariat"—and a hideous relish of violence.

I have mentioned foreign intervention, incompetent liberals, and clueless bankers. Let me not forget the fellow travelers, who were also there in 1917. John Reed, with his risible glamorizing of the revolution, would have many, many heirs. George Bernard Shaw's commentary on the show trials of the 1930s perfectly encapsulated this intellectual deformation. Even as the revolution devoured its own children, the fellow travelers cheered the executioners on. Not many went quite as far as the Cambridge spies, who shamefully betrayed their own country to Stalin. But throughout that long, *all-too-long*, short twentieth century, how many intellectuals turned a blind eye to the crimes of communism? Or rationalized away the mass graves and the Gulag? Because Hitler's crimes—which came later than Stalin's, of course—were in some way worse. Because the industrialization of Russia could be achieved in no other way. Because one had to crack an egg to make an omelet—and all the other cant.

In the summer of 1947, George Kennan published his anonymous essay in *Foreign Affairs*, "The Sources of Soviet Conduct." In it, he asked a question:

> Who can say with assurance that the strong light still cast by the Kremlin on the dissatisfied peoples of the western world is not the powerful afterglow of a constellation which is in actuality on the wane? ... [T]he possibility remains ... that Soviet power ... bears within it the seeds of its own decay, and that the sprouting of these seeds is well advanced.

Kennan was forty-three when he wrote those words. Yet he was eighty-seven when the Soviet Union was finally dissolved in December 1991.

Perhaps another reason that the communist virus continued to spread for so long—for the better part of twenty-five years after the policy of containment became the basis for US strategy in the Cold War—was this: that even good men underestimated the Soviet threat and were assailed by doubts about how much should be done to resist it. From the outbreak of the Korean War to the final confrontation in the early 1980s, even those, like Kennan, who considered themselves anti-communist, frequently lacked the stomach for the fight. Time and again, they succumbed to relativism. Perhaps this contest between the superpowers was really the fault of the United States. Perhaps the United States should simply withdraw its forces from the contested gray zones—from Southeast Asia, from Central and South America, from sub-Saharan Africa. And yet behold what happened when the US did that. It is now more or less orthodoxy that the Vietnam War was an unmitigated disaster—if you are tempted to doubt it, you may be forced to watch Ken Burns's new and widely acclaimed documentary series on the subject. I am of the unfashionable view that the real disaster was to abandon the people of South Vietnam to their cruel and entirely predictable fate at the hands of the communist North.

Have we learned anything from the history I have just summarized? Not nearly enough, I would say. It is not just the Che Guevara T-shirts I worry about. It is not just the bust of Lenin that is said to sit on the desk of the leader of the British Labour Party. It is not just the revival of "Anti-Fa" by young people presumably unaware of the cooperation between the German communists—the original antifa—and the Nazis who helped seal the fate of the Weimar Republic. It is not just the rising power of a China still ruled by communists—to say nothing of the sycophantic treatment I see their leader receiving in the West. It is not just the North Korean missiles, a stark reminder that communism is as ready as ever to kill people by the million.

No, what concerns me today is the entirely familiar response we see to a different but, to my mind, equally dangerous threat. Ask yourself how effectively we in the West have responded to the rise of militant Islam since the Iranian Revolution unleashed its Shia variant and since 9/11 revealed the even more aggressive character of Sunni Islamism. I fear we have done no better than our grandfathers did when the virus spreading around the world was Bolshevism. It is, indeed, the same old story.

Foreign intervention—the millions who have found their way from the Gulf to radical mosques and Islamic centers in the West. Incompetent liberals—the proponents of multiculturalism who brand any opponent of jihad an "Islamophobe." Clueless bankers—the sort who fall over themselves to offer "sharia-compliant" loans and bonds. Fellow travelers—the leftists who line up with the Muslim Brotherhood to castigate the state of Israel at every opportunity. And the fainthearted—those who were so quick to pull out of Iraq in 2009 that they allowed the rump of al-Qaeda to morph into ISIS.

A century ago it was the West's great blunder to think it would not matter if Lenin and his confederates took over the Russian Empire, despite their stated intention to plot world revolution and overthrow both democracy and capitalism. I believe that we are, incredible as it may seem, capable of repeating that catastrophic error. I fear that, one day, we shall awake with a start to discover that the Islamists have repeated the Bolshevik achievement, which was to acquire the resources and capability to threaten our very existence.

There are many good reasons to commemorate the tens of millions of people who lost their lives because of communism. Out of compassion, we should recall their sufferings. Out of intellectual consistency, we should not treat their deaths as less worthy of pity than the deaths of those murdered by Hitler and the other fascist dictators. But the best reason, in my view, to support the Victims of Communism Memorial Foundation is to learn from our past mistakes—so that we never again allow a renegade gang of fanatics to acquire the capacity to destroy Western civilization and individual freedom, which is its most cherished value. For we are not only anti-communists. As Natan Sharansky has illustrated with deeds and words, opposition to communism is merely a logical corollary of our faith in liberty: liberty of conscience, of speech, of association, of movement, of property ownership. Our forefathers were *for* these things before Lenin and his gang were against them. And those ideals of freedom will live on, long after the evil of communism has finally been consigned where it belongs: to the history books.

The Bolshevik Revolution and the Establishment of the Soviet Union

Marion Smith

It's been exactly a century since the Russian Revolution. That's more than a lifetime for most folks, and yet the Revolution's effects are all around us still. One-fifth of the world's population today still lives in a single-party state controlled by a communist party. Millions more live in post-communist states that still grapple with the legacy of decades of communism. The Revolution of 1917 has defined our world in innumerable ways, many of which will be addressed by the presentations in this conference.

We'll start by going back to the beginning—to the Revolution itself and the establishment of the Soviet Union. As Americans, it's easy for us to recognize the importance of a revolution: a revolution not just of arms but of ideas that overthrew a monarchy and established a new government in the name of the people. We can understand very well how a new regime proclaiming a new universal ideal could exercise a powerful attraction over intellectuals and common people around the world. We Americans had a revolution like that. And the Bolshevik Revolution can certainly stand alongside the American Revolution and the French

Revolution as one of the most decisive political events of modern history. In the twentieth century there are very few competitors.

The Soviet Union, the regime that the Revolution established, also has a strong claim on our attention. It was the world's biggest country, one of only two superpowers. It led a worldwide ideological movement. It helped defeat the Nazis yet enslaved and murdered millions of its own people and captured whole nations. It created, sometimes by force of attraction but mostly through conquest, carbon copies of its own regime around the world.

Why are these things important to understand one hundred years later? They're important because the nature of a revolution and the character of a government matter. Many American school children— unfortunately, I can't say *most*—can tell you about the Constitution of the United States, about our three coequal branches of government, our checks and balances, our system of democratic representation, and explain why we have a capacity for self-correction; and they can tell you how these features relate to our founding ideals. But few people, even highly educated adults, could explain to you the almost total concentration of power in the Soviet party-state; the way a single party penetrated every institution in a country spanning an entire continent; the way it ran a massive national economy like a single corporation; and its pervasive apparatus of surveillance, control, and punishment. All those characteristics stem from the Soviet Union's founding philosophy, too. That philosophy is communism.

The founding texts of Marxist Communism are incredibly arcane. For a vivid example of this, consider that Gareth Stedman Jones's new biography of Marx argues that Marx was not able to finish his famous book

Das Kapital because he could not figure out how to make it make sense.[1] But most communists around the world imbibed the philosophy of communism in a simplified form. Communism presented a promise of future justice; it provided a way to identify the friends of that justice (the Communist Party) and its enemies (the bourgeoisie). And joining that party allowed a person to become a warrior for that justice. Communism also provided a justification of power without constraint and the possibility of a strict social and moral code free from religion. In this sense, the communists were tactically shrewd about human motivations, even as they theoretically denied fundamental truths about human nature.

Therefore, they made mistakes about human nature of a type that our American founders did not. Communists ignored basic truths about the concentration of power; they ignored the foundational importance of individual liberty in the economic and cultural spheres; and their commitment to popular sovereignty, self-determination, equality, and solidarity eventually came to exist in rhetoric only. They explicitly believed they could alter human nature by altering human society through the coercive power of the state. These flaws went to the core of Marxist-Leninist Communism, and they defined the character and history of the Soviet Union, as well as all of the communist regimes founded, funded, imposed, or inspired by the USSR. And each of these governments, over the last hundred years, in some forty nations, either collapsed economically or turned into a totalitarian police state.

At this conference we will discuss and commemorate many aspects of Communism's hundred-year track record. We'll talk about the

---

[1] Gareth Stedman Jones, *Karl Marx: Greatness and Illusion* (Cambridge, MA: The Belknap Press of Harvard University Press, 2016), 537–540.

history of the Soviet Union, its imperial sphere, and its geopolitical impact. We will examine totalitarianism, its ideological roots, and its practical effects. We will discuss how historical clarity about communism's crimes can be established and how we can memorialize the disparate victims in a truthful way. And we will explore how communism's legacy still lingers in Russia and around the world one hundred years after the Bolshevik Revolution.

Vladimir Kara-Murza

I'm going to start right at the beginning in 1917 with the Provisional Government, the government that came to power after the abdication of Tsar Nicholas II in March 1917. The government was "provisional" in that its tenure was to last only until the election of the All-Russia Constituent Assembly, that dream of many generations of Russian liberals—a national parliament chosen by direct, equal, and universal suffrage on a secret ballot, with the powers to define the contours of a new democratic state. In the spring of 1917, the preparations for that election began in earnest, and a special commission tasked with drafting the election law was formed under the presidency of Fyodor Kokoshkin, a leading Russian jurist, cofounder of the Constitutional Democratic Party, and former member of the State Duma. The law was ready by August; it brought about what were at the time the most democratic election rules in Europe, with the minimum voting age set at twenty, suffrage for women, and no limitations or restrictions on suffrage based on property, education, ethnicity, or religion.

The vote was scheduled for September 17 (Julian calendar). But in August, Prime Minister Alexander Kerensky—fearing political instability and citing the need to clarify further some matters relating to electoral law—decided to postpone the election until November 12. This was probably the most consequential postponement in twentieth-century history. On October 25 came Lenin's "Yesterday was too early, tomorrow will be too late." The Bolsheviks, with the help of soldiers and sailors from the Petrograd Garrison and the Baltic Fleet, used force to seize physical control of key infrastructure in Petrograd. After a week of heavy fighting in Moscow, which included the shelling of the Kremlin by Bolshevik-controlled artillery, Russia's ancient capital succumbed, too. The Bolsheviks were now in control of the country's two most important political centers.

The expectations of a Constituent Assembly were so widespread, however, that the usurpers could not cancel the election straightaway. The vote on November 12 went ahead, and the Bolsheviks were humiliated, receiving just 22 percent of the vote. Even with their allies from the Left Socialist Revolutionary Party, they controlled only one-third of the seats in the newly elected Assembly. The election, the first ever held in Russia on the basis of universal suffrage, was won by the Socialist Revolutionary Party, a moderate democratic left-wing party that represented the interests of Russia's peasant class and advocated for a parliamentary republic, as opposed to the "dictatorship of the proletariat." The leading liberal reformist party in Russia, the Constitutional Democrats, won representation too, earning around 5 percent of the national vote and seventeen seats in the Assembly. They were unable to take them up, though: On November 28, Lenin's Council of People's Commissars banned the party, officially designating its members as "enemies of the people" (the first official use of this term by the Soviet government). Two

Constitutional Democrat legislators were arrested and later brutally murdered by sailors as they attempted to attend a session of the Assembly. One of them was Fyodor Kokoshkin, who had presided over the drafting of the electoral law.

The Assembly met for just one day: January 5, 1918. It refused to consider the Bolshevik proclamation of a "Republic of Soviets" and instead declared the Russian Democratic Federative Republic. Minutes after that—with the infamous words from Anatoli Zhelezniakov, "the guard is tired"—the Bolshevik guard shut down the Constituent Assembly. This was the end of Russian parliamentarianism for seven decades. Street demonstrations in support of the Assembly in Petrograd and Moscow were forcibly put down, with dozens of people killed. Vladimir Lenin called it "a complete and open liquidation of democratic forms for the sake of revolutionary dictatorship." His right hand, Leon Trotsky, was just as candid in his assessment: "We are not at all hiding or glossing over the fact that ... we have violated the formal law. Nor are we hiding the fact that we have used violence." It was only the beginning of the decades-long communist violence against the Russian people and other peoples subjugated under the Soviet empire.

It took more than five years of a bloody civil war for the Bolsheviks to take control of the country: a war that gave rise to several "innovations," including what is often considered the first concentration camp in Europe—opened on the Solovetsky Islands—and the first use of chemical weapons against civilian populations during the suppression of the anti-Bolshevik uprising in Tambov. And the violence did not stop with the end of the Red Terror and the Civil War. After that came the forced collectivization; the artificially created famines; the war against religion;

the deliberate targeting of entire segments of the population (the clergy, the military, the intelligentsia); the Great Terror of the 1930s and the hunt for "enemies of the people"; the mass deportations of entire nations; the anti-Semitic campaign against "cosmopolitanism"; and other chapters in the history of the Union of Soviet Socialist Republics. There is no consensus among historians as to the total number of victims of the Soviet regime, but the most oft-cited figure—which includes those who were executed, killed in the civil war, killed by famines, displaced by collectivization, deported, and forced to emigrate—is around thirty million people. This is more than one-fifth of the population of the Soviet Union of the early 1920s. History knows few crimes of such magnitude.

We have still not fully come to terms with this history in Russia. After the fall of communism in 1991, the new democratic leadership in Russia *did* take some steps to try to account for the Soviet past. Some of the Soviet archives were opened; the 1991 law "On Rehabilitation of Victims of Political Repression" recognized the "decades-long terror and mass persecutions" carried out by the communist regime and introduced criminal responsibility for those who had perpetrated them; and a 1992 ordinance by the Russian Constitutional Court, the highest court of justice in the Russian Federation, officially acknowledged that "the Communist Party of the Soviet Union was the initiator ... of repression directed at millions."

But the process stopped halfway. The archives were soon resealed; a full condemnation of the old regime never came; lustrations against former Communist Party apparatchiks and KGB operatives were never introduced; and just a few years later one of those KGB operatives,

Vladimir Putin, came to power in Russia, returning many of the symbols and methods of the Soviet past.

Dr. Paul Hollander

Growing up in Hungary after World War II created in me a predisposition to ponder the connections between Marxism-Leninism and the actual workings of communist systems—that is to say, between theory and practice. I had no idea at the time that those experiences would influence my eventual choice of occupation and that I would become a sociologist. I could have chosen political science, history, social psychology, or cultural anthropology and ended up with the same preoccupations which informed my lifelong professional interests. As is often the case, my professional interests were rooted in personal experiences.

I would like to begin my reflections with a proposition of Leszek Kołakowski's that I have cited on many occasions:

> Marxism has been the greatest fantasy of our century. It was a dream offering the prospect of a society of perfect unity, in which all human aspirations would be fulfilled and all values reconciled.... The influence that Marxism has achieved, far from being the result or proof of its scientific character, is almost entirely due to its prophetic, fantastic, irrational elements.... It is certainly not based on any empirical premises or supposed "historical laws," but simply on the psychological need for certainty. In this sense Marxism performs the functions of a religion, and its efficacy is of a religious character.... Marx, moreover, combined his romantic dreams with the socialist

expectation that all needs would be satisfied in the earthly paradise.[2]

The connections between Marxism and the nature of the Soviet system, and especially its political institutions and practices, were pondered and debated from the earliest days of the Soviet Union until its dissolution in 1991. There have been three major positions taken on the subject. Soviet leaders and ideologues insisted that their system was inspired, legitimated, and guided by the ideas of Marx (and more plausibly also by those of Lenin), and that his ideals were being implemented even under conditions he did not anticipate—*i.e.*, in an underdeveloped, largely agricultural country with a small working class, isolated from the far more advanced, highly urbanized, and industrialized societies of Western Europe. For the Western supporters of "the Soviet experiment" (as it was often called in its early years), it was important to believe that it was rooted in Marxist ideals, because that seemed to guarantee a respectable ideological basis. The latter seemed to ensure that the Soviet Union stood "for a good cause, indeed the only worthwhile cause"; and for the generation of intellectuals that included Eric Hobsbawm, this "mitigated its crimes."[3]

By contrast, many critics of the Soviet system argued that it had little, if anything, to do with Marxism, that it was a form of "oriental

---

[2] Leszek Kołakowski, *Main Currents of Marxism,* trans. P. S. Falla (New York: W. W. Norton & Company, 2005), 1206–1209.

[3] Tony Judt, *When the Facts Change: Essays 1995–2010* (New York: Penguin, 2015), 26–27. In an interview in 1994, Hobsbawm said he would have supported the Soviet system even if he had known about the mass murders of the 1930s because of "the chance of a new world being born in great suffering would still have been worth backing" (quoted in Robert Conquest, *Reflections on a Ravaged Century* [New York, W. W. Norton, 2000], 10–11).

despotism" or nationalistic dictatorship, heir to centuries-old autocratic traditions—and that its alleged Marxist ideological heritage was window dressing, a legitimating device.

There was also a third point of view, one I share, namely that Marxism inspired the Bolshevik revolutionaries and was a major influence on the character of the Soviet system without determining all of its features, while also helping to explain some of its defects and moral failings.

I believe that both the first and second propositions regarding the relationship between Marxism and the Soviet system are questionable. On the one hand, the Soviet Union (and other communist systems) were not defined and determined by Marxism. At the same time, it would also be totally untrue to claim that these systems had nothing to do with Marxism. There was an indisputable connection between Marxist ideas and Soviet (and other communist) practices, though the particulars and extent of this connection are subject to debate. Nevertheless, it is possible to specify some of these connections without holding Marxism as a whole responsible for all the deprivations and sufferings its attempted realization led to. To say the least, Soviet policies and institutions cannot be understood without an awareness of the influence of Marxism.

The major institutional expression of the influence of Marxism on the Soviet system was the state ownership of the means of production. Marx believed that the exploitation of workers could not be terminated without taking this measure. Public (in reality, *state*) ownership was also supposed to create a social system that would be not only just, but also highly productive and communitarian. The Soviet authorities faithfully implemented this idea; there was no gap between theory and practice in this regard. But it was a deeply flawed idea. State ownership of the means of production did not end exploitation; arguably it made it more thorough and efficient. Trade unions were abolished on the assumption that they were superfluous, now that the interests of the workers and the party-state coincided. Nor did nationalization make the economy more productive and the workers more highly motivated. Last but not least, it failed to create a new sense of community, or improve human nature. Again, as Kołakowski observed:

> Marx seems to have imagined that once capitalists were done away with the whole world could become a kind of Athenian agora: one had only to forbid private ownership of machines or land, and as if by magic, human beings would cease to be selfish and their interests would coincide in perfect harmony.... It turned out that, having nationalized the means of production, it was possible to erect on this foundation a monstrous edifice of lies, exploitation, and oppression.[4]

Especially unrealistic was the idea that public (or state) ownership of the means of production would create such social harmony that political conflicts would disappear, removing the need for the state—the organ that had previously regulated and moderated these conflicts. Lenin, too, subscribed to these beliefs, at any rate before the October Revolution. In *State and Revolution*, he quoted Engels approvingly:

> The state is the product and manifestation of the irreconcilability of class antagonisms.... When at last it becomes the real representative of the whole of society, it renders itself unnecessary. As soon as there is no longer

---

[4] Kołakowski, 1208–9.

> any social class to be held in subjection ... [and] nothing
> more remains to be repressed.... government of persons
> is replaced by the administration of things.

Equally unrealistically, Lenin further argued that

> the exploiters are naturally unable to suppress the people
> without a highly complex machine for performing this
> task, but the people can suppress the exploiters with a very
> simple "machine," almost without a "machine," without a
> special apparatus.... Only communism makes the state
> absolutely unnecessary, for there is nobody to be
> suppressed.... We know that the fundamental social
> [cause] of excesses, which consist in the violation of the
> rules of social intercourse, is the exploitation of the
> masses, their want and their poverty. With the removal of
> this chief cause, excess will inevitably begin to "wither
> away."[5]

This was the gist of the theory of the withering away of the state,
the utopian belief that the abolition of the private ownership of the means
of production would create such harmony and tranquility that social
conflict would altogether disappear, and with it, the state.

While Marx cannot be blamed for the one-party system, the cult
of personality, the creation of the Soviet political police (Cheka, GPU,
NKVD, KGB), the Gulag, or the show trials, his ideas about the necessity
of class struggle and the dictatorship of the proletariat helped to legitimate
regimentation, coercion, and political violence. However, the major,
indirect contribution of Marxism to political violence was the assurance it
provided for the revolutionaries, and later the powerholders, that by

---

[5] Vladimir Lenin, *State and Revolution* (1918; Lenin Internet Archive, 1993),
chaps. 1 and 5, https://www.marxists.org/archive/lenin/works/1917/staterev/.

embracing its ideals (and later those of Marxism-Leninism), they undertook to create an exceptionally praiseworthy and morally superior social system. Given this commitment, they were entitled to use any and all means that promised to help to accomplish these ideals and goals. As Solzhenitsyn wrote in *The Gulag Archipelago*, you cannot brutalize large numbers of people without an ideology of good intentions justifying it.

Despite its embrace of Marxism, the Soviet system violated or ignored various Marxist propositions and ideals as it embarked on major social, economic, and political transformations, without reliance on a large and politically conscious industrial working class, and without help from the more advanced Western European countries and their working classes. Nor did Marxism support or legitimate dictatorship by a single, immensely powerful leader, new forms of inequality based on political criteria, the vast increase in the coercive power of the state (embodied in huge new bureaucracies), or the increasing reliance on appeals of nationalism to bolster social solidarity.

The relationship between Marxism and the Soviet system may best be summarized by suggesting that while there was no conflict between Marxist ideals and Soviet political aspirations, the attempt to realize these ideals had numerous unintended and unexpected outcomes, including severe material scarcities, new forms of politically determined inequality, high levels of bureaucratization, and wide-ranging repression.

As has been noted on many occasions by many authors, Russia at the beginning of the twentieth century was not a suitable setting for the attempt to realize Marxist ideals and improve the human condition. Under these circumstances it is not surprising that the relationship between theory and practice turned out to be contradictory, unpredictable, and subject to manipulation by the self-appointed interpreters of the Marxist ideological legacy.

Dr. A. James McAdams

I would like to comment on communism as an international movement. This is a way of getting at the theme of this panel, which is the relationship between Marx, Engels, and other early communists to the movement itself. Simply put, I shall argue, in the same spirit of Paul Hollander's remarks, that it would be strange to imagine that two people, or a small group of people writing in the middle of the nineteenth century, would be able to formulate their arguments in such a way that they would directly and significantly influence later events.

What is the relationship between the writings of Karl Marx and Friedrich Engels and the Bolshevik Revolution? It would be a mischaracterization to say that it was ever straightforward. A better way of characterizing the connection with the events of 1917 is to say that these and the works of other early communists were creatively adapted and mythologized by later generations of revolutionaries into justifications for a global cause. This fact had a far greater incendiary potential than if the Bolsheviks and those who emulated their example had merely confined their messages to literal citations of the thoughts of their German predecessors. When one considers the broad sweep of the international communist movement from Russia to East-Central Europe to Asia during the early twentieth century, those figures who called for the overthrow of the status quo did not require *Das Kapital*, *The German Ideology*, or the *Anti-Dühring* to make their case for revolution. No matter how often they felt the need to quote the great works, they were primarily interested in something else. This was to convince their followers of their ability to lead them into the promised land. They set about accomplishing this task by invoking much simpler images of revolutionary inevitability that could be readily adapted to widely varying contexts. In turn, they and their successors used these claims to justify dictatorial policies that destroyed the lives of millions of human beings.

Karl Marx's *Manifesto of the Communist Party* is arguably the most illuminating example of this disjunction between a literal reading of foundational texts and their actual impact on the flow of events. Scholars of communist history routinely emphasize the empirical shortcomings of Marx's analysis. For example, contrary to his predictions, the revolutionary upheaval in the industrialized West never took place. When given the opportunity to revolt against the bourgeoisie before World War I, the proletariat of each nation chose to align itself with its oppressors against the workers of its country's enemies. Additionally, when a successful revolution finally came to Europe nearly seven decades after the appearance of the *Manifesto*, it was in a setting, Russia, that Marx and like-minded nineteenth century radicals considered inhospitable to such an event.

These truisms aside, I believe there is a more fruitful way of reading the *Manifesto*. As I have argued in a new book, *Vanguard of the Revolution: The Global Idea of the Communist Party*,[6] Marx provided future communists with three powerful reasons to sacrifice themselves— as well as the lives of others, including long-standing friends and comrades—for a seemingly noble cause. The first reason is the evidence

---

[6] A. James McAdams, *Vanguard of the Revolution: The Global Idea of the Communist Party* (Princeton: Princeton University Press, 2017).

they claimed to provide that every true communist was a participant in a progressive movement that was certain to achieve victory. In their characterization, this was a heroic movement that was destined to succeed. Conveniently, it was also one that could be understood in terms of a fairly simple dichotomy between ostensibly moral majorities and exploiting minorities. For true believers, there was a striking "family resemblance" (Ludwig Wittgenstein) between Marx's image of unremitting class conflict in nineteenth-century England and the equally devastating but different types of conflicts taking place in their own countries—between peasants and landowners, national liberators and colonial administrators, and patriots and invaders. If revolution was destined to come to the industrial West, non-western revolutionaries reasoned, surely the contradictions that transected their own societies would lead to similar uprisings at home.

A second reason for these figures' confidence is that the *Manifesto* offered them a sense of community and belonging in times when human relations were fractured by social unrest, economic hardship, and war. Marx's followers were emboldened by their hero's romantic image of the struggle of a heroic elite that, in his words, "cuts itself adrift" from the ruling class and is simply charged with "pointing out and bringing to the front the common interests of the entire proletariat."[7] In their eyes, this was a sacred cause. Hence, it made sense that all communists would work together unflinchingly to prove their fidelity.

Finally, the *Manifesto* encouraged these individuals to visualize themselves as agents of virtue. In rejecting their countries' social and

---

[7] Karl Marx and Friedrich Engels, *The Communist Manifesto,* with an introduction and notes by Gareth Stedman Jones (London: Penguin Classics, 2014), 342.

political conventions, they assumed that history itself had anointed them to educate the masses about their true interests. In effect, while many had been *called* to serve the communist cause, these agents were the enlightened few who were *chosen* to be at its head. In this capacity, these revolutionaries saw themselves as sacrificial individuals whose sole task was to liberate the proletariat from its chains. Far from serving their own needs, they would, in Marx's words, "always and everywhere represent the interests of the movement as a whole."

These were captivating ideas. Still, as I argue in *Vanguard of the Revolution*, they would never have taken root had equally powerful individuals not arisen with both the political skills to apply them to turbulent circumstances and the callous indifference to the wellbeing of their peers to force them into practice. Whether in the Soviet Union, China, or Cuba, communist parties thrived on the basis of the ability of personalities—such as Lenin, Stalin, Mao, and Castro—to instill in their followers a sense of inevitable victory, common identity, and virtuous calling.

Because these revolutionary leaders operated in diverse settings, it is important to appreciate there was nothing preordained about the formulas they chose to pursue their goals. In fact, the global communist movement was never monolithic, even in that part of the world that was dominated by the Soviet Union. A strategy based on a uniform conception of Marxism would have destined their respective parties to failure. For example, Stalin's despotism flourished because of his ability to convince the Soviet Union's citizens that his conception of Marxism would lead to the modernization of their backward country and fulfill Russia's centuries-old desire to become the equal of the great powers of the West. In contrast, in the face of opposition within the Chinese Communist Party, Mao used Marxism's dichotomous image of class struggle to champion a nationalist revolution in the countryside that made sense against the turbulent background of China's recent history. Finally, Castro took advantage of a century of economic inequality, government corruption, and patriotic resentment to justify a distinctively populist version of Marxism that elevated himself above the party. On balance, the extraordinary political longevity of all three dictators—Castro was in power for more than a half century! — suggests that these strategies served their purposes.

As we know, these leaders' success in monopolizing the language of revolution had tragic consequences. Acting with impunity at the top of his party, Stalin used a highly selective interpretation of Marxism in the 1930s and 1940s to rationalize the imprisonment, deportation, and execution of millions of people, many of them Old Bolsheviks. During the Cultural Revolution, Mao casually made decisions from the comfort of his swimming pool that eviscerated his party's Central Committee and threw his country into turmoil. Well before a unified communist party was established in 1965, Castro used the idea of a continuous revolution to eliminate his rivals and eradicate all forms of opposition.

These tragedies also had a perverse effect. In many cases, they led to the intensification of the devotion of their followers. For example, true believers in the Soviet Union did not regard the fierce resistance of the peasantry to collectivization as proof of their leaders' ineptitude or gratuitous cruelty. Rather, they viewed the opposition as a confirmation of what Marx, Lenin, and other revolutionary thinkers had consistently maintained about the class struggle. The ruling class would not voluntarily relinquish its supremacy. One needed to wrest political power from its hands by whatever means necessary. Likewise, the faithful did not regard Stalin's bloody purges of the Old Bolsheviks as a betrayal of the party. To the contrary, in their eyes, his campaigns confirmed that the threats to socialism—from hidden wreckers, saboteurs, and Western spies—were much greater than anyone had realized. To paraphrase Stalin's rationale, one could be certain that the class struggle would intensify before the party could ever make the full transition to socialism. According to this argument, true communists had no choice but to increase their repressive measures until their enemies were destroyed. As Paul Hollander has demonstrated, even Western "political pilgrims"[8] who journeyed to the homeland of the Bolshevik Revolution in the 1920s and 1930s were swayed by this reasoning.

What, then, are we to make of the fact that a majority of the communist regimes that dominated the twentieth century have vanished, and that even the few regimes that still bear this title—in China, Cuba, Vietnam, and Laos—have largely shed the distinctive attributes of Marxism and Leninism? We should not assume that the passing of a name is a guarantee that the atrocities of the old Soviet world will never recur. Quite the contrary. Given the right circumstances, it is possible that new despots will arise who are prepared to incite renewed violence in the name of an ostensibly noble mission and their claim to revolutionary certainty.

---

[8] Paul Hollander, *Political Pilgrims: Western Intellectuals in Search of the Good Society*, 4th ed. (New Brunswick, NJ: Transaction, 2009).

Discussion

Marion Smith: To begin with, I have a question related to your last comment, Dr. McAdams. When Xi Jinping or other nominally communist leaders are asked today why they are in charge, or why they have to be obeyed, how seriously do you take their fundamental claims of justice? It sounds like they fall back on the classic communist notion of the party as the guarantor of justice. How do you interpret that?

A. James McAdams: That's certainly their claim, that it's all about justice. I think if you look at the Chinese Communist Party, despite the remnants of its early revolutionary idealism, the focus is very much on keeping power, on having access to the benefits of that power, and justifying the organization that makes the access to these benefits possible. Of course, there are undoubtedly Communist Party members who take the idea of justice seriously; however, I don't think it's their leaders' main focus.

Paul Hollander: To add to that, I would remind you of Solzhenitsyn's famous remark that you need ideology in order to commit large-scale evil.[9] I think people like Stalin and Lenin and the rest of them were a peculiar mixture of power-hunger and idealism. They felt entitled to be ruthless and merciless because they had convinced themselves that the political project they were engaged in had an idealistic foundation.

Vladimir Kara-Murza: It's astonishing, but this quote from Solzhenitsyn has apparently been refuted by the current leadership of our country, by

---

[9] Aleksandr Solzhenitsyn, *The Gulag Archipelago,* 3 vols. (New York: Harper and Row, 1974), 1:174.

the Putin regime, because while they certainly commit a lot of evil, they have no ideology. Their only ideology is to grab as much money as possible, hide it in Western offshores, and stay in power to protect that money, because once they leave power, they'll be held accountable for everything they've done. It's astonishing to see a regime with not even a veneer or a façade of ideology. Obviously, whatever the Soviets proclaimed publicly had nothing to do with the substance of their rule, but at least they proclaimed something publicly. Putin's allies sometimes try to develop ideas like Eurasianism, the Third Way, or the Russian World; they come up with these pseudo-ideological notions because it doesn't sound very good to simply say "our ideology is to grab as much money and to keep power for as long as possible." It is cynical. It's not just a kleptocratic, corrupt, and authoritarian regime, it's also very cynical.

Paul Hollander: Putin does make some limited use of ideology—namely Russian nationalism, especially recalling the glories of the past, including the recent superpower status. It may be a cynical use of ideas, but the Russian masses resonate with it.

Marion Smith: Vladimir, what do you make of how the government of the Russian Federation is treating this anniversary of the Bolshevik Revolution?

Vladimir Kara-Murza: Officially, of course there is nothing. In fact, a few years ago, the holiday on November 7, which celebrated the October Revolution during Soviet days and remained on the same date for the first post-Soviet years, was moved to November 4, and is now supposed to commemorate the victory over the Poles in the seventeenth century. The only reason for that is that people were used to having some sort of a holiday at the beginning of November, so they looked at the calendar and said "OK, why not this one?" Nobody knows what it means.

A few days ago, I watched a two-hour documentary produced by Dmitry Kiselyov, who is the most prominent face of Putin's television propaganda, because I was interested in the very same question: How do they approach it? It was such a mixture. You could recognize all the messages that are the foundation of the regime today being projected back into history. Put simply, the main messages were, first of all, that the tsar was good, and any revolution is bad in itself; you can understand why that's the message they're trying to send. The second message was that the February Revolution, the real revolution—I actually hesitate to call what we're commemorating today a real revolution; it was a *coup d'état*—was bad. They badmouth it as much as possible. They used anachronistic terms like oligarch, which were not used at the time, and put the blame for that revolution on the oligarchs, the economic elite of Russia, who they said were in cahoots with the West, with Great Britain, with France, with the United States. Sounds familiar, right? They said that it was the political agents of these foreign powers in the Russian parliament, the Duma, who created the February Revolution. When they got to the Bolshevik *coup d'état*, the message was really confused. On the one hand, they said, "Well, yeah, that was a bad thing," but then they ended the film with the message that "then the USSR was created, and so many wonderful and good things happened because of it." As you know, Putin once called the dissolution of the Soviet Union "the greatest geopolitical catastrophe of the twentieth century." That gives you a notion of what he actually thinks about it.

Martin Palouš: The most visible materialization of the legacy of the October Revolution is Lenin's mausoleum on Red Square. Is there any discussion right now on the future of this symbol?

Vladimir Kara-Murza: There is. Boris Nemtsov once asked how we can talk about the future in our country when our main dead body is still not buried. It's a big attraction for Western tourists. My friends from Britain asked me to take them there twice. I went there as a school kid—we all had to—but I had to go there again just because I wanted them to enjoy the visit. But it's mind-boggling that we still have a dead body on the main square in our capital city.

It is known that President Yeltsin wanted on at least three or four occasions to get it over with, to bury Lenin. Actually, Lenin himself expressed his wishes on his burial. He didn't want his dead body to be lying on Red Square; he wanted to be buried in Volkovo Cemetery in Saint Petersburg, where his mother is buried. So it even goes against his own wishes, even if we forget everything else. But Yeltsin was never really able to do this, because for the entirety of his presidency, he faced a hostile parliament. He had a parliament that was controlled by the opposition, which was, of course, the Communist opposition. So he was unable to bury Lenin because of the political consequences.

In answer to your question, there is discussion in society, but there's no real discussion in the regime. Just in the last few days, there was a kind of fake argument between, on the one hand, Ramzan Kadyrov, who is Putin's viceroy in Chechnya and one of the most horrid and criminal representatives of the current regime in Russia, and, on the other, Gennady Zyuganov, who has been the head of the Communist Party of the Russian

Federation for the last 24 years and who in 2018 is going to run for president for, I think, the fifth time. They had this fake argument where Kadyrov said, "We should bury Lenin," and Zyuganov said, "No, we're never going to bury Lenin." But this is a distraction from the real public debate that is going on.

I have no doubt that when things change in Russia, and when we have a democratic government again, the mistakes that were made in the 1990s will not be made again and that we finally will bury that specter of communism, both literally and figuratively speaking.

Emanuelis Zingeris: Vladimir Kara-Murza, you spent years thinking about the difference between tsarist Russia and what the Soviets did to the Russian nation and its integrity. What, in your eyes, is the biggest difference between Russian imperialism and Soviet imperialism? And, after years of trying to restore the integrity of the Russian people along with Boris Nemtsov, what do you think is the most promising method for doing this?

Vladimir Kara-Murza: Thank you for the question and thank you also for drawing this distinction. It sounds really insulting to us when people in the West confuse the words *Russian* and *Soviet;* they're not the same thing. I remember reading about how, when Brezhnev invaded Afghanistan in 1979, the legendary Soviet dissident Vladimir Bukovsky, who was, at the time, already in the West, having been expelled in 1976 from prison and taken by a government plane to Zurich, wrote an op-ed, I think in the *New York Times*, objecting to this conflation. After the invasion of Afghanistan, you would read in Western newspapers about "Russian troops in Afghanistan" and "Soviet academician Sakharov" protesting about it. "Get your terms right," he said. Of course, our friends in the Baltic states never forget that there is a world of difference between *Russian* and *Soviet*. Numerically, the biggest victims of the Soviet regime were the Russian people; let's not forget that.

On your question of imperialism and on how we take this going forward, I don't think there can be such a thing as a "democratic empire." It goes without saying that when Russia finally becomes democratic, it will have to be a genuine federation or confederation or whatever other term you want to use, not the subjugation by a central government of all the regions and peoples and nations encompassed by our country. We have more than 120 different nationalities and ethnic groups. I don't think it is possible to govern such a massive and diverse country from one place. It's not even that it's *wrong*—although it *is* wrong—it's also *impossible*. We have seen in the last one hundred years that this empire collapsed twice, in 1917 and 1991. That should be a hint that this doesn't work. Those people who are now sitting in the Kremlin trying to recreate some sort of central structure will, I think, also find out one day that it doesn't work. But I don't understand why we have to fall into the same traps every time. Why not learn some lessons from history?

I think the only way Russia can function as a large democratic country, when it finally becomes democratic, is not as an empire, but as a federation or confederation based on subsidiarity, self-government, and genuine federalism, with as much power as possible at the level of the regions. When Putin does his annual TV show, the four-hour marathon where he is supposedly speaking to people who call in from across the country, he gets questions like, "Fix our road in Yekaterinburg," or "Please install a playground next to my house." This tells you how the current system is set up: everything is run from one place. That's not going to work.

Vytautas Landsbergis: This is only a little remark about terminology, but maybe with some substance. When we speak about the Bolsheviks after they took power—totalitarian power—we simply refer to them as "power holders." Maybe it would be better not to use such neutral language and instead call them "usurpers of power." There is no legitimacy in power gotten by subversion, *coup d'état*, and overwhelming terrorism, including the Great Terror, the Holodomor, and everything else—terrorism on a level never before seen, on the scale of the state.

Vladimir Kara-Murza: I try never to use the term "Soviet government." I say "Soviet regime." The same with Putin today: we never say "Putin government," we say "Putin regime," because I think the only acceptable form of legitimation for a government should be a democratic election. And neither the communists then nor Putin today gained power from democratic elections. The uprising of 1917–18 was one of the classic examples of usurpation. A small group of people forcibly seizes power, then loses an election, then forcibly disbands the assembly that was elected, shoots down the people who come out in support of this assembly, and then keep their power with blood and force for 70 years. I don't think there is a better definition of usurpation.

Audience: My concern is about all of the young people that seem to think that socialism or communism is the way forward. How do you argue with them? They will always tell you that there really has never been true communism or true socialism. And that is kind of true, because when the communists took power, it was the state that held the means of production, not the people, who were supposed to hold it, according to Marx. How do you argue with minds like that?

Paul Hollander: Your point reminds me of a major conclusion of much of my professional work, namely that human irrationality is profound and persistent. Even well-educated people are capable of believing absurd things. People believe what they wish to believe, and this includes dreams of authentic socialism.

Vladimir Kara-Murza: How many more times does it need to be tried, how many more millions of people need to die before everybody finally realizes that it does not work? I think that that should be self-evident, but you're right, there are still people who believe in this.

A. James McAdams: One thing I see in my students is that no matter how smart they are, they don't know about the past. Of course, it's my job, and that of others, to try to educate them. Socialism is a broad term. Historically, it means different things. But I think the attitudes you mention also speak to the fact that younger people are looking for something to believe in. Socialism, however one defines it, has many romantic ideals associated with it. Thus, the real question at this time in the history of the United States and the world is "What else do we have to offer?"

Audience: One of the things that strikes me about the history of communism is its international ambitions, beginning with Lenin and the Comintern, and continuing through the mobilization of Western opinion in very effective campaigns. Do you believe there is an ongoing threat of communism infiltrating Western societies?

A. James McAdams: Certainly, there was a proletarian international movement that lasted for nearly a century, though I don't see any reason to use that term to characterize the remnants of global communism today. I don't see any evidence that communists *per se* are trying to penetrate American society or the US government. Thus, I'm not too worried about this sort of eventuality. What does concern me more is the issue that I raised before: we don't have a well-articulated vision of what a democracy is. People are losing sight of that in the West, I think. For this reason, under the right circumstances, people can become captivated by similarly extremist beliefs and convictions. Just like during the communist era, the attraction of a sense of historical inevitability and the achievement of absolute justice for the people might lead people to question the merits of democracy. I see elements of this way of thinking in populist movements, both on the Right and on the Left, in the US and Europe today. This is what I worry about.

Paul Hollander: I agree with these comments, though I would phrase them somewhat differently, as I have done in my recent book, the subtitle of which is "Intellectuals and a Century of Political Hero Worship."[10] The beliefs and discontents noted by the previous speaker, especially as articulated by intellectuals, have much to do with the problems and discomforts of modernity, and foremost among them is social isolation.

---

[10] Paul Hollander, *From Benito Mussolini to Hugo Chavez: Intellectuals and a Century of Political Hero Worship* (Cambridge: Cambridge University Press, 2017).

People seek community and meaning, though no longer the kind of meaning communist systems claimed to offer. Western pluralistic societies, including ours, are consumed by somewhat novel forms of alienation and polarization, which are not caused by material deprivations. I wrote about these matters in the preface of my recent book, suggesting that the appeal (though not the policies) of Mr. Trump has been similar to that of Mussolini and Hitler, at least in the beginning of their popularity. Disillusionment with modernity is more a reflection of the decline of community than unmet material or consumerist expectations.

The Failure of Marxism and the Collapse of the Soviet Union

Dr. Marek Chodakiewicz

What is Marxism? Marxism is a materialist political ideology and philosophy that champions socialism and egalitarianism as a result of an allegedly scientifically predictable dialectic of history. However, if you take Professor Norman Cohn and Erik von Kuehnelt-Leddihn to heart, then Marxism is simply a heresy—a Gnostic heresy. There is an elect group that supposedly has a key to history, and we should follow the group to arrive at paradise on Earth. The elect has secret knowledge, esoteric knowledge, and paradise is inevitable. All this is naturally nonsense, but it's been tried for thousands of years with very, very similar results: widespread misery, death, and destruction. Marxism camouflaged itself—it's called in Russian *maskirovka*—as a materialist philosophy, yet it simply regurgitated the Gnostics' antinomianism—"all matter is evil"—concluding that private property is evil. We must absorb it; we must confiscate it.

There were also, among the various Gnostic sects, excesses that we have come to identify with cultural Bolshevism, including attempts to collectivize women. The Bolsheviks dropped it after a short while, but, as you see, this has now resurfaced in what Eric von Kuehnelt-Leddihn called the "freedom-below-the-belt" crowd—a metamorphosis of Marquis de Sade and his libertinism, which is a facet of cultural Bolshevism. Further, the Gnostics embraced Maccabean apocalyptic fantasies, namely, "If we'd only mass-murder the Roman elite, the Messiah would come and we'd have paradise on earth." That's called a revolution. The Bolsheviks and Marxists found their fulfillment in an orgy of red terror. That's absolutely the same thing; it's a heresy as old as the Earth. *Nihil novum sub sole*— Marxism was just a nineteenth-century manifestation of the same heresy. Science became God during the Enlightenment, displacing God, or so it was thought, so the heretics framed their proposition in appropriately fake scientific terms. So, if the heresy was wrong, as all heresies are, then it's not surprising that the product of the heresy—the Soviet Union— eventually collapsed.

There are two ways to end heresies; my preference is a crusade. Unfortunately, with nuclear weapons it was a moot point. We didn't do so well in Korea. We didn't help the Hungarians. We did not succeed in Vietnam, but in some other places we did. We enabled the freedom fighters in Poland, for instance, and in Afghanistan, Nicaragua, *etc.* Those were crusading days. But a second way for a heresy to end is via self-destruction. If there is an error in its genetic code, and there is, then it's only a matter of time before it falls. Heresies are unsustainable—they burn themselves out. And then they resurface yet again under a different guise. Today we have, for instance, Antifa and naked people in San Francisco. There were demonstrations of naked Bolsheviks in 1918 and 1919, when they were still trying the Kollontai option.

There are a number of theories for the collapse of the USSR. Conservatives like to talk about the "Holy Trinity": Reagan, Thatcher, and

Saint John Paul II. Liberals like Strobe Talbott claim that the USSR imploded through liberal kindness: the nicer the United States was to the communists, the more convergence and the more warm-fuzzies, hence Gorbachev. Some leftists say the Soviet Union imploded because Gorbachev really believed in socialist humanism. Well, socialist humanism is like a chair and an electric chair. The only thing that gives socialism its human face is its corruption.

China's socialism now is in the stage of the 1920s Soviet Union NEP (New Economic Policy). Most observers at the time of the implosion of the Soviet Union posited that it was nationalism that destroyed the Soviet Union. It was definitely a very important factor. But most also said it was a revolution. Until this very day, Estonians tend falsely to refer to their "Singing Revolution." I say no, and I think that anti-communism is a counter-revolution. Revolution is evil in itself. Counter-revolution is liberation from evil, bringing freedom to those who suffer under revolutions like the Nazi (National Socialist) revolution or international socialist revolution. They're related, but they're competitors.

There are quarrels over who gets the credit for ending communism. For example, the great Adda Bozeman claimed it was the East German people; they took to the streets, they breached the Berlin Wall. The Poles beg to differ. They say, "It was Solidarity!"—solidarity and its domino effect: once Poland went, everything followed. I tend to think that unrest in the peripheries of the empire and international anti-communist pressure caused Gorbachev to release the genie from the bottle. He was unable to put it back. The Soviet Union imploded, but communism did not collapse. This is what happened: Communism transformed into post-communism—not freedom, not sovereignty, not democracy. It was obvious from the very beginning.

Dr. Paul R. Gregory

I speak as a rare bird—an economist who specialized in the Soviet economy, which disappeared on us a while back. However, I find that if you want to understand modern Russia, if you want to understand China, if you want to understand repression, the best place to start is the Soviet Union, particularly under Stalin. We now have the state and party archives available to researchers, and I spend a lot of time reading these documents.

As an economist, I would like to talk about the economy and the role that it played in the Soviet Union's collapse. We're all familiar with the famous article by Francis Fukuyama, "The End of History."[11] Fukuyama wrote it shortly after the collapse of the Soviet Union, which appeared to be a clear victory for capitalism. We now have the famous YouGov survey which says that more than half of millennials would prefer to live under socialism or communism than capitalism. But when asked "What is communism?" or "What is socialism?" they don't seem able to answer the question. It puzzled me when, four or five years into the collapse, I would go online and see the number of new Marxist, Trotskyist, or communist groups throughout the world. As far as they're concerned, the battle is far from over and the decision is far from in.

This leads to what we economists call the "jockey versus horse debate." Why did the Soviet Union fail? Did it fail because it had a bad

---

[11] Francis Fukuyama, "The End of History?" *The National Interest,* Summer 1989, 3-18.

jockey, or did it fail because it was a bad horse? Those who continue to believe in communism or socialism (or variants thereof) say it was only the jockey. If the right person had been there, if Trotsky or whoever else had been there, everything would have turned out just fine. During the 1960s, in the midst of the Cold War, questions like these were a top priority, so many of us economists studied this very intensively. We didn't have access to the archives as we do today, but we learned a lot about growth, and we learned a lot about the horse.

The horse, it turned out, had a lot of illnesses, none of which were immediately fatal, but which eventually would combine to kill it. Just to list some: managerial incentives were all screwed up, and there was a form of very crude planning called "planning from the achieved level," in which each year's plan was just the previous year's plan, increased by some percentage, which means that year after year after year, they produced the same stuff, the only exception being some competition in the military.

What is happening today with Putin's Russia is very similar to what we saw during the 1970s and '80s with the Soviet Union. We knew it couldn't go on forever, but we couldn't figure out how it was going to collapse. The same is true of Putin. We think Putin's kleptocracy can't go on forever, but we can't quite figure out how it's going to end.

In the case of the Soviet Union, it actually ended in a very predictable way. The Politburo consisted of old men who were elevated during the Great Purge and who had no ideas. They would not live forever, so the question was who would replace them. Gorbachev came along in the guise of the great reformer who would know how to fix everything. He was advised by his own liberal economists and by Western economists who all gave him the same bad advice: "Make some small changes, destroy the power of the ministries, destroy the power of the departments of the Central Committee, give managers some more flexibility, and everything will be fine." He went ahead and pretty much destroyed the power of the planning system and created a system in which managers had much more flexibility. He created the opportunity to form cooperatives.

But the consequences were not exactly what was expected. Think of it: you're running an automobile plant and you're told you can create a cooperative. You get your best workers and say that one half of the factory belongs to the cooperative. You don't pay anything for the equipment. You steal the raw materials from the other side, which belongs to the state. And you still control export licenses and things like that. The result is the creation of oligarchs and of an enormous amount of corruption.

Dr. Alan Charles Kors

There was, and is, a great irony to communist states, the greatest slaughterhouses and charnel houses in human history: they maintained, in Marxist theory, the impersonality of historical forces, while in fact their histories have been dominated by leaders and individuals whose traits and decisions drove history into tragic dark ages. In *The Road to Serfdom*,[12] Friedrich Hayek argued that central planning had an ultimately totalizing logic, culminating in the total abolition of economic, intellectual, and moral liberty. The Bolsheviks professed to believe that with the abolition of capitalism and the supremacy of the proletariat, they would solve the problem of power in human affairs. Instead, they brought countless lives

---

[12] Friedrich Hayek, *The Road to Serfdom* (Chicago: The University of Chicago Press, 1944).

to ruin with a new history of the cruel exercise of a power that no one before them had ever attained.

Hayek explained this catastrophe in his chilling chapter "Why the Worst Get on Top." It was no accident of time or place that the concentration of power over all human life in a centrally planned society attracted and rewarded the aggressive, unscrupulous, and demagogic, who would attract around them the simultaneously submissive and ruthless. Central planning brought forth leaders who took power not as a necessary evil but as an end in itself. Economic power over the whole lives of other persons, centralized as political power, created a society of slave masters and virtual slaves in which a leader's decisions about the good of the whole overrode all individualist ethics and law. Those limited by ethical prohibitions would flee power, and those who were, in Hayek's words, "literally capable of everything" would rise to high positions under a ruler whose primary passion in life was to be obeyed. Indeed, George Orwell's *Nineteen Eighty-Four* presented history and human nature far more deeply than Marx's vision of the abolition of power itself: "One does not establish a dictatorship in order to safeguard a revolution; one makes the revolution in order to establish the dictatorship.... The object of power is power."[13]

The Bolsheviks understood that Marx was wrong about the ineluctable development of revolutionary class consciousness among the working class. They fully embraced Lenin's idea of "false consciousness." The necessary first stage of the revolution would have to be a "dictatorship of the proletariat," and for the Bolsheviks, given the absence of anything resembling Marx's revolutionary proletariat, they themselves, objectively

---

[13] George Orwell, *Nineteen Eighty-Four* (New York: Everyman's Library, 1992), 276.

and scientifically, if not modestly, were in fact that proletariat and that dictatorship. Those who seized centralized total power had a cold contempt for the lives of all those who could not comprehend the communist blueprint. When that mass of ordinary benighted lives opposed or resisted them, that contempt became a willingness to kill in numbers that the mind can barely comprehend. The best of them became merely cynics. The worst of them, who indeed would rise to the top, became willing despots and henchmen. In the beginning, at least, they believed that history would be the judge of what they did. And since they alone understood history, they absolved themselves before the fact, and, as Hayek understood, they were literally capable of everything.

Did they ever really believe their early pronouncements of worker-controlled industries or a worker-elected judiciary in any sense other than substituting "Bolshevik" for "worker"? Who knows? But as soon as they met resistance, their meaning crystallized clearly and quickly. The peasantry paid for that contempt most dearly. To gain power, promise them the land they worked, but true Marxists, of course, don't believe in private property, so coerce them onto hated and disastrous collective farms that served only the purposes of the communist elites and their plans. If peasants resisted, they exiled, imprisoned, killed, or starved them into oblivion. With only history to judge you by ends, the means matter little. As Lenin wrote concerning the kulaks of Penza in his celebrated epistle of August 1918,

> Comrades! The insurrection of five kulak districts should
> be *pitilessly* suppressed. The interests of the *whole*
> revolution require this because 'the last decisive battle'

with the kulaks is now under way *everywhere*. An example must be demonstrated.

1. Hang (and make sure that the hanging takes place *in full view of the people*) *no fewer than one hundred* known kulaks, rich men, bloodsuckers.

2. Publish their names.

3. Seize *all* their grain from them.

4. Designate hostages in accordance with yesterday's telegram.

Do it in such a fashion that for hundreds of kilometers around the people might see, tremble, know, shout: *they are strangling* and will strangle to death the bloodsucking kulaks.

Telegraph receipt and *implementation*.

Yours, Lenin.

Find some truly hard people.[14]

They found tougher people, and the mass murder proceeded apace.

The stated goal of communism was to reap the economic, cultural, scientific, creative, and communal rewards of abolishing private property and free markets and to end human tyranny. The Marxists, ironically, always asked that forms of human society be judged not by their ideals, but by their living incarnations. We shall have an accounting of that at this conference.

The people knew that their new lords, for all their jargon, were ruthless and indifferent to actual suffering. They could not have imagined, however, the kinds of leaders into whose posturing, unfeeling, shameless,

---

[14] Robert Service, *Lenin: A Biography* (Cambridge, MA: The Belknap Press of Harvard University Press, 2000), 365.

self-serving hands they were falling. It would be inconceivable if it hadn't happened. As Koestler noted, "With no imperatives but the historical, they sail without ethical ballast,"[15] which would be catastrophic, indeed an immolation.

Communism taught that people in the same relationship to the means of production would follow similar paths eventually, whatever the national culture, which turned out to be only true of the communist leaders who had "solved" the problem of power. Russia might have been historically unique, but Stalin was not. Mao, the Kims, Ceaușescu, Hoxha, Mengistu, Pol Pot, Rákosi, Castro, and on, and on. Having proclaimed the abolition of tyranny and the self-government of the workers whose objective interests they alone embodied, why would the communists ever concern themselves with checks, balances, or the separation of powers, all of which they had denounced as a bourgeois façade over human wage slavery? Neither they nor their heirs believed that the individual was an independent variable. They had no psychology or sociology of individual power. With nothing to stop them or the psychopaths in their midst, they brought into power cold-blooded sociopaths acting out their fantasies, resentments, and hatreds. The worst indeed got on top, and the centralization of power over all aspects of men's and women's lives placed all weapons possible in their hands. They tyrannized continents and unleashed poisons across the earth.

They believed that they could bring into being the most productive societies humankind had ever known, surpassing the bounty of what they derided as bourgeois exploitation and waste, but in fact they only

---

[15] Arthur Koestler, *Darkness at Noon,* trans. Daphne Hardy (New York: MacMillan, 1941), 260.

surpassed, and this exponentially, all other systems of production in turning out the dead. Communists demanded that we not judge a Christian society, for example, by its ideals, but by its historical reality. The communist reality has been a legacy of tyranny, untold suffering, scarcity, murderous inefficiency, arbitrary inequality, cronyism, enslavement, concentration camps, torture, terror, the destruction of civil society, ecological disaster, brutal secret police, and systemic tyranny. In that case let us always judge them by their own criteria. In the end, their own subjects began to do just that.

Dr. Russell Roberts

It would be an interesting experience to go around and ask people what we've learned from communism. One lesson might be that communism was unable to solve the central challenge that faces an economy: how much stuff to make, how to produce it, what prices should be set, and how to do it in a way that matches the desires of the people. Communism's failure to meet that challenge could be summed up in a few different ways: "Not enough toilet paper," or "Communism couldn't deliver the goods," or, my favorite, the ironic Soviet remark, "We pretend to work, and they pretend to pay us."

A second lesson, related to Alan Charles Kors's remarks, is that centralized power leads to corruption. It's not just that even well-intentioned people struggle to produce the right amount of stuff and to make the people happy. The worst get on top.

The problem with these "lessons" is that we live in a world where most of the leaders of democratic nations are not like Stalin; they're well-intentioned, at least on the surface, and this encourages people to believe that we just need socialism or communism with a human face. We need to put decent people in charge of the economy and let them design that economy to serve the people rather than serve narrow self-interest and profit. If the main lessons to be learned are that centrally planned economies don't work very well and that we've had bad people at the top, people just assume that we ought to improve the horse and the jockey. If we can just do that, everything would be great—we'd go faster and we'd go in the direction we want to go.

Paul Gregory's reference to the polling of young people reminds me of what Milton Friedman told me when I interviewed him for my podcast *EconTalk*. I was crowing about the fact that economists had made an important contribution to the world because we had shown people that price controls don't work very well, and how there's not much demand for price controls when, say, gasoline prices are high. He responded that this wasn't the result of good economics, unfortunately, but was simply a result of the fact that there are a lot of people alive today who lived through the 1970s, and who know what happens under price controls. When those people die there will be a demand for price controls again. Millennials' passion for these ideals called communism or socialism is a consequence of them not knowing much about them. That is the nature of the world.

I think it is important to really get at the more crucial lesson of the fall of communism. I think if you ask most economists—not the average person—what we learned from the fall of communism, they would refer to what's called the socialist calculation debate in which Mises and Hayek argued against Oskar Lange and others who advocated for "scientific socialism." Mises and Hayek won that debate. The socialists claimed that we could replicate the incentives and feedback loops of a market economy by just picking the prices correctly, and Mises and Hayek said that that wasn't possible, that the information required to solve the problem is too vast. Even with today's computers we couldn't solve that problem; it's too intractable.

But why? How many economists could put into words why that vision of socialism with a scientific face is likely to fail even with today's supercomputers? How many economics majors could make that case? How many American citizens? Unfortunately, in all those cases, the answer is: relatively few. That's because it is not fully understood that the problem is not a calculation failure. It's not simply that a socialist or communist top-down system fails to pick prices and quantities carefully. An answer like that betrays a failed model and a failed understanding of how our economy, in most of its sectors, actually works and what it achieves.

Economies are grown, not assembled. Markets are grown, not mandated. There's a temptation to take the visible outcome of a market process, the prices and quantities, and presume that we just need humane, wise leaders to pick those more carefully, and thus improve on the undirected chaos of the free market. But this is impossible, not because we have insufficient information about what people desire, but because what they desire is unknown to them. This would be true even if we had time to interview them and compile their answers.

For me, the best metaphor of this process is an ecosystem. Most modern economists see the economy as an engine or a machine with levers and dials to manipulate. A more specific metaphor is a prairie. If you tried to build a prairie by assembling the species and the plants, you would fail miserably, because there's a complexity to the evolution of a prairie that is not well understood and that cannot be replicated from the top down. In particular, you would not know the order in which the various species are to be introduced. Most importantly, you would also be missing the fire. Without fire striking at random times, destroying certain species and making room for others, you will not get a prairie.

I would suggest we also don't know how to make a thriving market. We failed in the many places where we expected markets to grow automatically, like the post-Soviet countries. We did not appreciate the full range of order and fire that was needed. We didn't appreciate the role of culture in creating a vibrant organic market. Markets do not function at the intersection of supply-and-demand curves—that's just the way we represent them in Econ 101. I'm a big fan of supply and demand, but they're the wrong way to think about the complexity of the process; they don't capture it in its entirety. The failure to understand this leads people to conclude that what makes a market is incentives and that we just need to pick the prices correctly. That's not the case.

I want to argue that the "order" of the market emerges only from the process of voluntary exchange among the participating individuals. The "order" is, itself, defined as the outcome of the process that generates it. Yes, markets do use prices to incentivize behavior, but they do much more than that, and they do it in a way that is embedded in culture. Otherwise Wikipedia would not exist. The incentives aren't there, yet Wikipedia is a beautiful thing. People would never tip in a restaurant they didn't expect to visit again, yet they do. These phenomena are crucial, and the richness of a market process is crucial. James Buchanan, the Nobel laureate, was the person who understood this best in modern times. He wrote:

I want to argue that the "order" of the market emerges only from the process of voluntary exchange among the participating individuals. The "order" is, itself, defined as the outcome of the process that generates it. The "it," the allocation-distribution result, does not, and cannot, exist independently of the trading process. Absent this process, there is and can be no "order."[16]

Now, this confusion over these ideas rears its ugliest head when we hear about market solutions to, say, prison provision (where a private prison contractor does the service), or to government schools (where a business is put in charge of a charter system), as if these are somehow market processes because there are prices involved. They're not markets; they're imposed by government, and so they don't work the way markets do. The worst example, of course, is healthcare, where the government's intervention in Medicaid and Medicare—the subsidization of private health insurance and the control over the number of doctors—creates a hodge-podge that makes people conclude that markets don't work, as if what we observe in the US healthcare system is a market process. And yet smart people will say that this proves that we need a government healthcare system. These are not market solutions. Market solutions would be for the government to get out of the business, not just of provision, but of financing and innovation.

The perspective I'm suggesting here is alien to the modern economist and the modern economic toolkit for making the world a better place. I think most economists are dangerous. We actually believe we have

---

[16] James M. Buchanan, in "Readers' Forum: Comments on 'The Tradition of Spontaneous Order' by Norman Barry," *Literature of Liberty* 5, no. 4 (1982): 5–18.

the tools to steer the economy and make people's lives better. And we forget that our incentives to believe in those systems are distorted by the fact that we are often the beneficiaries of that process. Something like 25 percent of the macroeconomists in the United States think they have a chance to be the head of the Federal Reserve—what is their incentive to be critical of the Fed as an institution? It is very small. The actual truth is there are only about five candidates. They hope to benefit from it someday. Economists are very good at analyzing the incentive effects of others but not so honest about their own incentives.

I will close with my favorite quote from F. A. Hayek, which I think summarizes the key lesson of what we have learned, and what we should learn from the failure of communism: "The curious task of economics is to demonstrate to men how little we know about what we imagine we can design."[17] Alas, most economists and policy makers have yet to learn that lesson.

Discussion

Audience: What part, if any, did the opening of the oil flood gates, that is to say, the increase in oil production in Saudi Arabia from two million to ten million barrels per day, have in hitting the Soviet economy? Conversely, what was the role of political will, the readiness to say, "We win, they lose"? Lastly, what was the role of the personal relationships between American and Soviet leaders?

---

[17] Friedrich Hayek, *The Fatal Conceit: The Errors of Socialism* (Chicago: The University of Chicago Press, 1988), 76

Paul R. Gregory: In 1980, fifty of the most distinguished specialists on the Soviet economy met at Airlie House and discussed the prospects of the Soviet Union through the year 2000. At that point, the answer was very unclear. But what was noted by Evsey Domar of MIT was that our economy was afflicted by stagflation at the time. This was only the beginning of the Reagan administration. In my view what made the difference was not Star Wars missile defense or anything like that but that, after that, the American economy took off. And had that not happened, had the US economy remained in the doldrums, I think we would not have had the success that we did have.

Russell Roberts: I think there is a mystery at the heart of your question. I'm an economist, so I don't have any problem saying that Reagan and Thatcher were extremely important, and the pope was extremely important. Obviously, that is all true. But I think it's really interesting that really smart people thought that it would never happen. Now we look back and laugh because they were wrong. But that doesn't change the fact that the fall of the Soviet Union really was unprecedented in human history— that people with great power did not fight almost to the death to maintain it.

My favorite personal story about the essence of the Soviet economy is that in the 1990s there was an exodus of Jewish families out of the Soviet Union. My family served as a host family for one of these families, despite the fact that we couldn't speak Russian and had a hard time communicating with them. We took them to the grocery store; the first thing we did, of course, was that we went to the produce section, where they wanted to linger. It was so beautiful to them; they treated it like it was a museum. At some point, it became clear to me that the wife wanted to make bread. We found the flour; now she needed yeast. Yeast is hard to find in a grocery store because it is very small. We looked around everywhere and couldn't find it, so I went over and asked an employee where it was. We found the spot where it was supposed to be, and it turned out that they were out. The employee says, "Well, let me go in the back and I'll check to see if there's any more there," and comes back with some yeast. Of course, I was relieved. But I looked over at the woman and I realized that she now thought that her host family was very important— the kind of people for whom they bring out the yeast from the back of the store.

That's a revealing story. You realize that she was accustomed to a situation where there were a bunch of people who got the yeast every day, but most people didn't get any because there wasn't enough yeast to go around. That kind of system usually sustains itself because the people who get the yeast also have the guns. To have a system like that end without bloodshed of the direct kind is an occurrence without historical analogue. I think we often fail to appreciate that. We believe the collapse was inevitable for economic or military reasons, but it was really quite extraordinary.

Audience: What do you think about the policy of détente that was a very fashionable part of political discourse in the years leading up to the collapse of communism, and about the language of "peaceful coexistence between states with different social and political systems"?

Alan Charles Kors: If détente meant doing what one must do to avoid nuclear war and looking for the remaining options, then it was in a sense successful. But détente was much more than that, culturally. It was the cause of the moment that made me most ashamed of being American: when Solzhenitsyn came to D.C. and, following Kissinger's advice, President Ford did not admit him to the White House for fear of upsetting the Russians. That was the disgraceful side of détente.

It was also a set of attitudes that could not, I think, have sustained and won the Cold War. In those days, all of academia was against the Reaganite prosecution of the Cold War, as well as all of our media, filmmakers, television stars, and shows. When *Red Dawn* came out, there were reviews accusing it of being political pornography. A culture that does not believe in itself will not push over even the most tottering of its competitive regimes. What won the Cold War ultimately was that ordinary Americans—not our elites, not our media, not our professors or textbooks—understood that there was a difference between freedom, in which you make an extraordinary number of decisions for yourself, and communism, in which thugs make those decisions for you.

Russell Roberts: There's a story that I used to think was apocryphal, but I now believe is probably true and probably even happened more than once. A Soviet delegation comes to the United States and is meeting with its counterparts—I heard this story from someone who was at this meeting—and at one point a Soviet minister of finance takes an American Treasury official off to the side and says conspiratorially, "Who really does set the prices? Obviously, you don't want us to know who it is, but I'd really like to get some suggestions." It is possible that the Soviets actually thought that our economy was so much more successful because we just had better jockeys, to use Paul Gregory's metaphor, and that they just had to figure out how to use the whip a little better. When the Treasury official laughed at them and said, "Nobody sets the prices. It's up to the individual entrepreneur and businesspeople, and they're forced by competition to set prices that make stuff available to people in great profusion," maybe that sowed some doubt in the visitors' minds about the soundness of their system. I wonder if the exposure to our economy—which must have been terribly educational for them—did not cause them to lose some faith in their system. It wasn't just a matter of executing better but rather that there was a fundamental flaw at the root of their economic worldview. With détente, too, while there were disgraceful things about it, I think that the cultural interchange that it involved had some impacts that we don't appreciate on the Soviets themselves.

Paul Hollander: I was among the many people who didn't expect the Soviet system to fall, and as a result, I devoted a book to trying to understand it better: *Political Will and Personal Belief,* which came out in 1999.[18] My main point was that the Soviet leadership's belief in the system had been undermined and weakened in a very gradual process that began with Khrushchev's speech at the 20th Congress. I argue that it was mainly an internal process, not caused by the good things the United States or the pope or Reagan did. Yes, of course there were these economic reasons that were aggravated by the arms race, but an internal decline in belief led to an internal decline in the will to repress.

Paul R. Gregory: The Soviet system committed suicide. It was not overthrown. The *nomenklatura*—which was in control of the resources,

---

[18] Paul Hollander, *Political Will and Personal Belief: The Decline and Fall of Soviet Communism* (New Haven: Yale University Press, 1999).

the oil fields, the metals, and so forth—understood that transitioning to another system would allow them to control these resources, and, in fact, to be even better off; they would be the billionaires of the future. Political scientists have studied the survival of this elite.

Alan Charles Kors: If we had seen the unraveling of the Chinese communist regime in the wake of Tiananmen, we would give all the same explanations: the failure of Mao's economics, the loss of belief among the Chinese *nomenklatura*. But I will go back to the point I made about what kind of human beings are generated by a system. And there, there was great fortune: Gorbachev and, above all, Alexander Yakovlev understood that there was something rotten at the center of Soviet life and the Soviet system. But if they had been willing to do what the Chinese leadership was willing to do—to kill as many people as they needed to, with no faith in Mao's economics, with no faith in the society that was around you, simply their own will to power—the Soviet regime, absent Gorbachev and Yakovlev, could easily have thrown up someone willing to let those tanks fire. And if those tanks fire, everything changes.

Russell Roberts: I want to make one more cultural comment, because I think it is really important as an economist to emphasize that material wellbeing is not the only thing that motivates people. I don't want anything I said today to be misunderstood to suggest that that's the case. I do think the American standard of living had an educational impact on the Soviets, but here's another side of it: A friend of mine from the former Soviet Union, when asked how he was doing, would say, "Fine, like all Americans." Russians don't say "fine"—they shrug, they make a face. I suspect there was a cultural impact from American life that went far beyond the size of our cars and houses and the profusion of fresh fruit and fresh vegetables in grocery stores, namely the vitality of our system and its rewards in terms of satisfaction and meaning. You can see that on the faces of Americans when you come from a society that is as gray and undynamic as the Soviet system of the 1970s and 1980s.

Don Ritter: I served in Congress during this historic period and was very much engaged as a senior ranking member of the Helsinki Commission. I want to suggest that, among all the factors we have discussed today, the war in Afghanistan proved to be extremely debilitating to this *nomenklatura*. They breathed the ether of superpower invincibility; they came home consistently in body bags. When Gorbachev came in in 1985, he promised to bomb the living daylights out of Afghanistan, and it started to work. We knew that you had to neutralize the Soviet air power, particularly helicopters, which would hover over the battle space and destroy the resistance. So we put Stingers in there. When the Soviets could not win in Afghanistan, when they left with their tail between their legs, with General Gromov going over the bridge at Termez, that was a seminal moment of their downfall militarily. The superpower was beaten by a fourth-world power (with our assistance, of course, and that of others). The rest is history. But the Afghan resistance, with 1.5 million Afghans dead in that war of terrible attrition, should be factored into our calculus regarding the downfall of the Soviet Union.

Audience: I'd like to ask how we should approach the destruction of the economy in countries like Venezuela and elsewhere in Latin America, which seems closely tied to a communist approach to governance.

Paul R. Gregory: Unfortunately, we have a new phenomenon, which is a decoupling of political power and economic performance. This has been demonstrated in North Korea, where you can have a subsistence economy along with a dynastic regime. I fear that the same is going on in Venezuela and other parts of Latin America. We can no longer count on economic collapse to bring down a dictatorial regime.

Russell Roberts: I argue that empty shelves always mean price controls—always. The Venezuelan government has tried to steer their economy and they've failed miserably. It is a tragically illuminating example of the civilizing force of voluntary exchange. Civilization is breaking down in Venezuela: people are killing other people and fighting to get bread in that system. We forget how thin the veneer is that protects us from that. That includes, among other things, our price system and our economy. It works and it is precious. We don't treat it that way.

Paul R. Gregory: But Russ, if the Venezuelan people were 100 percent economically literate, could they stand up to the dictatorial system?

Russell Roberts: No, they could not, which is why we are blessed to live here and not there. But it would be even worse if our citizens learned the wrong lessons from Venezuela and push us further in that direction.

Alan Charles Kors: I would just add very quickly that I don't think the Hugo Chávez or Maduro regime survives without Cuban secret police, Cuban organization, and Cuban advisors.

Yaroslav Martynyuk: During the 1980s, I worked for a unit of Radio Liberty in Paris called "Soviet Area Audience and Opinion Research." We did research interviewing Soviet citizens who found themselves in Western Europe. My findings revealed several factors that contributed to the fall of the Soviet Union that the experts at that time overlooked completely. Sovietologists and Kremlinologists looked at what was happening in the Soviet Union through the prism of the Moscow press, changes in the Kremlin hierarchy, *etc.* However, our public opinion research gave us information on what the Soviet people were thinking. The three overlooked factors included, first of all, the nationalities question. Very few people studied that because they believed the Soviet Union had solved the nationalities problem. The second factor that contributed immensely to the fall of the Soviet Union were the so-called "freedom radios," especially Radio Liberty and the Voice of America, which penetrated the Iron Curtain and had the effect of tunneling a fort. We all know the story, but the experts discounted the effect. The third factor, which based on my experience at the International Energy Agency I think was the last nail in the coffin, was the price of oil. After the 1973 oil crisis, crude oil quadrupled in price; the Iranian Revolution in 1979 tripled it; it reached a level of about $40 a barrel. For the Soviet Union, that oil revenue was a lifeline. But by the mid-1980s, the price dropped from $40 a barrel to $10, which made it impossible to continue the war in Afghanistan or to control Eastern Europe. That was probably one of the most important factors that contributed to the demise of the Soviet Union.

Soviet Totalitarianism,
the Captive Mind, and Uncivil Society

Dr. F. Flagg Taylor IV

In the spirit of some of the comments made during this conference, especially those of Professor Kors, I want to provide a quotation from an unjustly neglected Sovietologist named Waldemar Gurian. He once wrote, "A living lie—and that is the tragedy of human life—is superior, as force, to a dead truth."[19] It's a rather melancholy reflection, but I think it expresses something true about human life—and suggests the importance of the work that the Victims of Communism Memorial Foundation does.

Defined strictly, a totalitarian regime is one that bans all political and social activity that is not expressly approved by the state. Such regimes aspire to total control of their population in order to create a totally unified society. They do not permit any autonomous activity by societal or civil organizations. All such organizations are either banned or co-opted by the ruling party. Totalitarian regimes gain their legitimacy by claiming to be unerring actors in fulfilling historical laws. They claim in a sense to be

---

[19] Waldemar Gurian, "Trends in Modern Politics," *The Review of Politics* 2, no. 3 (July 1940): 336.

more lawful and even more rightly ordered than any regime in human history.

Once in power, such parties must demonstrate that their rule is justified. They must display for their citizens that the socialism once promised is being realized. Because reality proves to be recalcitrant, a vast and complex system emerges to engage people in a demonstration of socialism's presence and power. Only the pseudo-reality, or the ideological lie, is allowed public recognition. All public human interactions are infused by the dictates of ideology.

Václav Havel argued that this is what gives totalitarian regimes their distinctive brand of oppression. They force people to become pillars of the system that oppresses them. People must constantly conform their speech and actions to fit the demands of the party. This can mean publicly affirming the guilt of someone whom you know to be innocent, attending a May Day parade, or in Havel's paradigmatic example, placing a placard in your shop window that reads, "Workers of the World, Unite!"[20] Thus an elaborate network of appearances, rituals, and patterns of speech are developed to legitimate the fiction of a flourishing socialist regime. This is what the great philosopher and historian Alain Besançon identified as the moral destruction of communism.

Now the consistency and pervasiveness of the mendacity can be appalling, but only if one's faculties do not become numb and one is able to see the fictions for what they really are. This is how captive minds were fashioned and civil society was crushed. The philosopher Hannah Arendt once wrote, "The ideal subject of totalitarian rule is not the convinced Nazi

---

[20] Václav Havel, "The Power of the Powerless," in *Open Letters: Selected Writings 1965–1990*, ed. Paul Wilson (New York: Alfred A. Knopf, 1991), 132.

or the convinced communist, but people for whom the distinction between fact and fiction, and the distinction between true and false no longer exist."[21] Today we will hear about how some particularly courageous people sought to resist such systems and how and why they decided, in Aleksandr Solzhenitsyn's wonderful phrase, "to live not by lies."

Hon. Natan Sharansky

Looking back on the history of the Helsinki movement, many seem to think that it was so important that the Soviet Union had no choice but to follow it. But the dissidents of the Soviet Union did not consider the signing and publication of the Helsinki Final Act a victory. On the contrary, we saw it as one more proof of the betrayal by the Free World of their human rights cause.

Why? First, because it recognized existing borders. For the first time, the Free World recognized the occupation of Lithuania, Latvia, and Estonia, and all of what had happened with eastern Europe. They said, "That's yours—that's the Soviet Union and we're not going to challenge it anymore." The second aspect was the agreement on economic cooperation, when in reality the Soviet Union was so weak from the inside that it fully depended on the cooperation and assistance of the Free World. Finally, there was the third basket, on human rights, but we expected that any statements made about human rights would be nothing but lip service.

The Soviet Union had always won out when the West spoke of human rights. They would say, "You have your understanding of human

---

[21] Hannah Arendt, *The Origins of Totalitarianism,* new ed. (San Diego: Harvest Books, 1994), 474.

rights, and we have ours. You speak about freedom of speech and we speak about the freedom not to be hungry. We make sure nobody's hungry and everybody is employed. Your so-called freedom is the freedom to die of hunger under a bridge," or some other such phrase. This was the '60s and '70s, so we hoped that practically nobody still believed in the Soviet paradise, that awful dream that got so many people killed—the thought of a world of equality without any nations, religions, or opportunity. We were fairly sure that the Free World no longer believed in the nobility of these ideas. But they saw the Soviet Union as a bully, as an extremely powerful and nuclear-armed country, and decided that it was necessary to find a way to cooperate with it.

I started by having discussions with Andrei Amalrik and Yuri Orlov. Amalrik is the dissident who in 1969 wrote the book *Will the Soviet Union Survive Until 1984?*[22] *1984* was chosen because of Orwell but also because it was fifteen years from 1969. Amalrik described how weak the Soviet Union was from inside, how it spent all its energy controlling the brains of its people, and he argued it would inevitably fall apart. We felt how weak it was, but the West looked at the Soviet Union and saw how powerful it was. Yuri Orlov was one of the great Soviet scientists who followed Andrei Sakharov and whose success in science didn't stop him from speaking freely.

So, I proposed as a goal of our Soviet freedom movement that we try to involve the public opinion of the West in a discussion about how we understood the concept of human rights. We had to find common ground and make the topic so publicly discussed that there would be no way for

---

[22] Andrei Amalrik, *Will the Soviet Union Survive until 1984?* (New York: Harper and Row, 1970).

the Soviet Union to avoid it. We believed that in another month or two the Soviet Union would be able to take the conversation into a very dangerous place that would reduce any agreement on human rights to nothing but lip service. So, we started preparing such a letter, an appeal to the public representatives of other countries to start a sort of discussion club that talked about what the concept of human rights meant. And then suddenly the authorities gave Amalrik permission to leave.

I was meeting with Yuri Orlov and asked him how the letter was coming along, and he responded, "Natan, I don't want any letters. There will be more talk and more talk and more talk. If we really want to have influence, we need to declare that we are creating the Helsinki Watch and start publishing documents about specific cases within the Soviet Union. And if it is successful, if these documents related to the Helsinki Agreement draw attention, then we will show the real face of the Soviet Union and it will be more difficult for the West to deceive itself."

Yuri said, "Of course we will be arrested, and this time it will be for high treason, but at least we will make our statement; we will make our case." I told him, "I think you're wrong—I think they will arrest us for anti-Soviet activity"—which didn't incur the death penalty, only seven years imprisonment — "but you're probably right about the need to create it, so let's do it." In fact, a year later, we were all arrested. The irony was that I was arrested for high treason; he was arrested for anti-Soviet activity.

But during those eleven months between our arrest or exile and the creation of the Helsinki Group, what happened? First of all, our documents got a lot of attention, and the Ukrainian Helsinki Group and then the Lithuanian Helsinki Group were created. The documents also got a lot of attention in the American Congress. Congresswoman Millicent

Fenwick created her own Helsinki Group. At some point, I got a note from the American political attaché informing me that I no longer had to pass him these documents in secret, like before. He had received instructions from the Carter administration to receive these documents from our group and to bring them to the American administration. The other thing that happened, because Voice of America broadcasted not only our documents but also our names and addresses, was that people started coming from all over the Soviet Union with their problems straight to our homes.

There was no internet, so it took a lot of time to compile and disseminate each document. We were really working day and night. It suddenly changed the atmosphere. People started discussing these documents as the real face of the Soviet Union. There were documents about Jewish emigration, documents about Pentecostals, documents about Catholics in Lithuania, the Crimea and the Tatars, and many other human rights causes and violations. When we were arrested it was already very difficult to avoid the discussion of these issues. And ultimately, the Helsinki Process, which continued for years, ended up being primarily about not the first or second baskets, but all about human rights and linking the first basket and the second basket with the third.

Of course, the main question we had was whether the West would understand that the Soviet Union was not such a powerful superpower. It felt hopeless for every dissident. The best moment of my nine years in the Gulag was when President Reagan made his speech about the Evil Empire. Of course, we didn't hear his speech, but if you weren't in the punishment cell, you could read the Soviet newspaper *Pravda*. There was an article condemning President Reagan—how dare he make such an awful speech? It broke all the laws, all the rules of diplomatic relations, and so on. We were elated. Finally, the leader of the Free World had called the Soviet Union by its name. We thought that if the West understood the nature of the Soviet Union and the desire of its people to live in freedom, this would be a powerful non-conventional weapon against the Soviet Union. The days of the Soviet Union were numbered.

Three years later I was released, and I came to Washington and of course went to President Reagan to thank him for the role he played not just in my personal case but also in the fate of many others. When I told him how happy he had made all of us with this speech, he called all of his aides over and had them listen to what I was saying. Then I understood that he had been under strong criticism from his inner circle for making a speech like that because people had felt that it was a violation of all international norms. I think it is very important to remember that speaking the truth is important not only when you are a dissident in the Soviet Union, but also when you are the president of the United States of America.

Hon. Dr. Paula J. Dobriansky

What are the primary policy implications of the activities of various anti-communist and pro-freedom movements of past decades? There are eight lessons I would like to outline; these are derived from my experience as a foreign policy practitioner, having worked on the National Security Council at the White House in the Reagan administration. The key lesson from my experience—that the United States does not only espouse the principles of freedom but we also act on them—is as relevant today as it was then.

First, ideas and words matter. In this forum, you have already heard many references to President Ronald Reagan's speeches. They were quite inspirational. They fostered the hope that you heard Mr. Sharansky speak of: the hope that he felt when he was in the Gulag and was able to learn about Reagan's speeches. They provided hope to the activists and movements behind the Iron Curtain: hope that they were not alone in their struggle for freedom; that they were very much connected to the West; that we had not forgotten them; and that we would not stop protesting their imprisonment and the brutal treatment they were subjected to until they were released. The Evil Empire speech that President Reagan delivered on March 8, 1983, was one of his most powerful and memorable speeches because of its content, clarity, and directness. It was a speech that truly had an impact.

Second, human rights have been integral to US foreign policy from administration to administration. We have used many different mechanisms to shine continuously a spotlight on human rights issues. One example is the annual human rights report on the human rights performance of various governments, which is now well known and something that all countries look to for documentation. Although Moscow initially rejected a dialogue with the US on human rights, the report was something concrete that could be used to underscore the importance of the topic in our foreign policy discourse. There were countless times when the president, the secretary of state, congressional delegations, the assistant secretary of state for European affairs, or an ambassador in country would highlight a list of human rights cases. Over the years, the annual report has mattered greatly, because it documented and detailed cases and has demonstrated that these issues are integral to our foreign policy.

Third, there was the deployment of sanctions and establishment of conditionality. This definitely benefited dissident movements. In some cases, there were actual *quid pro quos*. For example, in the Jackson-Vanik amendment of 1974, preferential trade treatment for the Soviet Union and the lifting of trade barriers on certain goods was put forward to ensure the free flow of those Jews who wanted to emigrate from the Soviet Union and central and eastern Europe. Another example is the US response to the Polish regime's imposition of martial law between 1981 and 1983 and its attempt to crush the Solidarity movement. US sanctions were imposed not only against the Polish government but also against the Soviet Union. The most-favored-nation status of Poland was also suspended, and Poland's application for membership in the IMF was vetoed. These were tangible, concrete foreign policy measures that demonstrated that human rights issues and freedom mattered.

Fourth, effective foreign policy combines elements of realism and idealism. This was manifested during the Reagan administration's talks on arms control with Moscow. We conducted arms control negotiations with Moscow, but this did not sideline our human rights concerns. Moscow would frequently say, "This is not on our agenda, and we're not discussing it." Nevertheless, US officials persevered and always raised human rights issues. We successfully pursued a foreign policy at all levels that was both realistic and maintained our steadfast commitment to American values.

Fifth, multilateral diplomacy can be effective. The Helsinki Commission is a good example. This was a forum and a platform within which we highlighted the cases of dissident activists and the punishments they suffered. A chorus of nations and institutions speaking out collectively on behalf of human rights violations can make a real

difference. We even see it today. The Conference on Security and
Cooperation in Europe (CSCE) with its three baskets is now the
Organization for Security and Cooperation in Europe (OSCE), and it still
plays a crucial role in elections monitoring. The OSCE is also relied upon
by governments and human rights organizations to assess the current
conditions in Crimea—information that has been difficult to obtain, as
OSCE officials have been denied access.

Sixth, presidential statements and congressional resolutions
marking commemorative occasions or important historic dates have
mattered greatly. Human Rights Day on December 10 and Captive Nations
Week (the third week of July) are important. Starting with President
Eisenhower, every president, right up through the present, has issued a
Captive Nations Week Proclamation, which addresses the continued
repression of basic freedoms globally and deals with the very issues we're
discussing here today. From 1959 to the present, Public Law 86-90 has
been respected and implemented. Why does it matter? It keeps the issue
of human rights and freedom in the forefront of the global community. It
underscores that these issues are integral to US foreign policy: they matter
to us. Our strong and consistent voice buoys and motivates dissident
movements. Essentially, there has been a consistent policy framework
from 1959 to the present.

Second to last, assistance programs to opposition activists matter.
For example, when Solidarity was born, institutions such as CARE
(Cooperative for American Relief Everywhere) and the Catholic Relief
Service received funding from the US government at a very crucial time
during martial law. The National Endowment for Democracy, which
President Reagan launched and the creation of which he announced at

Westminster Palace during his visit to London in 1982, was absolutely crucial. What kinds of programs do they fund? One that I remember very specifically involved a dissident group in the Soviet Union that simply wanted the Universal Declaration of Human Rights translated into Russian so the text could be widely disseminated and people would know their rights.

Finally, consistent foreign policies maintained through consecutive administrations matter. With former President Landsbergis of Lithuania here today, I am reminded of one policy enunciated consistently decade after decade, administration after administration: the US non-recognition policy of the forced incorporation of the Baltic states into the Soviet Union. Former Undersecretary of State Sumner Welles issued the Welles Declaration in 1940, condemning the Soviet occupation of the Baltic states; this policy lasted through 1991 and continues to the present time.

These lessons demonstrate that democracy promotion and advancement of human rights causes is both doable and eminently workable. It is the key core component of any sound American foreign policy.

Hon. Dr. Martin Palouš

This year, I have had several opportunities to speak and write about Charter 77's fortieth anniversary, but I do so with certain feelings of absurdity about my situation—that of assuming the role of a guide in a museum in which I also function as one of the objects on display. Can someone who himself personally participated in certain events become a reliable observer capable of unbiased critical analysis? Having said that, I am well aware that I am not the only one who runs into such difficulties; it is a general methodological problem accompanying all attempts to examine phenomena belonging to the field of contemporary history, which are too close not only to their participants, but also to their historians. Thus it is difficult even for those historians to dissociate the object of their study from their own attachment to it, to look at it from a safe distance and tell— truly and reliably, *sine ira et studio—"wie es eigentlich gewesen ist."*[23] With this in mind, what I offer in this paper is not a comprehensive analysis of the history of Charter 77, but just a couple of personal remarks, historical reminiscences, and general observations.

What was Charter 77? I will start by recalling the basic facts leading to its creation. In a nutshell, it was the collective reaction of a relatively small group of Czechoslovak citizens to the reality and policies of the totalitarian regime in power in Czechoslovakia from the communist "Victorious February" of 1948 until its sudden collapse during the "Velvet Revolution" of November 1989. The initial declaration of Charter 77 was signed by 242 individuals, and the total number of signatories who joined this "civic initiative" between 1977 and 1990 was fewer than two thousand.

The key turning point in the history of this regime was a failed attempt to liberalize it—or at least "to endow this regime with a human face"—during the Prague Spring of 1968. As Václav Havel pointed out in his essay "Stories and Totalitarianism," there was a remarkable difference between the revolutionary ethos and terror of the Stalinist 1950s and the depressive, deadening atmosphere — "dull inertia, pretext-ridden caution,

---

[23] The famous dictum of Leopold von Ranke (1795–1886), the founder of German historicism in the nineteenth century.

bureaucratic anonymity, and mindless, stereotypical behaviour"[24]—of the "normalization" era of the 1970s and 1980s. The latter spread throughout Czechoslovak society like a plague after the defeat of the attempted "rejuvenation" of the socialist system—an attempt that Soviet leaders in Moscow and their local cronies considered a "counterrevolution."

In its original version, the defining feature of the totalitarian communist regime in Czechoslovakia was a combination of idealistic hopes for a better world with the use of brute force and physical violence:

> In the fifties there were enormous concentration camps in Czechoslovakia filled with tens of thousands of innocent people. At the same time, building sites were swarming with tens of thousands of young enthusiasts of the new faith singing songs of socialist construction. There were tortures and executions, dramatic flights across borders, conspiracies, and at the same time, panegyrics were being written to the chief dictator.[25]

A society that had been essentially "open" before World War II was forcibly "closed" after the communist constitutional *coup d'état* of February 1948 (the Nazi occupation of 1939–1945 had obviously already strongly undermined Czechoslovakia's "openness"). The building of the radiant socialist future foreseen in Marxist-Leninist ideology was accompanied by the ruthless and oppressive policies of the Communist Party, which had seized total power and had started to mercilessly

---

[24] Václav Havel, "Stories and Totalitarianism," in *Open Letters: Selected Writings 1965–1990*, ed. Paul Wilson (New York: Alfred A. Knopf, 1991), 331.
[25] Havel, "Stories and Totalitarianism," 331.

eliminate all its enemies, whether real or existing only in the wild revolutionary imagination of its members.

Of course, it was not only the immoderate lust for power or the blind conviction and commitment of the "young enthusiasts of the new faith"[26] that sent Czechoslovak democracy into the abyss. Czechoslovak communists certainly played their role, but the real historical force behind their success was the Soviet Union, the territorial and political gains of which had to be recognized in postwar Europe and the emerging global influence of which was also reflected in the American policy of "containment."

In Havel's description, however, in spite of the fact that the 1950s are, in retrospect, a "nightmare," there was something in this period that was surprisingly "positive." While the closing of Czechoslovak society— the systematic destruction of all its institutions, structures, and intermediary bodies, in Tocqueville's sense—was carried out by brutal and ruthless means, this "revolutionary transformation" took place in an environment that was still non-totalitarian.

The lifestyle and self-presentations of the communist leaders themselves—who enthusiastically assumed the role of "millenarian tyrants"[27] commissioned by history to destroy the bourgeois democracy of

---

[26] Havel, "Stories and Totalitarianism," 331.

[27] I am referring here to the taxonomy of tyrants presented in the recent book by Waller Newell, *Tyrants: A History of Power, Injustice & Terror* (Cambridge: Cambridge University Press, 2016). Newell distinguishes among three basic types of tyrants: the "garden variety" (who rule over entire countries as if they are their personal property); "tyrant-reformers" (rulers who rule their states with an iron fist in the intention of making them powerful, prosperous, and great again); and finally "millenarian tyrants": "These rulers are neither content to be mere garden-variety tyrants, gluttons, and exploiters, nor even to be reforming tyrants who make constructive improvements. They are driven by the impulse to impose a

the past—still bore some traces of the old, prerevolutionary world. It was this "ancestral" aspect that gave the beginning phase of Czechoslovak totalitarianism its specific "local color" and, if we can use this word in view of the enormous suffering experienced by thousands of innocent people, its "flavor":

> The song of idealists and fanatics, political criminals on the rampage, the suffering of heroes, these have always been part of history. The fifties were a bad time in Czechoslovakia, but there have been many such times in human history. It still shared something, or at least bore comparison with those other periods; it still resembled history. No one could have said that nothing was happening, or that the age did not have its stories.[28]

What was not entirely missing in the 1950s, and what took on more perceptible and socially significant forms after the Stalinist nightmare, was hope for the future. When people began to feel and perceive the signs of a new day, there emerged a dimension of the human condition that, despite everything, was still able to impart meaning to human life: the fundamental sense of historical continuity and the faith that the irreversible losses of the past could be healed, or at least saved from oblivion, by means of storytelling. It was this attitude that helped people see the light at the end of the tunnel, even when there was no real reason to believe that the communist regime would collapse and when it turned

---

millenarian blueprint that will bring about a society of the future in which the individual will be submerged in the collective and all privilege and alienation will forever be eradicated" (4).

[28] Havel, "Stories and Totalitarianism," 331.

out that the American intervention that so many speculated about during the 1950s was nothing more than sheer illusion.

This same state of mind nourished the social and political changes of the 1960s. During the Prague Spring of 1968, it made the vast majority of Czechs and Slovaks believe, even when they saw Soviet tanks in the streets of Prague and other cities in August of that year, that socialism— whatever this word meant for them—was reformable after all: central Europeans were not doomed to remain forever—as Milan Kundera wrote in 1984, reflecting on Czechoslovak experience of 1968—the "victims and outsiders" of world history.[29]

The 1970s and 1980s saw the end of this hope, the unpleasant discovery that there was no saving bridge over the gap between the past and the future, that central Europe had indeed found herself at a dead end of history. The bipolar political architecture of the Cold War turned out to be much more influential in shaping her destiny than the desire of central Europeans to actively participate, at least in some limited way, in its creation. The period of "normalization" in Czechoslovakia started not at the moment of the Soviet occupation, but when the huge majority of Czechs and Slovaks simply gave up and conformed to their historical lot— by either willingly cooperating with a rehashed ruling power or retreating to the private sphere of their lives and succumbing to passivity. The spirit

---

[29] Milan Kundera, "The Tragedy of Central Europe," *The New York Review of Books*, April 26, 1984: "Central Europe, as a family of small nations, has its own vision of the world, a vision of deep mistrust of history ... history, that goddess of Hegel and Marx, that incarnation of reason that judges us and arbitrates our fate, that is the history of conquerors. The peoples of Central Europe are not conquerors. They cannot be separated from European history. They cannot exist outside of it. But they represent the wrong side of history. They are its victims and outsiders."

of 1968 was eclipsed in 1969 by the "captive mind" named and analyzed by the Polish poet Czesław Miłosz.[30] The regime that emerged under these circumstances served, as Václav Havel pointed out in 1986, "as a textbook illustration of how an advanced or late totalitarian system works."[31] It depends "on manipulatory devices so refined, complex, and powerful that it no longer needs murderers and victims. Even less does it need fiery utopia-builders spreading discontent with dreams of a better future. The epithet 'Real Socialism,' which this era has coined to describe itself, points a finger at those for whom it has no room: the dreamers."[32] In other words: in a desperate effort to adapt itself to given geopolitical conditions, specifically the influence of an external totalitarian power, Czechoslovak totalitarianism dramatically changed its style and external manifestations.

First, what was lost entirely was the revolutionary character of totalitarian government. Although politically it uncompromisingly adhered to the dogma of the "leading role of the Communist Party," it dropped its intention to transform the existing social and political order according to the Marxist-Leninist blueprint. It "set itself a single aim: self-preservation."[33] Acts of open violence intended to physically destroy the defeated social classes and draconian policies intended to build a new world were no more. The "normalization" regime was created by unprincipled opportunists who simply desired to keep themselves in power by any means necessary and were ready to make practically any turn, as far as the system of their beliefs was concerned, to achieve this goal.

---

[30] Czesław Miłosz, *The Captive Mind,* trans. Jane Zielonko (New York: Knopf, 1953).
[31] Havel, "Stories and Totalitarianism," 331.
[32] Havel, "Stories and Totalitarianism," 332.
[33] Havel, "Stories and Totalitarianism," 331.

With the exception of a relatively small group of "counterrevolutionaries," who incurred exemplary punishment, the population was offered the possibility of preserving their own wellbeing and a relatively safe and undisturbed existence. The ticket one had to buy to ride this train was quite cheap, and the vast majority of people were easily persuaded. No class origin, no conviction, no commitment, not even difficult moral choices, were required to get on board—just a formal agreement with Soviet occupation and an at least tacit consent to the basic goals of "normalization": the readiness to give up all ideals and noble visions and to just play the game and be flexible enough to adapt oneself to the requirements of the new situation.

The ruling power simply offered to the ruled a kind of bizarre "social contract"—a contract in a way comparable to the arrangements that political philosophers describe as being behind the modern state: a relatively undisturbed private life and even some personal benefits in exchange for loyalty to the regime and acceptance of its understanding of what political order means.

Here the history of totalitarianism made a remarkable full circle. It began in the 1920s by critiquing the "bourgeois" ideal of private liberties and the liberal claim for freedom from politics.[34] First, the Italian Fascists and the German Nazis emphasized the necessity of building a strong state and strived to impose a new concept of politics on the "decadent" Western societies and to resolve the crisis of European civilization by reviving

---

[34] The following part of this text expresses my own analysis of Czechoslovak "late totalitarianism" (a term coined by Václav Havel). See Martin Palouš, "Totalitarianism and Authoritarianism," in *Encyclopedia of Violence, Peace and Conflict,* 2nd ed., ed. Lester Kurtz (Oxford: Elsevier, 2008), 3:2129–2142.

ancient virtues and values. The communist revolutionaries, departing from the progressive teachings of Marx, Engels, and Lenin, also wanted to see the oppressive bourgeois state "wither away" and be replaced by a new political order, characterized by the "new form" of administration of human matters—based in this case not on the mythologized past but on a future-oriented, unknown and thus utopian project. However, what the disciples and heirs of the totalitarian "founding fathers" of the communist avant-garde got, and what they found themselves actively supporting after the power of their ideological premises and political enthusiasm burned out, was quite the opposite of their original millenarian intentions: a farcical imitation of the "rotten" and supposedly outdated "bourgeois" political regime.

The politics that pursued the idea of the total state ended in the "Lessons of the Years of Crisis,"[35] which used the old revolutionary slogans, but the message of which had an entirely different meaning:

1. Any effort to open up the socialist system and to reform its form of government was considered dangerous and would lead to destabilization—intolerable to the ruling forces of this world.

2. Only fools and martyrs could be so crazy as to act against this fundamental and invincible "law" of human history.

---

[35] "The Lessons of the Years of Crisis" ("Poučení z krizového období ve straně a společnosti po XIII. Sjezdu KSČ") was an infamous document adopted by the ruling Communist Party in 1970 that formulated the basic framework for the policies of so-called "normalization," namely, to punish the counterrevolutionaries, to perform a comprehensive "screening" of party membership, and to eradicate all the elements of freedom that appeared in Czechoslovak society thanks to the Prague Spring.

3. In the era of Real Socialism being built in Czechoslovakia, politics should be understood not as a sphere of human responsibility and agency, but as a mechanistic, empty ritual. The principal aim of the normalization policies of the time was not to take care of human matters in the open field of human history, but to stay in line, to keep them in their current state, and to fiercely suppress anything that might signal the need for change.

4. It was perfectly acceptable that under given circumstances, not everybody had the ambition—or the stomach—to become involved in the public matters of the ritualized socialist state—a state that didn't "wither away" but became bigger than ever. In that case, he or she was not to be rebuked, or even punished, but simply advised to mind his or her own business and to stay away from politics.

There is no doubt that such a "liberalization" of the traditional elements of totalitarianism—the reinterpretation of the above-mentioned "social contract"—made life much easier and more bearable for the enslaved citizens. At the same time, however, it obviously did not mean an increase of their freedom, but, on the contrary, their further enslavement. A society ruled by an advanced or late totalitarian system was no longer decimated by the revolutionary "reign of terror and virtue," and some socialist governments even managed to offer to their populations a high standard of living. But it did not save its members from the destructive effects of a "radiation of totalitarianism."[36]

There was no unmanipulated public space available for them, no ideologically undistorted language to address the relevant social issues and

---

[36] Havel, "Stories and Totalitarianism," 349.

to formulate and discuss new political ideas. There was no substantive communication between the organs of the state and its citizens regarding the public good and matters of common interest. There were no events other than various anniversaries to make the news and to form stories; no social movements to be seen; no experiences to be transformed into political knowledge; no hope, at least for living generations, that the political situation could ever be changed.

What remained was a society, relatively well fed, surviving under a kind of socialist welfare state, but suffering a strange disease that Havel compared in this essay to asthma: still alive, but permanently struggling for air to oxidize the blood:

> It is not true that Czechoslovakia is free of warfare and murder. The war and killing have assumed a different form: they have been shifted from the daylight of observable public events, to the twilight of unobservable inner destruction. It would seem that the absolute, "classical" death of which one reads in stories (and which for all terrors it holds is still mysteriously able to impart meaning to human life) has been replaced here by another kind of death: the slow, secretive, bloodless, never-quite-absolute, yet horrifyingly ever-present death of non-action, non-story, non-life and non-time; the collectively deadening, or more precisely, anaesthetizing, process of social and historical nihilization. This nihilization annuls death as such, and thus annuls life as such: the life of an individual becomes the dull and uniform functioning of a component in a large machine, and his death is merely something that puts him out of commission.[37]

---

[37] "Stories and Totalitarianism," 329–330.

What could people do under the given circumstances? How should they react to the existing political conditions in Czechoslovakia—certainly not bad enough to decimate its population and thus to outrage again "the conscience of mankind," to use the language of the Preamble to the UN Universal Declaration of Human Rights, but penetrating "only" to the depth of their personal lives and destroying their human identity? There was an option here, for sure, used by many: to leave. More than eighty thousand Czechs and Slovaks decided to emigrate, and they found new homes in Western Europe, the United States, Canada, Australia, South Africa, or other foreign countries.

Václav Havel, however—in contrast to Milan Kundera, for instance, who decided to emigrate to France—opted for another way to protect his human identity. Having decided to stay home, in April 1975, he wrote an open letter to the secretary general of the Communist Party— and soon also president of the republic—Dr. Gustáv Husák.[38] Here, as if inspired by his great English predecessor in the theater who once had a character clearly state the elementary "purpose" of all "playing"—"to hold, as 'twere, the mirror up to nature, to show virtue her own feature, scorn her own image, and the very age and body of the time his form and pressure"—Havel decided to do something unprecedented: to submit to the attention of the current Czechoslovak ruler a clear description of the state of public affairs in Czechoslovakia under his leadership. Here are the opening paragraphs of Havel's submission:

---

[38] Gustáv Husák (1913–1991) was a Slovak politician, President of Czechoslovakia (1975–1989), and Secretary General of the Communist Party of Czechoslovakia (1969–1987).

Dear Dr. Husák,

In our offices and factories work goes on, discipline prevails. The efforts of our citizens are yielding visible results in a slowly rising standard of living: people build houses, buy cars, have children, amuse themselves, live their lives.

All this, of course, amounts to very little as a criterion for the success or failure of your policies. After every social upheaval, people invariably come back in the end to their daily labors, for the simple reason that they want to stay alive; they do so for their own sake, after all, not for the sake of this or that team of political leaders.

Not that going to work, doing the shopping, and living their own lives is all that people do. They do much more than that: they commit themselves to numerous output norms which they then fulfill and over-fulfill; they vote as one man and unanimously elect the candidates proposed to them; they are active in various political organizations; they attend meetings and demonstrations; they declare their support for everything they are supposed to. Nowhere can any sign of dissent be seen from anything that the government does....

One must ask seriously, at this point, whether all this does not confirm your success in achieving the tasks your team set itself—those of winning the public's support and consolidating the situation in the country....

I may be so bold as to answer, No; to assert that, for all the outwardly persuasive facts, inwardly our society, far from being a consolidated one, is, on the contrary, plunging ever deeper into a crisis more dangerous, in some respects, than any we can recall in our recent history....

Why are people in fact behaving in the way they do? Why do they do all these things that, taken together, form the impressive image of a totally united society giving total support to its government? For any unprejudiced observer, the answer is, I think, self-evident: They are driven to it by fear.[39]

And here is what Havel wrote in the conclusion of his letter—his blunt and audacious advice, or warning, to Dr. Husák:

> So far, it is the worst in us which is being systematically activated and enlarged - egotism, hypocrisy, indifference, cowardice, fear, resignation, and the desire to escape every personal responsibility, regardless of the general consequences.
>
> So far you and your government have chosen the easy way out for yourselves, and the most dangerous road for society: the path of inner decay for the sake of outward appearances; of deadening life for the sake of increasing uniformity; of deepening the spiritual and moral crisis of our society, and ceaselessly degrading human dignity, for the puny sake of protecting your own power....
>
> As a citizen of this country, I hereby request, openly and publicly, that you and the leading representatives of the present regime consider seriously the matters to which I have tried to draw your attention; that you assess in their light the degree of your historic responsibility, and act accordingly.[40]

I am sure that Havel was not surprised that Dr. Husák didn't react to his letter—aside from passing it to the organs of State Security, which he certainly did, since in his mind such "subversive acts of civic disobedience" fell primarily under their discretion and responsibility. This

---

[39] Václav Havel, "Dear Dr. Husák," in *Open Letters: Selected Writings 1965–1990*, ed. Paul Wilson (New York: Alfred A. Knopf, 1991), 50–52.
[40] Havel, "Dear Dr. Husák," 82–83.

unusual communication between the dissenting playwright and his ruler, however, had another very significant effect. It was received by the public at large, thanks to its open nature, as a wake-up call. Havel's letter to Dr. Husák hit a nerve in Czechoslovak society and mobilized at least some of its members. It was copied and disseminated among an ever-growing number of people. They finally heard the voice of someone who dared to speak, loud and clear, the opinions they themselves were carefully hiding in the depth of their hearts.

Of course, not every reader of Havel's letter was ready to join him in his ceaseless efforts to break the deadening silence and speak the truth. But his plain and simple argument, coming in the middle of the spiritual crisis Czechoslovak society experienced during the 1970s, shattered society's "collective soul," opening the path to Charter 77, which would be published twenty months later. The summer 1976 trial of the Plastic People of the Universe, an iconic rock band of the emerging Czech underground movement, was the catalyst for the unification of many hidden currents surviving in various spheres of Czechoslovak society composed of people trying to resist Husák's normalization on their own terms and for their own reasons. By December 1976 these "conspirators," Havel included, were drafting the first Charter 77 declaration and gathering signatories.[41]

---

[41] An incomplete list of the members of the informal collective who wrote the Charter 77 Manifesto, and who also, beginning in December, collected the first signatures for the document, would include Jan Patočka, Jiří Němec, Václav Havel, Ladislav Hejdánek, Zdeněk Mlynář, Pavel Kohout, Petr Uhl, Ludvík Vaculík, and Jiří Hájek. Pavel Kohout came up with the name "Charter 77."

Let us remind ourselves now once more of the principal arguments and main messages of the Manifesto of Charter 77 dated January 1, 1977. It began with the following legal reasoning:

> In the Czechoslovak Register of Laws No. 120 of October 13, 1976, texts were published of the International Covenant on Civil and Political Rights, and of the International Covenant on Economic, Social and Cultural Rights, which were signed on behalf of our Republic in 1968, reiterated at Helsinki in 1975 and came into force in our country on March 23, 1976. From that date our citizens have enjoyed the rights, and our state the duties, ensuing from them. The human rights and freedoms underwritten by these covenants constitute features of civilized life for which many progressive movements have striven throughout history and whose codification could greatly assist humane developments in our society. We accordingly welcome the Czechoslovak Socialist Republic's accession to those agreements.[42]

The text continued with a list of grievances, openly addressing the facts that all Czechoslovak citizens experienced in their daily lives. The rights and freedoms guaranteed by these covenants existed currently in Czechoslovakia on paper alone. It stated that the Czechoslovak government was systematically violating them and thus had to be reminded of its international obligation to refrain immediately from such unlawful behavior.

---

[42] "Charter 77 Declaration," in *The Power of the Powerless: Citizens against the State in Central-Eastern Europe,* ed. John Keane (New York: M. E. Sharpe, 1985), 217–221.

This was, indeed, a harsh criticism of a government not used to hearing such from its own enslaved population. The worst, in the eyes of its representatives, however, was still to come. The announcement following the list of grievances could be understood by the Czechoslovak authorities as a group of reactionary outcasts' declaration of war on the very foundations of the Czechoslovak "socialist" state:

> Responsibility for the maintenance of rights in our country naturally devolves in the first place on the political and state authorities. Yet not only on them: everyone bears his share of responsibility for the conditions that prevail and accordingly also for the observance of legally enshrined agreements, binding upon all individuals as well as upon governments.

> It is this sense of co-responsibility, our belief in the importance of its conscious public acceptance and the general need to give it new and more effective expression that led us to the idea of creating Charter 77, whose inception we today publicly announce....

> Charter 77 does not aim, then, to set out its own platform of political or social reform or change, but within its own field of impact to conduct a constructive dialogue with the political and state authorities, particularly by drawing attention to individual cases where human and civic rights are violated, to document such grievances and suggest remedies, to make proposals of a more general character calculated to reinforce such rights and machinery for protecting them....

> We believe that Charter 77 will help to enable all citizens of Czechoslovakia to work and live as free human beings.[43]

---

[43] "Charter 77 Declaration," 217–221.

The 242 original signatories of the text, which sounded something like a Czechoslovak Declaration of Independence, would eventually swell to nearly 2,000. What were their motivations for joining this bold, ambitious, but very dangerous "civic initiative"? What were the aims of this amazingly heterogeneous group of people—Christians of various denominations, Jews, ex-communists expelled from the party after 1968, independent liberal intellectuals, and many people with no specific background, creed, goals or expectations? Each had his or her own specific personal reasons for signing, yet together they sent one and the same message to the Czechoslovak authorities: We cannot remain silent in a country where hypocrisy is an accepted norm, where all basic human rights "exist, regrettably, on paper alone,"[44] and where many people have become "victims of a virtual apartheid."[45] We want to speak the truth again, no matter what, and we will!

The arguments made by Václav Havel in his letter to Dr. Husák were right on target and, as the emergence of Charter 77 persuasively demonstrated, they worked. The political significance and true meaning of Charter 77 were actually demonstrated right away by the near-hysterical reaction of the communist regime. State media immediately launched a massive smear campaign. The repressive apparatus of the state opened a criminal investigation to discover the main culprits of this "hostile and subversive activity"—allegedly inspired by Western reactionary circles and coordinated by US intelligence services.

The instructions from the highest echelons of power in Czechoslovakia were swift and clear: the signatories of Charter 77 were to

---

[44] "Charter 77 Declaration," 217–221.
[45] "Charter 77 Declaration," 217–221.

be selectively punished for their "anti-socialist" behavior—if not imprisoned right away, then interrogated by the organs of the Czechoslovak Secret Police, exposed to public condemnation and harassment, and deprived of their jobs, passports, and driver's licenses.

There is one aspect of this broad counter-offensive launched by the Czechoslovak state against a small group of dissenters that deserves our special attention: the way the communist government dealt with the introductory legal arguments of the Charter 77 Manifesto, which referred to two major international human rights covenants endorsed by Czechoslovakia, and in particular to the fact that these commitments were unambiguously reiterated in the Final Act of the Helsinki Conference.

It was not only the regime's propagandists and ideologues who offered their expertise in the struggle against the reactionary elements who were aiming to "disrupt the Czechoslovak socialist system of government"—they were joined by the honorable lawyers of Charles University, who not only departed in their reasoning from the ideological dogmas of Marxism-Leninism, but actually tried to tie their arguments to the venerable normativist legal traditions of the pre-war "bourgeois republic," which unambiguously subscribed to the principle of supremacy of constitutional law over international law.[46]

---

[46] According to Zdeněk Neubauer, a disciple of František Weyr and Karel Engliš, the founding fathers of Czech normative and teleological legal theory, which had a decisive influence on the legal and political thought of pre-war Czechoslovakia, for the founding fathers of this state the supremacy of constitutional over international law in the Czechoslovak legal order was not a matter of choice, but a necessity corresponding to the current historical situation: "In contrast to state law, there was not a common subject of norm-creation in international law and the probability of correspondence between the requirement of its norms and the reality of their execution even against the will of those who have obligation to obey them was practically non-existent." (Zdeněk Neubauer, *Státověda a teorie*

First of all, according to this legal philosophy, international agreements signed by the Czechoslovak government and ratified in due constitutional process could not be seen as a legitimate source of rights for Czechoslovak citizens. Czechoslovak citizens thus could not lawfully appeal to these agreements when seeking redress for their grievances or expressing their personal opinions about the state of public affairs, as the Charter 77 Manifesto suggested. Their fundamental human rights were fully articulated and guaranteed, according to the law professors at Charles University, by the Czechoslovak Socialist Constitution only. The socialist legal order based on it was wholly sufficient for any complaint or constructive criticism Czechoslovak citizens might have. The signatories of Charter 77—bypassing all the existing provisions and mechanisms the Czechoslovak socialist state was generously offering them (in the context of the aforementioned "social contract," one hastens to add!)—were simply undermining the state. They were openly engaging in reactionary and treasonous, and thus punishable, activities, either driven by their own malicious designs and intentions or, in the more positive case, seduced by others, not clearly aware of the consequences of their actions.

Second, the international conventions on human rights to which Czechoslovakia was now a party could never sideline or impair the

politiky [Prague: Sociologické nakladatelství, 2006], 82, trans. Martin Palouš). Consequently, when defining the place of international law within the legal order of the new state, the writers of the Czechoslovak Constitution of 1920 decided to use a dualistic model: the domestic legal effects of international treaties could arise only by the means of domestic legislation. Czechoslovak courts of justice were obliged to apply international treaties in their adjudication only by the means of application of the norms of domestic law (cf. Jiří Malenovský, *Mezinárodní právo veřejné, jeho obecná část, a jeho poměr k vnitrostátnímu právu, zvláště k právu českému*, 4th ed. (Masaryk University, 2004). See esp. section 14, "Poměr mezinárodního práva a vnitrostátního práva v České republice," pp. 409–467.)

existing Czechoslovak legal order and undermine the sovereignty of the Czechoslovak state. What everyone had to be reminded of—primarily the diplomats of the Western capitalist countries participating in the Helsinki Process—was Article 2(7) of the UN Charter, clearly recognized in and confirmed by the Final Act, rejecting implicitly any intervention in the domestic affairs of UN member-states. The repressive actions taken by the organs of the Czechoslovak state against the group of "losers and self-appointed politicians"[47] who had signed Charter 77 was an internal matter and no one else's business; no one from the outside world had a legitimate right to step in and criticize or support in any way their dirty, destructive, and selfish political cause.

Taking these legal positions into consideration, and also the fact that the communist regime possessed all the necessary means to enforce them, with its own survival ("the defense of socialism against all enemies") as its number-one goal—Charter 77's almost unsurmountable obstacle comes into focus. Under the given circumstances, how were they supposed to conduct a "constructive dialogue with the political and state authorities," as proposed in their manifesto? Given the totalitarian nature of the communist regime, wasn't this sheer fantasy, the ultimate proof that, despite their personal heroism, Chartists were just utopian dreamers, entirely out of touch with political reality? Even worse, didn't their readiness to engage in "dialogue" with a totalitarian communist government imply its legitimacy?

---

[47] The title of a famous article in *Rudé Právo*, the Czechoslovak Communist Party's daily newspaper, published a couple of days after the Charter 77 Manifesto appeared in the Western press, that launched the official smear campaign against it.

The central—in fact, the *only*—institutional feature of Charter 77 was its nomination of Jiří Hájek, Václav Havel, and Jan Patočka[48] as its spokespersons — "endowed with full authority to represent it vis-à-vis state and other bodies, and the public at home and abroad." Their signatures were to "attest to the authenticity of documents issued by the Charter." Hájek and Havel deserve great credit for their roles in Charter 77's beginnings and their contributions to this "civic initiative" during its whole existence. It was, however, the philosopher Jan Patočka who turned out to have the decisive influence as far as Charter 77's spiritual grounding and public identity were concerned. Patočka was indispensable in the formation of Charter 77, and his death only a few weeks after its creation—caused by the harsh police treatment he was subjected to due to his role—only sealed the fact that it was classical philosophy revived in our times that was at the very center of the Charter 77 story and still remains the core of its legacy.

It was quite surprising at first that it was he, out of all other possible candidates, who assumed this challenging role, and stood in the forefront of the dissidents' revolt. Patočka had theretofore enjoyed, even among his Marxist opponents, a reputation of being a profound theoretical thinker and a renowned scholar. He was highly regarded in informed circles of the intelligentsia as a master in his field and a great teacher, endowed with an exceptional capability to elucidate the history of

---

[48] Jiří Hájek had been minister for foreign affairs in 1968 and had been expelled from the Communist Party in the aftermath of the Prague Spring. Jan Patočka (June 1, 1907–March 13, 1977) was an eminent Czech philosopher who made significant contributions to phenomenology and the philosophy of history. He studied in Prague, Paris, Berlin, and Freiburg and was a student of both Edmund Husserl and Martin Heidegger.

philosophical ideas and to open to his students the gates of the wonderful—veritably wonder-awaking—world of Western philosophy. Forced to retire from his post at Charles University in 1972, he kept lecturing smaller circles of his disciples in private seminars organized in private apartments—still primarily engaged in his own phenomenological investigations and studies of other fundamental problems of contemporary philosophy.[49]

If for most of his life Patočka was in the habit of approaching his topics *more philosophico*, from the perspective of a distanced observer of the world of human existence (the *Lebenswelt*, in the terminology of his principal teacher, the founding father of phenomenology Edmund Husserl), his acceptance of the role of spokesperson for Charter 77 was an apparently radical change in course. He decided, metaphorically speaking, to step down from his philosophical observatory to enter the public realm of his *polis*. At the time he underwent a deep spiritual crisis and set himself—on the basis of his specific philosophical reasoning—into action.

And what happened? Charter 77's signatories—most of them certainly not trained in philosophy and unable to make sense of the subtle intricacies of contemporary philosophical discourse—found Patočka's reasoning comprehensible and attractive!

Patočka's reasoning is laid out in six short texts he wrote in the last weeks of his life, clearly under conditions somewhat different from the tranquil isolation of the "well-spoken path of the Goddess ... lying far

---

[49] Patočka's last great lecture cycle was on Plato and Europe. In the fall of 1976, when Patočka was already involved in the discussions that resulted in the creation of Charter 77, he and a small circle of his students read Heidegger's *Grundprobleme der Phaenomenologie*.

indeed from the beaten paths of humans" recommended by Parmenides. Quite the contrary: Patočka wrote them in a period during which he was interrogated daily by the secret police and threatened by the State Prosecutor with charges of subversion and "antisocialist activities." However, these texts are distinctly philosophical in that, while they clearly focus on matters connected to the extremely difficult first weeks of Charter 77's existence, they speak to the entire *polis*, all of Patočka's fellow citizens. Given this civic audience, Patočka speaks not as a Parmenidean or Platonic scholar, with his spiritual eye turned to the sphere above the heavens, but after the fashion of Socrates, the first person who, as Cicero put it in his *Tusculan Disputations*, "called philosophy down from heaven, and placed it in cities, and introduced it even in homes, and drove it to inquire about life and customs and things good and evil."[50]

Was this re-orientation of philosophy, attributed by Cicero to Socrates, something entirely new in the context of Patočka's philosophy, imposed by chance or sheer necessity? Taking into consideration the basic mission that he had already set for his philosophical activities in 1930, as a twenty-three-year-old incipient scholar with his adult life in front of him, I would respond in the negative. In one of his first articles published in a philosophical journal, he explained what philosophy meant for him: it was not merely speculation *in abstracto*, as philosophy often presents itself in the human world, but a discipline with the ability "to criticize life in all its components and manifestations,"[51] willing "to give expression to what society still rudely wants to say, to give its voice to still mute tendencies,

---

[50] Cicero, *Tusculanarum disputationum*, ed. C. F. W. Müller (Leipzig: Freytag, 1904), bk. 5, sec. 4.
[51] Patočka, "Kapitoly z současné filosofie" (Chapters from Contemporary Philosophy) in *Sebrané spisy*, vol. 1, Péče od duši 1, p. 96.

but also to expose what is behind them, to demonstrate their genesis, to mark cross-roads, to identify problems, even to try to resolve them."[52]

As Patočka repeatedly stated in his Charter 77 texts, by publicly defending human rights, Charter 77 was not intended to interfere in politics *sensu stricto*—with politics conceived as a power struggle, the basic aim of which has always been and must always be to replace those who are momentarily in government by others with different policies. Charter 77's activities had to be limited to a non-political goal: by pointing to individual violations of human rights and proposing the dialogue about it to the ruling power, to resist the devastating consequences the late totalitarianism of the 1970s had for those exposed to its "radiation."

Charter 77's activities were to be based, according to Patočka, on things that should not be given up by humans under any political circumstances—on the moral claim made on each of us striving to live in unity with ourselves; on the claim which not only turned all participants of the Charter 77 movement into "dissidents" against the communist regime but brought them at the same time from the world of sheer lies, deceptions, false pretentions, and endless manipulation back to the search for the truth and the care for the soul; the claim which opened for them the door into the largely forgotten and abandoned realm of classical political philosophy.

In the text "What Charter 77 Is and What It Is Not," Patočka decided to bring "to everyone's clear awareness" the "truths of which we are all in some sense aware"—his own philosophical definition of human rights:

---

[52] Patočka, "Kapitoly z současné filosofie," 92.

The idea of human rights is nothing other than the conviction that even states, even societies as a whole, are subject to the sovereignty of moral sentiment: that they recognize something unconditional that is higher than they are, something that is binding even on them, sacred, inviolable, and that in their power to establish and maintain a rule of law, they seek to express this recognition.[53]

According to conventional wisdom, the concept of human rights elaborated in the international covenants the authors of the Charter 77 Manifesto were appealing to is rooted in the European Enlightenment of the late eighteenth century. Patočka's moral argument, however—his cautious references to "the truths of which we are all in some sense aware"—sounded rather like a voice coming to the present from a distant past, bringing to life something that does not fit well in the contemporary discourse on human rights but belongs to premodern and largely abandoned spiritual traditions. His argument that respect for human rights represents the moral foundation of any human society—and that it is our recognition of the sovereignty of moral sentiment that constitutes them— shifted the focus from the modern, emancipated individual who simply possesses human rights as an entitlement to the ancient conflict between politics and philosophy. It turned attention to the trial of Socrates, who seems to have been the inspiration for Patočka's approach to political matters in general, and, for his own activities in the public realm, his great example and predecessor.

---

[53] Jan Patočka: "What Charter 77 Is and What It Is Not," in *Jan Patočka: Philosophy and Selected Writings*, ed. Erazim Kohák (Chicago: The University of Chicago Press, 1989), 341.

Where, actually, does any just political order emanate from? What enables a political body, notwithstanding its customs, its valid laws, its form of government, and all practical aspects of its daily politics, to exist as a political body? No matter what politicians themselves have to say on this point, their answer is, from the Socratic-Patočkian perspective, insufficient or even irrelevant. The adequate response to this question simply cannot come from their realm; it must come from the sphere outside politics. Even states endowed with the sovereignty to create binding laws, to execute them and to supervise their observance, must first honor something above them. Even sovereign states have to respect the elementary fact that being human precedes any political role one may be assigned as citizen. Not only individual human beings, but states and whole societies must be "subject to the sovereignty of moral sentiment."

Signing Charter 77 could not then be perceived, Patočka argued in his capacity as Charter 77's spokesperson, as a "political act in the strict sense." Charter 77 constituted "no competition or interference with political power in any of its functions." That is why it could be "neither an association, nor an organization" but just "an outgrowth of the conviction that any society cannot function without a moral foundation."[54]

To sum it up: Patočka not only reopened the basic question of Socrates in his Charter 77 texts, but also revived his spirit. When he said that the Charter 77 Manifesto was "an expression of joy" of our citizens and "also an expression of [their] willingness … to do their part in bringing about the realization and public fulfilment of the principles proclaimed,"

---

[54] Patočka, "What Charter 77 Is," 341–342.

he said it with a Socratic irony that had to fly directly in the face of the communist powerholders.[55]

Patočka's observation that after all their ferocious onslaughts against the Charter 77 signatories, "our people have once more become aware that there are things for which it is worthwhile to suffer, that the things for which we might have to suffer are those which make life worthwhile,"[56] had to be perceived by them not just as an empty, moralizing proclamation, but as a kind of declaration of war on them. And when the organs of State Security went after him openly, interrogating and trying to intimidate him day after day until he died, his speaking out was a clear act of Socratic courage.

Joshua Rubenstein

Just over thirty years ago, sometime in the middle of 1986, Soviet Premier Mikhail Gorbachev decided "to turn off the lever of repression." The regime stopped arresting prisoners of conscience and began the process of releasing those it was already holding. With this step, a highlight of the long-ago era of *glasnost* and *perestroika*, the human rights movement as we had come to know it, ceased to exist.

The movement had lasted for two decades, emerging for the first time in 1965 in response to the arrest of two Soviet writers, Andrei Sinyavsky and Yuli Daniel, who had taken the extraordinary step of sending essays and short stories to the West, where they were published under pseudonyms. It was the public nature of how their friends and

---

[55] Patočka, "What Charter 77 Is," 341–342.
[56] Patočka, "What Charter 77 Is," 346.

supporters responded—with appeals and petitions, a nonviolent demonstration, and the circulation of an unofficial but reliable transcript of their trial—that set the pattern for many events that were to follow.[57]

The dissident writer Andrei Amalrik once commented to me in an interview in December 1977 that "even now the regime exists, perhaps not only, but mainly, on the interest from the capital of fear amassed under Stalin." The achievements of the human rights movement can best be understood against this background of enforced silence. In 1968, following a series of political trials, three dissidents, Ilya Gabay, Yuli Kim, and Pyotr Yakir, wrote a letter to Soviet cultural and scientific figures, warning against the rebirth of Stalinism. They understood that the regime relied "on our own passivity, our short memory, and the bitter fact that we are accustomed to an absence of freedom." Only exposure, it seemed, could restrain the authorities. Recalling the country's isolation under Stalin, when it seemed as if the West had no knowledge of his crimes, Pyotr Yakir described the movement's principal goal: "They tried to make public every illegal act committed in our country so that all the world may know. This is a great stride forward by comparison with Stalinism. Under Stalin there was always an iron curtain, and no one knew what was going on here. Millions of people were destroyed, and nobody knew anything about it. Now we try to publicize every arrest, every dismissal from work. We consider this the main task today."

---

[57] Further information on the events discussed in this essay may be found in Joshua Rubenstein, *Soviet Dissidents: Their Struggle for Human Rights* (Boston: Beacon Press, 1980) and Joshua Rubenstein and Alexander Gribanov, eds., *The KGB File of Andrei Sakharov* (New Haven: Yale University Press, 2005).

The human rights movement reflected and reinforced a breakdown in the political and cultural isolation of the Soviet Union. As unsanctioned poetry circulated, then novels, and finally detailed information about political trials and conditions in the labor camps, the regime's control of information grew less effective. Through correspondents, diplomats, and tourists, the West also learned about Soviet life in greater and more vivid detail. The regime could not ignore this development. For the most part, the authorities responded with arrests and other reprisals, but the repression inflicted on the dissidents should not obscure the tangible changes they accomplished.

For the first time, individuals did not have to submit, through inertia, to the regime's lawlessness but could decide for themselves how to act. In his book *The Challenge of the Spirit*, Boris Shragin described their predicament: "Instead of having to decide between parties and political programs, the choice is between two ways of life. One consists of obeying one's own conscience with all the suffering that is bound to ensue; the other, of avoiding anxiety by renouncing one's freedom."[58]

No moral dilemma existed under Stalin because the consequences of open dissent were so certain and often so final. There was also a complete lack of information about the scale of repression. But once the regime relented after Stalin's death, it was only natural that at least some people would test the limits of free expression and by their example encourage others to do the same.

---

[58] Boris Shragin, *The Challenge of the Spirit* (New York: Alfred A. Knopf, 1978), 10.

By the late 1960s, this makeshift collection of individual activists—liberal Marxists, Orthodox believers, democrats, writers, scientists, would-be Jewish émigrés—could be said to constitute a movement, or perhaps parallel streams within a movement, because they shared certain fundamental beliefs and possessed sufficient moral and political solidarity. They had learned, as Shragin again commented, that "moral and legal demands are a force in themselves"[59] that could drive the physically omnipotent but spiritually bankrupt authorities into a corner.

Gorbachev's program is what finally broke down the political and cultural constraints of Soviet life. But as much as the dissidents helped to prepare the groundwork for Gorbachev's reforms, historians are likely to debate the role of the human rights movement in provoking his initiatives altogether. Gorbachev himself has denied that the human rights movement had any discernible impact on the development of *perestroika*. Neither in his memoirs nor in the memoirs of his closest advisers is there more than a passing reference to Andrei Sakharov or the slightest acknowledgment of the dissidents' role in the post-Khrushchev period in promoting liberal, democratic values. When he lectured at Harvard University on November 11, 2002, Gorbachev insisted that reforms could never have emerged "from below," primarily because virtually all the dissidents were either in jail or in exile by the mid-1980s. How could they be credited with initiating change when they never had access to levers of power in the ordinary political sense?

Gorbachev and his advisers liked to claim that they found their inspiration within the very communist system they were determined to

---

[59] Shragin, xiv.

reform. For them, the image of Vladimir Lenin as a more tolerant political leader (in contrast to the murderous Stalin), the limited economic and cultural achievements of the New Economic Policy of the 1920s, the political alternatives that Nikolai Bukharin offered the country, and most immediately the example of Nikita Khrushchev and the Twentieth and Twenty-Second Party Congresses—when Stalin was denounced as a tyrant—offered a legitimate political legacy and the basis for a political program that included respect for fundamental rights and historical truth, economic reform, integration into the world economy, more open borders, unfettered debate within the party itself, and an end to censorship in society at large.

Nonetheless, this revolution "from above" should not obscure the role of the human rights movement in shaping Gorbachev's priorities. It was the dissidents who first relied on international agreements to explain and advance their cause. It was the dissidents who first made human rights an international issue and added such words as *gulag, glasnost,* and *samizdat* into the world's vocabulary. (Vladimir Bukovsky once insisted that "Mr. Gorbachev did not invent Glasnost—he borrowed it from the Soviet human rights movement.") And it was their courage and sacrifice that helped to set the moral agenda for Gorbachev's reforms and the terms for his acceptance in the West. They may have been relatively few in number, but as Sakharov recognized during his exile in Gorky, what was important was "the qualitative fact of breaking through the psychological barrier of silence." His own essays and memorandums, Amalrik's pathbreaking book *Will the Soviet Union Survive Until 1984?*, Valentin

Turchin's *The Inertia of Fear and the Scientific Worldview*,[60] and the many reports of the Helsinki watch groups explored issues that affected all or a substantial number of Soviet citizens. The movement did focus on the defense of individual victims—a matter of principle that also served to raise legal consciousness—but it continually pointed to the country's economic and social problems and insisted that they could be adequately addressed only in a framework of open, democratic reform.

This was, essentially, Gorbachev's program, and though an argument can be fashioned that *any* thoughtful person who took the time and energy to examine Soviet society would have reached the same conclusion as Gorbachev did, the fact is that the dissidents attempted to articulate it *out loud* at a time when the regime could respond only with arrests and other reprisals.

Sakharov never lost his moral compass or succumbed to the naïve, wishful belief that Gorbachev's initiatives meant that the Soviet Union was now fundamentally a different country, that its misery was over, that a prosperous democracy would emerge out of the decayed garden of Russian despotism. Gorbachev's unexpected and startling reforms may have lulled Western leaders into complacency over the prospects for democracy in the Soviet Union. Sakharov, for one, never entertained such illusions.

Regrettably, several close advisers to Gorbachev and other government officials exhibited an ugly condescension toward the human rights activists of the Brezhnev era, an attitude that reflected a certain self-

---

[60] Valentin Turchin, *The Inertia of Fear and the Scientific Worldview,* trans. Guy Daniels (New York: Columbia University Press, 1981).

important arrogance. *They* were in charge; the levers of power were in *their* hands. For them, the sacrifice of so many dissidents was a mere footnote in the country's history.

Two dismal wars in Chechnya, the annexation of Crimea and ongoing fighting in Ukraine, an increasingly controlled press, official corruption, frequent killings of Kremlin critics, the lack of genuinely free elections or democratic institutions in virtually all of the former Soviet Union—these conditions speak more of a country that has yet to dig out "from under the rubble" of Bolshevik and Stalinist dictatorship than of a country inspired by the human rights movement.

The human rights movement provided a consistent and reliable means for the West to see and understand the reality of Soviet life. No other manifestation of open dissent would have been possible without the example set by human rights activists. The dissidents created the first independent channels to the West, the phenomenon of political *samizdat*, the example of courage in the struggle against fear. They proved that one could challenge the regime and survive, that truth provided its own strength, that law was worth defending.

Their setbacks did not mark the triumph of a heartless, arrogant regime over an oppressed, intimidated people but rather a courageous struggle, however quixotic or doomed to failure, between two Russias: the Russia of violence and deceit and the Russia of justice and humanity. It is a struggle that continues.

Sir Roger Scruton

I have been asked to reflect on my experiences in the anti-communist underground in Eastern Europe, and on the lessons to be drawn from it. Young people—and there are many such in this room—will have had no experience either of communism or of the Cold War, or of the deeper civilizational confrontation through which we all lived in Europe during the period following the Second World War. There is a natural desire to forget times of hardship and to move on. But although there is a need to move on, there is also, as this institution testifies, a need to remember. We remember not in order to repeat our mistakes but in order to learn from them.

Looking back on it now, people downplay the cruelty, the suffering, the privations, the midnight arrests, and the prison camps. Of such things they are inclined to say "Well, that was the aftermath of the war, and luckily it is all in the past." The countries where those things happened are now part of the European Union and have joined in the enterprise of creating a new and united Europe. So, "Let's forget about communism: it is no longer relevant."

But the project of forging a new and united Europe has faltered. And the legacy of communism has become suddenly clear, as we see the populations of the former communist countries fleeing to the West. We should learn from these things, and we should do so by looking back at circumstances that we did not understand at the time but which have become clear in retrospect. Poland, Czechoslovakia, Hungary, Romania, and Bulgaria, after their liberation from the communist grip in 1989, found themselves rootless and lost. They were searching for the identity that the communists had buried. They needed to rediscover what they had been, in order to move on from the immediate past. Not finding what they were looking for, young people decided instead to flee.

It became apparent that the real evil of communism, apart from the cruel treatment of individuals, lay in the systematic destruction of civil society. Under the communist system, however mildly exercised, the Communist Party had refused to distinguish civil society from the state. It had regarded all gatherings of people with suspicion, unless it was itself in charge. Family reunions, the meeting of friends in bars and restaurants, attendance at church or synagogue—all such things were regarded as conspiracies against the ruling power, to be forbidden or controlled.

Of course the Communist Party was, nominally, distinct from the State; it had concocted a fiction of its independence. But since it had no corporate personality, could not be sued in law, and dictated who was and was not to be a member, there was no way in which the citizen could really treat it as an independent body. In practice, the Party was the State and enjoyed the use of all the powers of the State, while not itself subject to them. Any part of civil society that threatened to escape from the Party's control had to be infiltrated and, if necessary, suppressed. This meant the associative instinct of the citizens was destroyed. It became dangerous to join things, dangerous to share any kind of social ambition or any sphere of private interests. Charities—which are the core of civil society in America—were forbidden. To collect money or assets for the good of others branded you as a criminal. Hence there was no way in which social initiatives could begin. The result was a society locked in the dead agenda of the sclerotic Communist Party, which lacked the means to adapt to the changing circumstances of the modern world.

We adapt to change by getting together with our fellow citizens and turning the change toward our common good. But when we cannot associate, that process does not occur, and society stagnates. That was why communism entered its period of collapse. The rise of global communications, the mass culture of consumption, the accelerating pace of the surrounding world—all these enormous changes lay beyond the wall, and nobody could begin the process of adapting to them. So a fracture opened between the Party and the citizens, and neither had the means to change in response to it.

Many people, young people especially, in eastern Europe today, look around at their social and political inheritance and ask themselves "How do I belong to that?" Everything distinctive, everything that makes Poland *Poland* and Hungary *Hungary*, has been wiped out. History is at an impassable distance, separated from the present by the sterile desert of the communist years. The natural response is not to pick up the burden of belonging where the grandparents had been forced to relinquish it, but to emigrate to some place where civil society still exists, where it makes sense to join things, to pursue shared adventures, and to live at the pace of the new communicative world. And no place exemplifies those desirable features more appealingly than my own country of Great Britain. As a result, Great Britain has a huge immigration problem, while eastern Europe has an equally devastating *emigration* problem, as the young, the industrious, the educated, and the talented flee to more promising climes, leaving behind them a sparsely populated ruin.

We are therefore living through a continent-wide crisis, caused partly by the legacy of communism, and partly by the EU's insistence on the free movement of peoples. In a way this result is the opposite of what

I and my colleagues, in the days when we joined the anti-communist underground, hoped to achieve. We sought to reunite the young people of eastern Europe with their cultural inheritance, in order provide a light in the communist darkness. The EU offers them, instead, an escape route from their past. It offers to complete the work of the communists, in wiping away forever the memory of the European nations.

Rather than lament this new turn of events, however, I shall reflect on some of the lessons to be drawn from my own experience. The first and most important lesson is that the countries that had fallen victim to Soviet domination were not all affected in the same way. In particular, Poland stood out as a place of defiance. The Polish Catholic Church had refused to concede victory to the communists and recognized throughout the postwar period that it was engaged in a battle for the souls of the Polish people. Its hierarchy—the priesthood and bishops—were resolutely Christian, dedicated to the mission of their church, which remained a largely communist-free zone, under whose aegis people could associate in the old way, without fear of arrest. The Church had its local reading groups and youth groups, and the Communist Party had long since given up the attempt to control what was said or done when these groups got together. There was in Poland the only independent university in the eastern bloc, the Catholic University of Lublin, which the Church had fought successfully to retain, even though it had lost most of its property and buildings to the communists, who managed to confine the University to a tiny corner of Lublin where it was thought to do no harm. The Catholic University was a great benefit to those of us who wanted to establish relations with the Polish educated class, since it was an institution where you could meet your fellow intellectuals as *people* rather than as delegates of the communist system.

At that time there were also many vocations, especially in the Dominican Order, which offered to young men a way of life outside the official structures, and in honorable relation to the past and the identity of Poland. The election of Pope John Paul II, and his pilgrimage to his homeland, was a crucial event, which was to remind Poles that they owed their allegiance to a higher power than any that could be invented or imposed by the Communist Party. And the Solidarity union was, in those days, more like the secular arm of the Catholic Church than a trade union on the Western model.

All that is recorded in the history books, and no one disputes it. But other countries were radically different, and it is important to understand that each had its own way of resisting communist annihilation. Hungary, for example, had won for itself a comparative freedom in 1956. Prior to the Soviet invasion of that year, the Hungarian Communist Party had installed a government committed to reform, in which Hungarian national feeling took precedence over Soviet foreign policy. That government was unacceptable to Moscow, and the tanks were sent in. But to the surprise of everyone, the Hungarian people fought back. This was a shock to the Communist Party and also to the Russians, and the immediate consequence was to identify Hungarian national feeling with the rejection of communism, rather than acquiescence in the face of it. Hungary became a country where communism was regarded as a necessary evil, and the Party itself, while reassuming power, was forced to allow negotiable freedoms to a populace that it was frightened to antagonize further.

In Czechoslovakia the reform communist movement of 1968 was also put down by Russian tanks. Unlike the Hungarians, the Czechs and the Slovaks did not resist. They complained and refused to cooperate; a young student, Jan Palach, burned himself to death by way of protest. But resistance was confined to such symbolic gestures, and the Communist Party continued on its miserable way, by a process of "normalization" that involved ejecting everyone with talent from the educational and artistic institutions.

It was not until 1977 that resistance began again, with the Charter movement that began in that year. The Charter, drafted by a group of intellectuals largely under Václav Havel's leadership, declared the rights and freedoms of the Czech and Slovak people as guaranteed under the Helsinki Accords, signed by the reform government in 1968 and subsequently ratified for fear of precipitating a diplomatic crisis. The Charter was a call to the Czechoslovak government, and therefore to the Czechoslovak Party, to obey the law that it had been trapped into signing. Unlike the Polish case, in which opposition was shaped by a nationwide religious spirit, the Czechoslovak opposition was led by a group of legally minded secular intellectuals—though it is true, also, that mass pilgrimages of the youth in Slovakia, based on the Polish model, did much to give the Charter the support of a populist movement.

In Romania and Bulgaria, the Communist Party exercised the powers of an oriental despotism, backed by a ruthless, secret police. Some of our network tried to extend their activities into those countries—notably Jessica Douglas-Home, who set up a trust to support the anti-communist networks in Romania.[61] But the work was much, much harder, even if, in the long run, just as effective.

Our principal activities, in all the countries where we worked, involved offering support to private initiatives in education, and encouraging people, by visits and the supply of books, printing equipment, and small stipends, to maintain and expand the underground universities that existed, in one form or another, throughout the communist bloc.

In the circumstances that prevailed in eastern Europe there was no advantage to the individual in being educated, at least not in the way that we encouraged. There was no career to look forward to as a result of the underground seminars, except possibly a career in jail. True, the seminars created an arena of friendship and a center of conversation. And they had an inspiring effect, not only on the students, but also on the foreigners who visited them as teachers and colleagues. They illustrated the ancient thought that true education is not a means to an end but an end in itself. The students were acutely aware that they were studying something that had to make sense in itself and had to be valuable in itself, otherwise there was no point in attending the seminars. And through this thought our students became aware also, just as we did, of the radical distinction between useful nonsense and useless knowledge.

This is a lesson for us today. Much of the education in humanities in our universities consists of useful nonsense. Consider gender studies, which teaches young women how to look on the other sex with suspicion and hatred, while deconstructing the literary and cultural heritage of our

---

[61] More information can be found in her memoir, *Once Upon Another Time: Ventures Behind the Iron Curtain* (Norwich: Michael Russell Publishing, 2000).

civilization. Such a subject, with its heap of nonsensical jargon and belligerent prejudice, is immensely useful, pointing female students toward a career in the wider world. Spouting this nonsense, you get to the head of the queue for an academic job. Study real knowledge, by contrast, such as the language of Chaucer or the meaning of German Romanticism, and you will leave the university with something of great value to *you*, but of no use whatsoever in your career. In just that way we were able to teach in the underground seminars with no other goal than to replace nonsense—the Marxist waffle that formed the official propaganda, and which was the pathway to a career—with real and useless knowledge, which was the knowledge of the cultural heritage that the communists had wished to destroy.

How did we operate? I will give the briefest of summaries. A friend of mine, Kathy Wilkes, alas now dead, had—in her office as secretary of the board of Literae Humaniores in Oxford—received a request from a Czech dissident, saying "Why don't you visit us? Why do you visit only those official universities where they teach nothing but Marxist drivel?" Notwithstanding the fact that a large part of Oxford education at the time consisted of Marxist drivel, she took up the challenge, and did what was necessary if radical aims are to be accomplished—she fell in love, in fact, with the dissident whom she visited. *His* cause then became *her* cause. So energized was she by this that she persuaded her Oxford colleagues, and me, too, though I was not part of the Oxford world, to travel to Prague and lecture to the underground seminar that she had discovered. The aim was ostensibly to bring our Czech colleagues up to date with Western scholarship in philosophy and related disciplines. It looks somewhat quaint, in retrospect, to think that there is such a thing as the "latest scholarship" in the humanities. But it did not look so quaint then, in 1979, because there really was true scholarship in philosophy, literature, and the arts, in those days before deconstruction, gender studies, and the like had wiped away the curriculum. Moreover, it became quickly apparent that our Czech colleagues really did want to know about this scholarship, and whether it was relevant to their great cause: that of maintaining a culture of debate in their homeland.

We worked out a curriculum and began to make contacts through the underground networks in Prague and Brno, discovering more and more initiatives that were, or at least seemed to be, invisible to the secret police. Our procedure was ostentatiously to support, with visits and books, those open discussion groups that were visible to the police, and which would be regarded as the main centers of subversion, while concentrating our work on other initiatives that were to remain unobservable. Visitors to the open seminars risked arrest. But behind the scenes, if you had arrived on a tourist visa and studiously shaken off the person who was following you, you would contrive to arrive as though by accident in a little room where four or five people were waiting in silence. And in that room you enjoyed an educational experience that was quite unlike anything that you would have known from your university back home.

We ran seriously structured courses for such groups of students, on the nature of analytical philosophy, on social and political theory, and on central European history—the search for history being vital for our Czech colleagues, who had inherited the long-standing question of Czech identity. In a series of *samizdat* publications and discussion groups they pondered the relation of this place where a Slavonic language and a headless Protestant culture had survived in the midst of a German-speaking and Roman Catholic empire.

Gradually our courses expanded to include art, architecture, and music—with a circle of young composers in Brno whom we provided with regular visits from their British peers. Work in Brno was greatly facilitated by the "Theatre on a String," under the leadership of Petr Oslzlý, which served as a front organization for many initiatives reaching across the entire province of Moravia.

For a full account of our work in Czechoslovakia you should consult Barbara Day's definitive history, *The Velvet Philosophers*. Barbara Day was secretary to the Jan Hus Trust, and party to all its decisions in those exciting and difficult years. As for our work in Poland and Hungary, that still awaits documentary treatment, and I hope that one day it will be provided.

What is important now is to recall the encounters with people for whom education really mattered. This was inspiring to our Western visitors, most of whom came from universities where they had to deal every day with students for whom nothing mattered at all. Even if you were arrested and expelled—indeed, *especially* if you were arrested and expelled—you were given the rare experience of seeing education as a coveted asset, and also a threat. At a certain stage the Czech secret police made a useful mistake, which brought the arrests of our speakers to an end. They had decided to make an example of our next visitor to Dr. Hejdánek's open seminar. The plan was to plant drugs in the visitor's suitcase and arrest him at the airport for drug smuggling. The visitor in question happened to be Jacques Derrida, a prominent leftist philosopher and personal friend of President Mitterrand. The secret police had not done their homework and, by arresting Derrida, precipitated a diplomatic crisis that caused them to retreat in ignominy from all that they had planned. The experience improved Derrida immensely: his night in jail with a drunken gypsy cured him of his leftism. It also improved the secret police, who thereafter left our visitors alone.

Those private seminars in apartments were often conducted, in Czechoslovakia, by highly educated people: former professors who had been purged from the universities during the period of "normalization" in 1971. The purges were renewed in 1977 in the wake of the Charter. As a result, Czechoslovakia was unique among communist countries in containing a large class of unemployed and unemployable intellectuals who were also, such being the nature of the system, maintained in fictional employments, usually as stokers in large centrally heated buildings. This provided us with a trained workforce of a kind that no Western university enjoyed, since it was a workforce without personal ambition, and with no temptation to pretend to knowledge that it did not possess. In order to facilitate their work, we supported a *samizdat* press and were constantly pushing the *samizdat* houses towards semiofficial publication. In that world where books were a threat to the ruling power, they acquired a value that they no longer had in the West. After fruitlessly trying to get your British students to read a book, it was a refreshing experience to arrive in this place where books were forbidden, therefore dangerous, therefore precious and loved. There was no difficulty in sharing your love of books with your students, nor was it strange to these students to seek to belong to the traditional culture of their homeland.

We made a point of not being partisan. That was easy for me, because I am a conservative, and conservatives are not partisan, as you know. However, my colleagues were for the most part leftists, even '68ers, and it was difficult for them to refrain from making propaganda for the causes that were dear to them. But even the leftists came to see that, in this situation, what was sought by the students was knowledge, not opinions, and that the whole operation was an exercise in the art of shutting up, so that writers greater than yourself could take the floor.

As mentioned, we branched out toward music, architecture, and art. The First Republic of Czechoslovakia was the fountainhead of the modernist movement in architecture. Mies Van der Rohe's first attempt at a work of art in concrete and glass stood, then in a derelict state, on the edge of Brno—though it has now been revived as a museum and has become the subject, too, of an interesting novel, *The Glass Room* by Simon Mawer. The Czechs were intrigued by the thought that some architects in the West were turning their backs on the modern movement and trying to rediscover and apply the classical orders. And we were able to send them architects and critics who could give them firsthand knowledge of this anti-modern movement. This had particular significance, too, on account of the association between the early modernists—the Bauhaus in particular—and Marxism-Leninism. If you could recover from modernism in architecture, maybe you could recover from Marxism in politics.

The question arose, around 1985, whether we could not teach our students for a degree course that would be validated by a Western university. We enquired of the various universities that had been set up outside the traditional system—the Freie Universität in Berlin, the Open University, the University of Buckingham—and asked if they would cooperate. They all said no, concurring with our Foreign Office in the view that we were acting outside the received protocol and threatening good relations with our communist neighbors. However, one of our group was a professor in the Divinity Faculty at Cambridge, which had since the Middle Ages had the right to grant its own degrees, which the university would be obliged to authenticate. He agreed to set up a degree course that would be examined by his Faculty.

Theology is a wonderful subject that can be used as a cover for virtually any form of humane speculation. We put together a course that gave to our students all that they wished for, the price being merely ancient Hebrew and New Testament Greek—a price they enthusiastically paid. At the end of the course they sat for the Cambridge degree examinations in a basement, and their papers were smuggled in the diplomatic bag to London. There were three finalists: two received an upper second-class degree, and one, Jiří Schneider, subsequently deputy foreign minister, was awarded a first.

What about the wider agenda? I worked very closely with Jiří Müller, a factory worker who had been five years in prison and who worked from a tiny cupboard in Brno, running a *samizdat* press and a spider's web of networks devoted to defeating the communist assault on his country. He kept quiet about this work, and would not talk to foreigners, so it took me some time to win his confidence. Through him we were able to provide tapes of lectures for schoolchildren on Czech history and literature, and these were distributed to schools across Moravia. To build networks in schools was, of course, especially dangerous, since schoolchildren belonged to the Communist Party. The rule was that nobody should know the identity of anybody else in the network, while Jiří knew them all.

Our rapid expansion was greatly aided by the invention of the portable computer and the floppy disk. One of our collaborators, working in the gray zone between the official and the underground circles, invented a Czech language program for PC, before any such program existed in the hands of the secret police. This greatly facilitated communication and made it clear, in due course, that something in the system had to give: we were running ahead of our oppressors, and they would have to become either *more* frightening or *less*. By default, they chose the latter course.

Those experiences taught me that there is a link, in the end, between humane education, focused on what is intrinsically valuable, and the consciousness of identity—of what I am and to what I belong. Our students had been torn from their roots by the communist system, and they wanted to rediscover those roots, to repossess the past and the culture to which they belonged. Only if they could do this would they have the courage to go on, to recognize that being in the place where they found themselves was not an accident, not a meaningless joke on the part of history, but a call to duty. They wished one day to give back to their country the soul that the communists had stolen.

I draw the lesson that the business of building a collective identity, which is not the business of the state but an aspect of national consciousness, is the enterprise that makes education worthwhile. This is increasingly relevant for us now. It is tempting to say "Totalitarianism is finished; there is no longer the desire or the power to control people's thoughts and words and communicative actions. We now have social media, which will bypass all attempts to dictate to us." But it has not happened that way. We have social media and the internet, and they bring new freedoms; but they also bring new controls. They are as much used to intimidate, to silence discussion, and to propagate orthodoxies as they are used to foster educated debate. And the desire to intimidate has its home, now as then, in the universities. It was the student revolutionaries who led the charge in Russia in 1917, and the university Brownshirts who silenced opposition to Nazism. The totalitarian impulse manifests itself in education before it is observable elsewhere. And this is happening again in our universities. It is precisely in educational institutions that the instinct to control opinion is strongest. Lest, by chance, students should hear a forbidden thought, they must now even be provided with "safe spaces" in which to hide from opinions that might irreparably damage their psyches.

Consider the question of gay rights, as this has been treated in our universities. No sooner was the question raised than a firm orthodoxy emerged in liberal circles, and only one view was thereafter to be heard on the campus. Anyone who disagreed or hesitated, and certainly anyone who was passionately opposed, would be targeted on social media and even "disinvited" from the campus. There is only one view that is now tolerated concerning homosexuality: namely that it is a "legitimate option." All dissent is branded as "homophobia," a state of mind that must be excluded at all costs from polite liberal society. To be guilty of this crime it is sufficient to be accused of it, and once accused, your career as an academic or public figure is in jeopardy. I do not say that dissent in this matter is right or justified; I do say that it is no longer possible freely to express it.

There are many views which have been suddenly projected into prominence as icons of an emerging orthodoxy. We do not know what the next undiscussable issue will be—who could have foretold, for instance, that the divide between good and evil would be suddenly discovered to lie between rival views about bathrooms? Of course, all this has an air of comedy, compared with the censorship exercised by the fascist and communist students of the twentieth century. The penalty administered to the dissident who believes that men who define themselves as women should nevertheless be excluded from women's bathrooms is comparatively mild compared with that administered to the one who argued for the humanity of the Jewish race in a Nazi classroom or the one who taught the truth about Lenin in a Czech university. Nevertheless, the "totalitarian temptation" is with us today as it has been with us for over a century, and we should take note of it.

In the face of that, we ought to be ready to begin a new underground university, in order to defend freedom of thought against the new forms of belligerent ignorance. I cherish the hope that people in our democracies will wake up to the fact that degrees are worthless if no knowledge, but only prejudice, is required in order to receive them. When that thought has become widespread we should begin again, as we began in communist Europe, to teach to small groups of volunteers the things that they wish to know. Bit by bit, our new underground university might grow, and as fast as it grows, the appeal of the old universities will dwindle, until the last student of gender studies wakes up one morning with an urge to read Dante, and signs up for the underground course on *The Divine Comedy*.

Discussion

Emanuelis Zingeris: I have a question for my dear friend Natan Sharansky: You know very well that in '68, when the Czechs were attacked by the Soviet Union, eight people protested in front of the Kremlin. In Yeltsin's time, the numbers increased somewhat. And since

Bolotnaya there have been more and more people protesting. You live in Israel now, but your background is as a refusenik; you come from the democratic forces in Russia. How do you feel now about the growing numbers of independently thinking people in Russia today, and their growth from eight to something more substantial after Yeltsin chose Mr. Putin rather than Boris Nemtsov as his successor?

Natan Sharansky: Back then, eight people was a lot. In our demonstrations of Jews who demanded emigration, ten people participating in a demonstration, standing for five minutes with their slogans, was a lot. The more people who participated in a demonstration, the greater the chance that the KGB knew—and that put demonstrators in real danger. Today we have tens of thousands demonstrating against Putin. We have to understand that even with all the desire to make comparisons between the Soviet Union in Stalin's or Brezhnev's time and today's Russia, there is really no comparison with the totalitarian regime at a time when there was no internet, no satellite TV, no opportunity to speak to people openly, and five million people working as KGB informers. It took us months back then, but today we can reach millions of people in seconds. I think that today it is impossible to create that type of totalitarian regime simply because it is impossible to stop the flow of information. That was our major struggle back then: how to reach people inside the Soviet Union and how to reach people in the West. That's why today, even those who want to create this type of regime cannot, and that is why I have an optimistic side. On the other hand, while I'm praising the internet and saying that you can use it to reach so many people, they say that today the KGB, or its successors, can use the internet to control people, even without millions of informants.

Paul Kamenar: Yesterday, in a major speech in South Korea before its National Assembly, President Trump referred to North Korea as a rogue regime, a sinister regime, a dictatorship, and a cult, all of which is true. But he failed to put an ideological label on it by not calling it a *communist* regime. Did the president miss an opportunity to educate the world about the evils and horrors of communism, as he described the difference between life in North Korea versus the freedom and democracy in South Korea? Or do you think that if he'd done so, he might have offended the Chinese communist leaders that he's also going to meet?

Paula Dobriansky: First, I thought that the speech was striking, because it went into rather strong detail about the human rights atrocities. Was it a missed opportunity on the other front? Earlier this year, President Trump issued a Captive Nations Week proclamation, a statement I mentioned earlier, the historical origins of which are strongly tied up with communism. Each president since Eisenhower to the present, whether Republican or Democrat, has delivered such a statement. So I think he has addressed it on other occasions.

Natan Sharansky: I *do* believe it is very important for the president of the US and the other leaders of the Free World to speak about violations of human rights in China, in Russia, and, if possible, in North Korea. It's very unfortunate that often the leaders of the Free World make strong speeches on Capitol Hill, but when they meet with the leaders of totalitarian regimes, they somehow forget or decide that it is politically incorrect to mention it.

Audience: In the nations of the former USSR, the Czech Republic, and many other eastern European countries that directly suffered the deprivations of communism, there is a surprisingly large part of the public that no longer understands the realities of the regimes of the past and how horrible they were. There seems to be a nostalgia, probably more in Russia than anywhere else. With reference to Russia and the Czech Republic today, could you explain why that has happened, and also what we in the West and specifically in the United States can do about it?

Martin Palouš: I spend most of my time with American students, teaching at Florida International University, but I also know the situation in the Czech Republic. I think we can endlessly complain that young people are not interested enough in important historical lessons, but it is also up to us and our willingness and capability to communicate the message. My experience in Florida is that not very many, almost none, of my twenty-year-old students have ever heard the name Václav Havel or about central Europe. But it is possible to engage them in a meaningful communication about the situation today. I think it's our responsibility. In the Czech Republic the case is the same. I also want to bring us back to the times of the Charter 77 movement, to what was called "independent public space." It was full of educational activities. We could not engage in politics, but we could read classic books, and we could engage ourselves in meaningful conversations. And these conversations were an important part of our resistance. I am certainly not 100 percent pessimistic; I think it's doable. This institution has a great task and all other friendly institutions should do the same. I am also a member of the board of the Havel Library in Prague, which is kind of a presidential library in Prague (it was George W. Bush who inspired Václav Havel in his last visit). And I can tell you for certain that every day, the average age of visitors is somewhere between twenty and thirty. So I'm optimistic.

Natan Sharansky: Whether it is sad or not, people have a short memory about things that are not connected to their daily life. I remember the celebration of the fiftieth anniversary of the Bolshevik Revolution. I was a young student in Moscow and then in St. Petersburg. It was a huge, imperial celebration. It was clear that communism would exist for the next 1,000 years and shape the world. What's interesting is that on the one hundredth anniversary, not only does the USSR no longer exist, but it doesn't even interest anybody except those who study it professionally. I speak a lot with young people in Israel on different issues, and for them, the Bolshevik Revolution is somewhere between the French and American Revolutions—well, it's very, very old history, anyway. It's very similar when you look at Russia and switch on some official programs and see how people express their nostalgia for the days of Stalin. But nobody thinks seriously about any of the facts—about the Gulag for instance— only that they were the times when we were respected by the world, when we had a strong army, and when everybody thought it was a great honor to sign an agreement with us, and they wonder where those times have gone. In order not to repeat the mistakes of the past, we must learn from the past. But unfortunately, as they say, we cannot change human nature.

Audience: I wanted to ask Mr. Sharansky about the relationship between Russia and Israel today and the Putin-Netanyahu relationship.

Natan Sharansky: Well, I'm not present in meetings between Putin and Netanyahu. I was an activist in two movements: the Jewish and human rights movements, and I am involved in the connection between Israeli and Jewish communities, regarding emigration and so on, and am also involved with Russia. I can say that the attitude of Putin personally to Jews is very positive. He is not an anti-Semite. This may be the first time in history that Russia or the Soviet Union has a leader who is not an anti-Semite at all and whose attitude toward the Jews is maybe even positive. As a democrat, I can say the situation is very negative. Putin reversed a lot of democratic changes that had happened. It's sad, it's unfortunate, and of course, we cannot accept it. As for Israel, on one hand, Israel does appreciate the fact that there is no problem with immigration. We have a huge *aliyah* from the former Soviet Union, and as the one responsible for this, I can say that 50 percent of all new immigrants coming to Israel are from Russia and Ukraine and come without any problems. And those who want to live as Jews in their communities in Russia and in Ukraine have absolutely no problems. And we appreciate it. On the other hand, there is no doubt about the role of Russia in arming Hezbollah. Putin personally said that the weapons he gave to Syria would never be used against Israel. Well, during the Second Lebanon War, many of our soldiers were killed by Kornets produced in Tula. Regarding Iran, I personally had many conversations with Putin and others on Iran fifteen or twenty years ago, and everything that was said was wrong. Russia did actively participate in helping Iran to be where it is now. Should we be concerned about the fact that there is a Russian military base in Syria? Of course, we should. But can it be our concern without it being a concern of the United States? It cannot. It is very difficult for us in global issues to be stronger in criticism of Russia than the United States. It's a delicate balance.

Vytautas Landsbergis: The main thing we have talked about today is human rights. Actually, we may have spoken more about the *enemies* of human rights. But the spirit of evil in the world attacks not only human rights, but the human as such—the human soul, the human essence, humanity. If it succeeds in changing the human soul, what will be the point of speaking about human rights? If the human soul is changed, remade as a zombie, or as what was once called *Homo sovieticus* or *Homo hitlerus,* then we are speaking about the dehumanization of humanity. This goes against human rights, but more than that, against human civilization!

Paula Dobriansky: President Landsbergis, if we had had time, I was just going to read from President Reagan's "Evil Empire" speech, where he says, "The source of our strength in the quest for human freedom is not material, but spiritual." It's the very essence of what you just said, and I couldn't agree more.

Martin Palouš: I also fully subscribe to this view, because today there is a kind of misleading concept that human rights is an ever-expanding catalog of our entitlements, which is getting more and more complicated. The point is that it's about human dignity. If you're old-fashioned, and I am, you say "soul." This is the tradition about which we should be reminding ourselves, and this is the central point of our educational activities.

Soviet Imperialism, the Captive Nations, and Global Revolution

Dr. Jeremy Friedman

Global communism. World revolution. Proletarian internationalism. For some people, these are terms conjured by fevered McCarthyite imaginations, or worse, cynical tools employed in the name of rapacious American capitalism and imperialism. For others, they are idealistic glosses on a nefarious, centralized conspiracy directed towards world domination by the Kremlin.

For the first group, communists in Asia, Africa, and Latin America, the regions that made up what was often called the "Third World" during the Cold War, were above all nationalists, fighting for the interests of their people: for independence, national dignity, economic development, and social progress. Their vocal adherence to communism was either a reflection of their idealism or simply a product of the fact that the Western powers that opposed communism also seemed to oppose the independence and progress of Third World states. At times, it reflected the willingness of the Soviets, Chinese, and others to provide aid to their struggles for freedom. When people such as Ho Chi Minh, Fidel Castro, or Mengistu Haile Mariam enacted policies reminiscent of Stalinist Russia or Maoist China, some in this group expressed shock and surprise, and others continued to assert that these leaders were truly motivated by the best interests of their people. Claims that these figures were somehow tied to an international conspiracy was either a tragic mistake leading the United States to undertake costly crusades that were doomed to failure or a cynical ploy on the part of the military-industrial complex to sell its wares.

For the second group, the activities of communists around the world were coordinated from Moscow in a way that differed little from the earliest days of the Comintern. Soviet officials picked locations for revolutionary disruptions that would deprive the West of key raw materials or provide specific strategic advantages. Soviet aid to Angola was an attempt to put a Soviet naval presence astride the routes of oil tankers from the Persian Gulf to Western Europe when the Suez Canal was closed. The Soviet invasion of Afghanistan was the first step toward a Soviet takeover of the Gulf itself. In this model, revolution was exported by Moscow, Beijing, Havana, and sometimes other capitals as part of a concerted plan for world domination, and local communists were either dupes or cynical sub-contractors. Revolutionary disruptions, then, were less the product of local circumstances than they were the manifestations of a new type of imperialist expansion, one made all the more dangerous by clothing itself in the language of justice.

In order to understand the threat that communism represented, it is important that we gain a proper understanding of the relations between communists around the world during the Cold War. Fortunately, the opening of archives and publishing of memoirs allows us windows into these relationships—windows that would have been unimaginable during the Cold War. The issue of the relationships between communist parties was central to their legitimacy. Opponents, both domestic and foreign, often attacked communists as agents of a foreign power who put the interests of international communism, or the Kremlin, above those of their compatriots, or the working masses they claimed to represent. Communists often countered by claiming that they were nationalists, authentic representatives of the people. Moreover, they were often the people's truest advocates because of their opposition to foreign imperialism, bolstered by the prominent role that communists often played in anti-colonial struggles. They claimed that their policy choices were their own, and that their sources of support and funding were domestic. The truth, however, lies somewhere in between.

Despite the disbanding of the Comintern in 1943 and the Cominform in 1956, communist parties around the world remained in very close contact. The International Department of the Central Committee of the Communist Party of the Soviet Union took over many of the activities and responsibilities of the Comintern. These included regular consultations, the dispensing of advice and direction, ideological instruction, and the provision of textbooks, propaganda materials, printing presses, cash, and much more to communist parties around the world.

Contact was much more frequent than many observers understood at the time. For example, the Indonesian Communist Party, the world's third-largest in the late 1950s and '60s and a popular object of study among Western scholars at the time, claimed to be charting its own unique path based on Indonesian conditions and national interests. This claim was bolstered by scholars who relied on interviews with Indonesian communist leaders and published documents. The truth was more complicated. Indonesia's strategy for taking power through peaceful means was actually crafted with significant guidance from the Chinese and from Joseph Stalin himself between 1950 and 1952. Indonesian communist leaders remained in nearly constant contact with the Soviets and the Chinese through both embassy and International Department contacts, and factions within the leadership of the Indonesian Communist Party used contacts with Moscow and/or Beijing for leverage in internecine struggles.

   This is not to say that the Indonesian Communist Party, one of the loudest voices in the international communist movement for the independence of individual parties, was simply a tool of outside powers. Rather, it demonstrates that the relationships among communist parties during the Cold War were something like a franchise. Moscow felt itself in a position to decide who would and would not be allowed to lead the local franchise of the international communist movement, and it enforced this through attempts to control individual leaders and policy positions. The nature of this relationship became clearest in limited cases such as that of Indonesia, where a communist party that was powerful enough to seek independence nevertheless found itself constantly having to explain, justify, and protect itself from its ostensible benefactor, often by calling on the support of the Chinese.

   Unlike business franchises, however, money tended to flow from the headquarters to the local franchisers rather than the other way around. Funding of communist parties was a central issue in these discussions over whether the parties were really "nationalist" or not. Despite claims, again using the Indonesian Communist Party as an example, that funding sources were all domestic, we now know that funding communist parties abroad was a regular function of the Soviet Communist Party. In fact, there was something like a regular appropriations process, in which funds were allocated to parties and movements in good standing with Moscow. Anyone who wanted an increase in funding would request it from the International Department, which would combine these requests into an annual budgetary proposal for foreign communist funding. Delivery of the money often required a greater deal of creativity, but the appropriations process seems remarkably routine.

While the ties between communist parties during the Cold War were more robust than many at the time imagined, this does not mean that international communism functioned according to a plan drawn up by the Kremlin. Contrary to visions of Soviet strategists plotting revolutions on a map, most of the time Soviet leaders found themselves responding to events rather than creating them. Places like Angola, Ethiopia, Nicaragua, and Vietnam were not locations chosen to expose the vulnerabilities of the free world, but rather revolutionary opportunities that Soviet leaders felt obliged to support. In the imagination of Soviet leaders, the historical processes described by Marxist-Leninist theory leading to the worldwide victory of socialism were inevitable. Their job was therefore not to export revolution, but to make room for history to take its course by preventing "imperialism" from artificially delaying the historical process of revolutionary transformation. This led the Soviets to find themselves devoting massive amounts of resources to places they found strategically inconvenient and politically useless, since it meant that any would-be revolutionary had some kind of legitimate claim on the resources of the socialist motherland.

Often, this put the Soviet Union at the mercy of its supposed clients. Moscow's worries that Cuban adventurism would create unwelcome problems in Latin America led to the Soviets telling the

Bolivian communists not to help Che Guevara—and might have even gone as far as to play an active role in his death. Most significantly, it meant that the Soviet Union often found itself at the mercy of the North Vietnamese leadership, which was determined to prosecute a war that many in Moscow thought it could not win. Nevertheless, Hanoi maneuvered between Moscow and Beijing during the Sino-Soviet split to gain the maximum amount of aid from each while simultaneously maintaining as much policy autonomy as possible. A large part of Hanoi's leverage, though, came from the fact that the North Vietnamese leaders were such devoted communists, and that both they and their communist patrons understood their cause as being central to the fate of international communism, rather than being simply a Vietnamese nationalist struggle. It was therefore the sincere belief in the communist cause, rather than strategic calculation, that led the Soviets and others to see involvement in the Third World as not just an opportunity but an obligation.

This understanding can help us resolve certain questions arising from the nature of Cold War geopolitics. First of all, the "Domino Theory," though much mocked as the province of paranoid anti-communists, contained a great deal of substance. Since communist parties relied so heavily on external help, it made sense that the fall of one country to communism would make its neighbors more susceptible to communist insurgency: it would open paths for the supply of men and matériel and provide strategic depth. Taking this view, the fact that the rest of Southeast Asia did not become communist after the fall of South Vietnam does not invalidate the theory: it just means that the dominoes were stopped in Thailand rather than in South Vietnam. The importance of territorial contiguity to communist insurrection was also demonstrated in Indonesia, where the desire of the Indonesian communists to start a guerilla insurgency was countered by Stalin and the Chinese on the simple grounds that Indonesia was an archipelago. If Indonesia had shared a land border with China, it almost certainly would have had a communist guerilla insurgency.

Similarly, this can help us understand the failure of détente. Détente seems to have been doomed ultimately because the two sides had different understandings of its meaning. For the United States, détente seems to have been understood as something like a ceasefire, in which both sides would stop their advances and leave things as they were. But for the Soviets, freezing the world in place was not only impossible; it was not their choice to make. Who were they to stop history? They could not prevent revolutionary explosions in Angola, Ethiopia, or elsewhere, and they were obliged to support them when they occurred.

In sum, the evidence that has become available in the wake of the Cold War helps us to see that Soviet communism was indeed an international phenomenon, not because the Soviet Union was run by a power-hungry clique bent on world domination, but rather because the ideological underpinnings of the revolution required it to be international and to remain so, whether or not that ultimately redounded to the advantage of either the Soviets or other communists around the world.

Dr. John Earl Haynes

Earl Browder, leader of the Communist Party of the USA (CPUSA) from 1930 until 1945, claimed in 1960 that an article in the April 1945 issue of *Les Cahiers du Communisme* constituted "the first public declaration of the Cold War."[62] He was particularly sensitive because if this early 1945 article was the first shot in the Cold War, he was the one who took the bullet. As a result of its publication, his colleagues ousted him from the leadership of the CPUSA.

The background for Browder's claim is as follows. After the Nazi-Soviet Pact of August 1939, the CPUSA dropped its Popular Front policy and its support for President Franklin Roosevelt and the New Deal. The CPUSA and its allies, particularly strong in the Congress of Industrial Organizations (CIO), harshly attacked FDR's program of assisting those nations fighting Nazi Germany and opposed FDR's reelection in 1940, denouncing Roosevelt as an imperialist and fascist. Communists and their allies took a fierce antiwar stance and opposed passage of the Lend-Lease Act and military conscription.

On June 22, 1941, however, Hitler invaded the Soviet Union. American communists knew they would be dropping their antiwar policy and shifting to defending the Soviet Union. However, they were initially unsure as to what line Moscow wanted toward Britain and those other nations fighting Nazi Germany. Consequently, the initial statements by the CPUSA, while calling for an all-out defense of the Soviet Union, were cautious about any assistance toward those, such as the British, who had been fighting Hitler since 1939. The day after the invasion, for instance, the *Daily Worker* warned that the Nazi attack on the USSR set up the conditions for a new "Munich," a peace between Nazi Germany and Great Britain leaving the Soviet Union alone to face the Nazis.[63]

---

[62] Earl Browder, "How Stalin Ruined the American Communist Party," *Harper's Monthly*, March 1960, 45.
[63] *Daily Worker*, June 23, 1941, 1.

The Communist International (Comintern) in Moscow, however, quickly provided different instructions, and on June 26 sent the CPUSA the outline of a more far-reaching change in policy. The message, labeled "please decipher at once," stated that "the aggression of German fascism against [the] Soviet Union has basically changed [the] whole international situation and [the] character of the war itself." Georgi Dimitrov, chief of the Comintern, told the CPUSA that the anti-capitalist and anti-imperialist phraseology that had dominated communist rhetoric during the Nazi-Soviet Pact period no long applied, explaining that the war was now to be seen as "neither a class war nor a war for socialist revolution," but a "just war of defense."[64] Another Comintern message reinforced the point that Marxist-Leninist concepts would be dropped for the time being. It told American communists to "keep in mind that at the given stage the question is about defense of peoples against fascist enslavement and not about socialist revolution. Acknowledge receipt. Transmit this directive to the Latin-American comrades."[65]

Dimitrov also explained that

> this basic change of situation and of character of the war requires also a change in tactics of the Party. The main task now is to exert every effort in order to secure the victory of the Soviet people and to smash the fascist barbarians. Everything must be subordinated to this main task. From this follows; first that the Communists and the

---

[64] Dimitrov to New York, "The aggression of ...", 26 June 1941, RGASPI 495-184-3 (1941 file). RGASPI: Russian State Archive of Socio-Political History.
[65] "Perfidious attack against ...", RGASPI 495-184-3 (1941 file). Internal evidence dates this message to approximately the same time as the document cited in ibid. The Comintern often used the CPUSA as a conduit for instructions to Latin American Communist parties.

working-class in America ... with all forces and all means, must resolutely raise struggle against German fascism. Secondly, they must demand from the American government all aid to the Soviet people.[66]

Dimitrov also dealt with the issue of aid to Britain in his June 26 message. He ordered the CPUSA to drop opposition to assisting Britain, explaining that communists must "support all measures of the government which makes possible the continuation of the struggle of the Anglo-American bloc against fascist Germany; because this struggle itself is actually a help to the just war of the Soviet people."[67]

Once the Comintern's orders arrived, the CPUSA adjusted its position as instructed. On June 28, the Party adopted a "People's Program of Struggle for the Defeat of Hitler and Hitlerism" that accorded in full with Dimitrov's message. The statement denounced Nazi Germany as a menace not only to the Soviet Union but also to "the American people, the British people and the people of the world." Prior rhetoric opposing aid to Britain vanished; instead, the new line demanded all possible aid to anyone fighting Hitler. The party then set about reviving its Popular Front policies and presenting itself as an ardent backer of President Roosevelt.

The Comintern's orders to the American party were not, of course, unique. As soon as Germany attacked, Stalin instructed the Comintern "not to raise the issue of socialist revolution but rather to stress the common threat of fascism to the peoples of the world," according to historian Eduard Mark. "In addressing the secretariat of the Comintern on the evening of June 22, the Comintern's head, Georgi Dimitrov, elaborated

---

[66] Dimitrov to New York, "The aggression of ..."
[67] Dimitrov to New York, "The aggression of ..."

the new policy, directing, *inter alia*, that movements of national liberation be created that should include not only workers but [also] the petite bourgeoisie, intellectuals, and peasants; calls for world revolution were to cease—for the time being."[68] Orders then flowed to individual parties such as the CPUSA about how to implement the new policy, as well as broad statements directed collectively to all communist parties around the world.

Stalin's new National Front policy served his immediate goal of a stance by which communists around the world could rally broad support for assisting the USSR's defense. But as the war proceeded it also served Stalin's need to deepen the wartime "Grand Alliance" with the United States and Britain by reassuring the latter that the Soviet Union and communism no longer represented a revolutionary threat to democratic societies and capitalist free-market economies.

Earl Browder's problem came from over-interpreting Stalin's policy. In late 1943, Browder decided that this wartime convergence of communist interests and those of the United States and Britain was not temporary. Pointing to the November 1943 agreements between Roosevelt, Churchill, and Stalin at Tehran as evidence that the ruling classes of the US and Britain had put aside hopes of destroying communism and had come to accept the Soviet Union as a full partner in world affairs, Browder decided that "the greatest, most important turning point in all history" had occurred.[69]

---

[68] Eduard Mark, "Revolution by Degrees: Stalin's National-Front Strategy for Europe, 1941–1947," Working Paper No. 31 (Washington, DC: Cold War International History Project, Woodrow Wilson International Center for Scholars, 2001), 15.

[69] Earl Browder, "Teheran—History's Greatest Turning Point," *The Communist*, January 1944, 3.

Stalin's dissolution of the Communist International in 1943 further persuaded Browder that the USSR would not renew the drive for world revolution in the foreseeable future. Nor did he see any prospects for social revolution in America after the war; he was also convinced that postwar Europe "probably will be reconstructed on a bourgeois-democratic, non-fascist capitalist basis, not upon a Soviet basis."[70] It is easy to understand how Browder reached such a conclusion. As Mark observed,

> From the Atlantic Charter onward the Soviet Union signed every agreement promising democratic self-determination to the occupied nations of Europe; it even tendered unilateral assurances of its own. Soviet diplomats routinely explained to Western colleagues that Moscow "did not want to Sovietize the Eastern European states," though it "would insist on Governments whose policy was friendly to the Soviet Union, which did not preclude equally friendly relations with Britain and [the United States]." Stalin himself made light of world revolution at Teheran, saying "We won't worry about that. We have found it is not so easy to set up a Communist society."[71]

In light of his understanding of world conditions and his reading of Stalin's intent, Browder felt American communists should assign the dictatorship of the proletariat to the distant future and focus on preventing reactionaries from sabotaging long-term Soviet-American cooperation. In order to promote that end, the CPUSA should not "raise the issue of socialism in such a form and manner as to endanger or weaken national

---

[70] Browder, "Teheran," 7.
[71] Mark, "Revolution by Degrees," 16.

unity" and was "ready to cooperate in making this capitalism work effectively."[72]

However, Browder went further than a standard restatement of the National Front policy. What made his "Teheran doctrine," as he called it, unique was that Browder added a new (for communists) analysis of America's domestic political system. Rather than seeing the Democratic and Republican parties as representing the political interests of the bourgeois class, he said:

> These parties are parties only in a formal and legal sense; they are not parties in the sense of representing well-defined alternative policies. They are coalitions of local and regional interests, diverse tendencies of political thought, and institutionalized politics ... that in most other countries would be separate parties.[73]

Although communists had worked within the New Deal coalition in the late 1930s, the CPUSA had been careful to maintain its formal independence and its claim to be the only legitimate representative of the working class. In the minds of American communists, the Popular Front stance of the 1930s had been a tactical alignment, not a permanent strategy, and the party's formal independence was a sign that it kept its options open. Browder called for a change, saying, "If the lesser group takes the name of party and become one of the so-called minor parties it is regarded as a sect which has withdrawn itself from the practical political

---

[72] "Browder, "Teheran," 19.
[73] Earl Russell Browder, *Teheran and America: Perspectives and Tasks*, pamphlet (New York: Workers Library Publishers, 1944), 29, 40.

life of the nation."[74] Browder in effect rejected the CPUSA's policy of claiming to be an independent political force as ineffective and implicitly rejected the Communist Party's traditional claim to be the only legitimate representative of the proletariat.

In line with his revision of orthodox Marxist-Leninist political analysis of the American political system and the communist role in it, Browder ordered a sweeping restructuring of the American communist movement. The Young Communist League dissolved and reformed as the American Youth for Democracy (AYD). The AYD presented itself as a broad liberal-left organization of progressive youth and did not advocate Marxism-Leninism or even socialism. The most striking change came in May 1944, when the Communist Party of the USA itself dissolved and re-formed as a non-party organization entitled the Communist Political Association (CPA).

Browder envisaged communists as the militant left-wing of a broad progressive coalition and the CPA functioning as an energetic left advocacy group within the existing Democratic and Republican two-party system. In Browder's view, full integration into the existing two-party system was the most effective way for communists to support the Roosevelt administration's policies of a New Deal at home and a Soviet-American alliance abroad.

Browder's reorganization of the CPUSA and his revision of Marxist-Leninist political analysis, if sustained over time, would have thoroughly transformed the nature of the American communist movement. Browder, however, had gone well beyond what the Comintern and Stalin

---

[74] Browder, *Teheran and America*, 40.

had in mind with the National Front policy. Stalin had never intended the National Front policy to be a permanent stance. In many forums Stalin emphasized that the goal was always the same: socialism (defined as the totalitarian state Stalin had created). How to get there, however, was a matter of tactics and changed when necessary. For example, Stalin, in a speech to German communists just after the war, urged avoidance of disruptive immediate Sovietization in East Germany, remarking "you should advance toward socialism not by taking a straight road but by moving in zigzags."[75]

What Browder thought was a permanent change in Stalin's policy was, alas for Browder, a zigzag. Later a number of historians would make the same error. As Mark observed, "A common mistake of historians is to suppose that the national fronts that Stalin put in place late in the war and just after it were ends in themselves and not means to a preordained end. To a considerable degree, Cold War revisionism has been based upon that error."[76]

World War II had cut off close contact between the CPUSA and the Communist International. The yearly visits by numerous CPUSA officials and cadres to Moscow to report on American affairs and to undergo Comintern training and the dispatch of Comintern representatives to the United States—standard practice in the 1920s and 1930s—were not practical after wartime restrictions on travel began in late 1939. The shipment of CPUSA documents to Moscow also declined to a trickle from

---

[75] From Vladimir K. Volkov, "German Question as Stalin Saw It (1947–1952)," paper for the conference "Stalin and the Cold War, 1945–1953," Cold War International History Project, September 1999, quoted in Mark, "Revolution by Degrees," 17.

[76] Mark, "Revolution by Degrees," 17, note 33.

the thousands of pages prior to the war. And, of course, in 1943 the Comintern itself dissolved. With the war on, supervising foreign communist parties was low on Moscow's priority list, but it was still on the list. And the Comintern's central staff, although officially dissolved, lived on in several secret "institutes" that were eventually absorbed by the International Department of the Communist Party of the Soviet Union (CPSU) and carried on the tasks of the Comintern, although in a more discreet manner.

In early 1944, Browder sent Georgi Dimitrov, head of the nominally no-longer-existing Comintern, a report on his plans to reform the American communist movement. Within the confines of the CPUSA's National Committee, Browder's plans had been criticized by William Foster. Although a leading figure in CPUSA since the early 1920s, he had clashed with Browder over the years and was by this time isolated and no longer commanded a party faction. Browder brushed aside Foster's criticism but did agree to forward his plans and Foster's objections to Moscow. Browder later told his colleagues that Moscow supported his views, and he forced Foster not only to withdraw his objection but also to preside over the expulsion of Sam Darcy, a veteran CPUSA official who had supported Foster. Foster's criticism was known only to a small circle of high party officials, there was no significant dissent to Browder's plans, and when the CPUSA met in convention on May 20, 1944, Foster, the figurehead chairman of the party, presided over a unanimous vote to dissolve the party. The delegates then constituted themselves as the founding convention of the Communist Political Association and unanimously elected Earl Browder as the president of the CPA. (His

CPUSA title of "general secretary" was dropped as part of a nomenclature change to make the organization sound more American.)

Browder, however, had deceived his colleagues about Moscow's attitude. In *The Soviet World of American Communism*, Harvey Klehr and I quoted a March 1944 coded cable Dimitrov sent Browder. His message was not an endorsement of Browder's views. Instead, it was a warning. Dimitrov said:

> The new theoretical, political and tactical positions developing among you somewhat disturb me. Aren't you venturing a little far in adapting to changes in the international situation, in fact right up to negation of the theory and practice of the class struggle and the necessity for the working class to have its own political party? I ask you to think over all of this again and report your reflections.

To underline the seriousness of the matter, he added, "Please confirm your receipt of this telegram."[77]

Browder, who believed fervently in his own ideological sagacity, appears to have thought that he understood better than Dimitrov where history and Stalin were going. Confident that Stalin's 1941–45 stance of putting world revolution on the back burner and seeking alliance with the United States and Great Britain was a long-range strategic policy and not

---

[77] Harvey Klehr, John Earl Haynes, and Kyrill M. Anderson, *The Soviet World of American Communism* (New Haven: Yale University Press, 1998), 106. The message is in Georgi Dimitrov's diary, 7–8 March 1944, RGASPI 146-2-13. The message is also reproduced in Georgi Dimitrov, *The Diary of Georgi Dimitrov, 1933–1949,* ed. Ivo Banac (New Haven: Yale University Press, 2003), 307. This telegram is also discussed in James G. Ryan, *Earl Browder: The Failure of American Communism* (Tuscaloosa: University of Alabama Press, 1997), 229.

just a temporary wartime tactic, Browder ignored Dimitrov's warning and carried out his plans. Browder was confident that when the postwar world developed on the basis of continued American-Soviet friendship, Dimitrov would recognize that Browder's reforms had reshaped the American communist movement to fully support that situation.

Nothing, however, worked out as Browder anticipated. The postwar period brought the Cold War, not the era of American-Soviet comity that he had anticipated. And, before the Cold War was even publicly underway, he had been removed as leader of the CPA in response to an indirect signal of Moscow's disapproval of his course.[78]

The April 1945 issue of *Les Cahiers du Communisme*, a journal published by the Communist Party of France, included an article by Jacques Duclos, a senior French party official, entitled "On the Dissolution of the American Communist Party." The Duclos essay stated flatly that Browder's views were "erroneous conclusions in no wise flowing from a Marxist analysis of the situation" and that his "notorious revision of Marxism" had led to the "liquidation of the independent political party of the working class." The essay denied that the wartime Soviet-American agreements could be interpreted to lay the foundation for "a political platform of class peace in the postwar era" or that there was "the possibility of the suppression of the class struggle in the postwar period." Instead, the article said the Tehran agreement of the Soviet Union with Britain and the United States was only "a document of a diplomatic

---

[78] Browder's ouster is discussed at length in Ryan's *Earl Browder*.

character."[79] Put another way, Browder had confused a zigzag with a permanent change of doctrine.

The Duclos article became public in the United States in May 1945. American communists concluded that Duclos's essay was a Moscow message; Duclos had no reason to concern himself with the American movement without Moscow's prodding. Moreover, he had also quoted Foster's critical comments, but Foster's comments that had been sent only to Moscow, not to the French.

Earl Browder had been the supreme leader of the American communist movement since the early 1930s. Most major and minor officials in the CPUSA owed their position to his approval. Most rank-and-file members had joined the party subsequent to his taking the leadership and had no memory of any party leader prior to Browder. None of this counted when Moscow, even by the indirect means of the Duclos article, indicated its disapproval. In June the Communist Political Association stripped Browder of his executive power and in July 1945 an emergency convention dissolved the CPA and reconstituted the Communist Party of the USA. Later the CPUSA denounced its former leader as "an unreconstructed revisionist ... a socialimperialist ... an enemy of the working class ... a renegade ... an apologist for American imperialism" and in early 1946 expelled him from the party.[80]

Browder's argument that the Duclos article was the first declaration of the Cold War (and he the first casualty) rested on this logic:

---

[79] Jacques Duclos, "A propos de la dissolution du P.C.A.," *Les Cahiers du Communisme,* Nouvelle Serie, no. 6 (April 1945), 21–38. An English translation can be found in *Political Affairs* 24 (July 1945), 656–672.

[80] *Daily Worker*, April 30, 1946, 2.

He had reorganized the Communist Party into a movement tailored for an era of peaceful Soviet-American coexistence, not one prepared for Soviet-American rivalry. In light of the criticisms contained in the Duclos article, the CPUSA in the late summer of 1945 changed its strategy from Browder's policy of integration into mainstream politics to a post-Browder policy of positioning itself for possible confrontation with those who did not support American accommodation to Stalin's postwar goals. Browder assumed that the Duclos article had been largely written in Moscow and that it was intended to prepare the CPUSA for an anticipated Soviet-American confrontation.

Browder was not alone in taking this view. In mid-1945, long before Browder offered his retrospective judgment, Raymond Murphy, a senior State Department official, suggested to his colleagues that the Duclos article might be a harbinger of increased Soviet aggressiveness. Other commentators have echoed Browder's and Murphy's view that the Duclos article signaled Stalin's Cold War intentions.[81]

Browder's argument presumed that the Duclos article was largely written in Moscow. Since 1945 most scholars have judged the Duclos article to have been a Moscow message, although a few have had doubts.[82]

---

[81] Raymond E. Murphy memorandum, "Possible Resurrection of Communist International, Resumption of Extreme Leftist Activities, Possible Effect on United States," June 2, 1945, in *Foreign Relations of the United States: The Conference of Berlin (The Potsdam Conference)*, 1945, vol. 1, (US Department of State, Washington, DC: Government Printing Office, 1960), 267–280; Arthur Schlesinger, Jr., "Origins of the Cold War," *Foreign Affairs* 46 (October 1967), 43–44; Philip J. Jaffe, *The Rise and Fall of American Communism* (New York: Horizon Press, 1975), 206–210, 230.

[82] For example, M. J. Heale in *American Anticommunism: Combating the Enemy Within, 1830–1970* (Baltimore: Johns Hopkins University Press, 1990) would allow only that the Duclos article was "apparently reflecting the views of Moscow," 134. Ellen Schrecker skeptically called the Duclos article "supposedly

Opinions differed more widely about whether the article was actually written by Soviet officials or whether Moscow only encouraged the attack on Browder's ideological presumption but left the details of the theoretical analysis and criticism to Duclos. If the latter, then the view that the article was a harbinger of Soviet Cold War intentions would have been weakened because the harsh attacks on the "political platform of class peace in the postwar era" and its narrowing of the significance of the Tehran agreement to only a "diplomatic" meaning could have been only Duclos's gloss.

In *The Soviet World of American Communism,* Klehr and I show that the Duclos article was not only written in Moscow but was first published in Russian in the January 1945 issue of the *Bulletin of the Information Bureau of the CC RCP(b): Issues of Foreign Policy.*[83] This secret journal circulated only among high officials of the Soviet government and the CPSU. The article listed no author, indicating it was a collective and authoritative editorial product. Only then was it translated into French and sent to Paris for publication under Duclos's name. The differences between the January 1945 translation we found and the final French published version are minor. Someone, presumably the French, revised occasional phrases into more idiomatic French and added a few opening sentences attempting (unconvincingly) to give a plausible reason for Duclos to concern himself with the CPUSA, as well as a few closing

---

Moscow-inspired." Ellen Schrecker, *Many Are the Crimes: McCarthyism in America* (Boston: Little, Brown, 1998), 132.

[83] Klehr, Haynes, and Anderson, 91–106. Some of the same evidence is also discussed in Alexander Dallin and Fridrikh Igorevich Firsov, *Dimitrov and Stalin 1934–1943: Letters from the Soviet Archives* (New Haven: Yale University Press, 2000), 257–60.

paragraphs seeking to immunize the French Communist Party from charges that its own policies were similar to those of Browder.

While documentation that the Duclos article was written in Moscow and was an authoritative statement of the CPSU's International Department strengthens the case that it was "the first public declaration of the Cold War," the issue is more complicated. Dimitrov's March 1944 cable showed his doubts about the ideological propriety of Browder's plans. Browder's theoretical stance and organizational reforms, when taken to their conclusions, set aside the communist movement's vanguard role and as a practical matter so integrated communists into mainstream American pluralist politics that over time their distinctive identity (and their ability to be used as an instrument of Soviet policy) would be lost. Even without anticipating a postwar Soviet-American confrontation, Kremlin ideologists might have found Browder's revisionism too much to stomach.

Dimitrov's March 1944 warning, while clear, was mildly phrased and did not contain the unalloyed condemnation of the later Duclos article or its suggestion of an approaching era of Western-Soviet confrontation. Soviet officials may have found Browder's disregard of Dimitrov's warning and his decision to go ahead with his program an intolerable presumption by the head of a national communist party. The Comintern as a mechanism of Soviet control had been abolished, but the reality of Soviet suzerainty had not. Additionally, by the time the article was written in late 1944, the possibility of a postwar break with the West may have loomed larger in Soviet thinking.

The reconstitution of the CPUSA in 1945 repudiated "Browderism," but it did not repudiate the Popular Front strategy of the

CPUSA and was fully in line with Stalin's still reigning National Front policy. There was no revision to the harsh partisan stance of the Nazi-Soviet Pact period and certainly not to the overtly revolutionary stance of the late 1920s and early 1930s. American communists, after ousting Browder, continued to emphasize working with liberal and left allies within the CIO and within a number of ostensibly non-communist organizations, such as the National Citizens Political Action Committee; the Independent Citizens Committee of the Arts, Sciences, and Professions; the Progressive Citizens of America; and, ultimately, the 1948 Progressive Party that nominated Henry Wallace for the presidency.

From a Soviet perspective, in one sense the Progressive Party and Wallace's candidacy demonstrated the success of the Duclos article. As relations between the West and the Soviet bloc deteriorated in 1946 and 1947, the reconstituted CPUSA maneuvered to promote criticism in liberal and labor circles of President Truman's developing Cold War policies. And when it became clear that Truman would persist, communists maneuvered to pull their allies and friends out of the Democratic Party and create a third-party challenge, the Progressive Party, for the leadership of the liberal-left in America. In contrast to Truman, Wallace blamed the West for the increasing tensions with the USSR and advocated America accommodating Stalin's foreign policy goals. If Browderism had prevailed, communists might well have found themselves so well integrated into the two-party system that mounting a third-party campaign might have been impossible and a challenge to Truman muffled. On the other hand, Wallace and the Progressive Party's overt support of Stalin's foreign policy goals and their poor showing in the 1948 election resulted in the CPUSA losing most of its liberal allies and being driven from the

CIO. The 1948 election broke the back of the Popular Front in America and put the CPUSA on a downward spiral from which it never recovered.

The CPUSA's continued Popular Front stance from 1945 to 1948 paralleled Stalin's policy for postwar Europe. During the war Stalin desperately needed Britain and the United States as military allies fighting Nazi Germany in the west while the Soviets fought Germany in the east, as well as needing the massive economic and military aid of American Lend-Lease that sustained the Soviet military machine and even the USSR's ability to avoid starvation. Stalin's wartime National Front policy supported this vital alliance by reassuring the United States and Britain that the USSR and its communist subordinates were no longer an existential threat to Western democracy. Victory over Germany, however, did not immediately end Stalin's desire to sustain the Grand Alliance.

Victorious though the USSR was, the war left it economically devastated and, without Lend-Lease, facing a difficult trade-off between sustaining its military machine and rebuilding its economy. The continuation of the wartime alliance would reduce the threat to Soviet security and allow more resources to be transferred to economic rehabilitation. Additionally, continuation of the alliance might mean American aid in the form of loans and credits to assist in economic rebuilding. As Mark noted, Stalin had "every reason to suspect that if he followed in Eastern Europe and the Balkans anything like the program he had applied to the Baltic states, Eastern Poland, Bessarabia, and Bukovina during 1939–41—immediate revolution through massacre and deportation—there would follow in the West so sharp a reaction" that all hope of maintaining the Grand Alliance as well as any prospect of American economic support would be ended.[84]

Stalin's alternative to the blood-soaked repression of 1939–41 was a continuation in the postwar period of the National Front policy as a transitional mechanism to full Sovietization. In the short run, this would reassure the West and at least partially meet the multiple promises the Soviets had made of respecting the national independence and supporting democratic institutions in the liberated states of Eastern Europe. Stalin envisioned the postwar governments in Eastern Europe as regimes where the institutions of "bourgeois" democracy would be maintained and some space allowed for non-communist political entities. In his view, communist parties would be the dominant political actor in broad-ruling National Front coalitions with social democratic, liberal, and peasant political parties that deferred to communist leadership. (Fascists, rightists, and monarchists, however, would be repressed.) Over time, the success of communist leadership of the National Front coalitions would see the withering away of non-communist entities and the eventual implementation of total communist regimes. And, in fact, from 1945 and for a few years thereafter, the regimes of Eastern Europe imposed under Soviet occupation were built on this vision, with National Front coalition governments that allowed limited but real political space for non-communist socialist, liberal, and peasant political formations.

However, Stalin's confidence that his National Front policy would lead eventually to Sovietization while simultaneously reassuring the West had been based on faulty premises. He assumed the postwar communist

---

[84] Mark, 14–15. Here and below follows the argument Mark advances.

parties of Eastern Europe would be popular and have electoral success. In fact, while certainly much stronger than they were before the war, the postwar communist parties fell well short of electorally dominating their rivals, despite the patronage of Soviet occupation authorities. Soviet assumptions that the new National Front governments would achieve rapid economic success that would build popular support for communist leadership also proved faulty as mismanagement was widespread and economic rehabilitation slow. The leaders and cadres of the Eastern European communist parties, while voicing the pieties of National Front compromise and civil behavior, found it much harder to restrain their repressive instincts. Their thuggish behavior did little to increase communist electoral appeal. Non-communist political formations also failed to defer to communist leadership and aggressively competed for popular support and political influence.

Stalin soon realized that his postwar National Front policy was failing to work as he had anticipated. He also realized that ending the National Front policy likely meant forfeiting the postwar continuation of the wartime alliance. But it was a price he was willing to pay. As Eduard Mark stated:

> From his Marxist-Leninist perspective, moreover, it was
> obviously more prudent that the military security of the
> USSR should ultimately be entrusted to a glacis of
> socialized states in Eastern Europe than to agreements
> with capitalist states that he viewed as intrinsically
> predatory potential enemies.... The chief deterrent to
> Stalin's reordering of Eastern Europe unilaterally after the
> fashion of 1940 was the expectation that significant
> advantages would accrue in the shorter term from
> continued association with the West. Two processes,

which began to work almost simultaneously soon after the war, disabused him of this hope. The weakness of the national fronts became apparent, presenting him with a stark choice of either seeing Eastern Europe fall into the hands of non-communist political parties or else resorting to repression inimical to continued alliance with the United States and Britain. At the same time, Western positions at the meetings of the Council of Foreign Ministers and at the Paris Peace Conference increasingly showed Stalin that he had invested excessively in his hopes for continued alliance with the Western democracies. Washington soon decided that it would not extend economic aid or even credits to the USSR.... Stalin's reasons for maintaining the alliance gradually evaporated. That, in turn, removed the chief inhibition against the use of methods to consolidate the faltering "popular democracies" of Eastern Europe that were faster and cruder than Moscow had envisioned in its wartime instructions to the region's Communists.[85]

By 1947 or 1948, depending on the country, the political space provided to non-communist entities was erased and replaced by a far more repressive regime modeled directly on the Soviet police state example. By 1950, the liberated nations of 1945 had become the captive nations of the Cold War.

Mark Kramer

In the closing months of World War II and the latter half of the 1940s, the Soviet Union oversaw the establishment of communist regimes throughout Central and Eastern Europe. Over the next four decades, those

---

[85] Mark, 45–46.

regimes constituted what was informally known as the Soviet bloc. Initially, China, which fell under communist rule in 1949, was also part of the bloc. The first major breach in the Soviet bloc occurred in 1948, when Yugoslavia was expelled amid a deepening rift with the Soviet Union. A more serious breach occurred at the end of the 1950s, when a bitter dispute erupted between China and the Soviet Union and soon became irreconcilable. The Sino-Soviet rift also inspired Albania to leave the bloc. Aside from these three breaches, however, the Soviet bloc remained intact until 1989, when the collapse of East European Communism put an end to the bloc once and for all.

The establishment of communism in Eastern Europe proceeded at varying rates. In Yugoslavia and Albania, the indigenous communist parties led by Josip Broz Tito and Enver Hoxha had obtained sufficient political leverage and military strength through their roles in the anti-Nazi resistance to eliminate their opposition and assume outright power as World War II drew to a close. In the Soviet zone of Germany, the Soviet occupation forces and control commission enabled the Socialist Unity Party (*Sozialistische Einheitspartei Deutschlands*, or SED) to gain preeminent power well before the East German state was formed in 1949. Similarly, in Bulgaria and Romania, communist-dominated governments were imposed under Soviet pressure in early 1945.

Elsewhere in the region, events followed a more gradual pattern. Exiles returning from Moscow played a crucial role in the formation of what initially were broad coalition governments, which carried out extensive land redistribution and other sweeping economic and political changes. The reform process, however, was kept under tight communist control, and the top jobs in the Ministry of Internal Affairs were reserved exclusively for Communist Party members. From those posts, they could oversee the purging of the local police forces, the execution of "collaborators," the control and censorship of the media, and the ouster and intimidation of non-communist ministers and legislators. Supported by the tanks and troops of the Soviet Army, the communist parties gradually solidified their hold through the determined use of what the Hungarian Communist Party leader Mátyás Rákosi called "salami tactics."

Moscow's supervision over the communization of the region was further strengthened in September 1947 by the establishment of the Communist Information Bureau (Cominform), a body responsible for binding together the East European communist parties (as well as the French and Italian communist parties) under the leadership of the Soviet Union. By the spring of 1948, "People's Democracies" were in place all over East-Central Europe. Although the Soviet Union withdrew its support for the communist insurgency in Greece and refrained from trying to establish a communist government in Finland or even a Finno-Soviet military alliance, Soviet power throughout the central and southern heartlands of the region was now firmly entrenched.

Within a few weeks, however, at the June 1948 Cominform summit, the first—and, in Eastern Europe, the largest—crack in the Soviet bloc surfaced. Yugoslavia, which had been one of the staunchest postwar allies of the Soviet Union, was expelled from Cominform and publicly denounced. The rift with Yugoslavia had been developing behind the scenes for several months and finally reached the breaking point in the spring of 1948.

Tito, far from giving in to Soviet pressure, struck a posture of firm defiance. The split raised concern in Moscow about the effects elsewhere in the region if "Titoism" were allowed to spread. To preclude further such challenges to Soviet control, the Soviet leader, Joseph Stalin, ordered the East European states to carry out new purges and show trials to remove any officials who might have hoped to seek greater independence. The process took a particularly violent form in Czechoslovakia, Bulgaria, and Hungary.

Despite these purges, the split with Yugoslavia revealed the limits of Soviet military, political, and economic power. Stalin attempted to use economic and political coercion against Yugoslavia, but these measures proved futile when Tito turned elsewhere for trade and economic assistance, and when he liquidated the pro-Moscow faction of the Communist Party of Yugoslavia before it could move against him. Stalin's aides devised a multitude of covert plots to assassinate Tito, but all such plans ultimately went nowhere. The failure of these alternatives left Stalin with the option of resorting to all-out military force.

If Yugoslavia had bordered on the Soviet Union, Stalin undoubtedly would have sent in troops almost immediately. But the prospect of invading the country through Hungary, Romania, and Bulgaria was complicated. From 1950 to early 1953 the Soviet Union actively geared up for a full-scale military incursion into Yugoslavia, but Stalin's death in March 1953 brought an end to those preparations. With the military option no longer under consideration, the Soviet Union was forced to accept a breach of its East European sphere and the strategic loss of Yugoslavia vis-à-vis the Balkans and the Adriatic Sea.

Despite the loss of Yugoslavia, the Soviet bloc came under no further threat during Stalin's time. From 1947 through the early 1950s, the East European states embarked on crash industrialization and collectivization programs, causing vast social upheaval yet also leading to rapid short-term economic growth. Stalin was able to rely on the presence of Soviet troops, a tightly-woven network of security forces, the wholesale penetration of the East European governments by Soviet agents, the use of mass purges and political terror, and the unifying threat of renewed German militarism to ensure that regimes loyal to Moscow remained in power. He forged a similar relationship with communist China, which adopted Stalinist policies under Moscow's tutelage and subordinated its preferences to those of the Soviet Union. By the early 1950s, Stalin had established a degree of control over the communist bloc to which his successors could only aspire.

After the communists came to power in 1949, China had been very much part of the Soviet bloc, even though it was in Asia, and the Sino-Soviet alliance was one of the closest. Mao, despite fancying himself also a world communist leader, was nonetheless willing to subordinate himself to Stalin. After Stalin died, Mao became increasingly uneasy about China's subordination to the Soviet Union, which eventually led to the full-scale rupture between the two countries at the end of the 1950s. Subsequently, in 1961, Albania ceased taking part in any of the activities of the different institutions of the Soviet bloc and then in 1968 formally left the Warsaw Pact. The Soviet bloc was not, strictly speaking, a Hotel California where "you can check out any time you like, but you can never leave": there were a few countries that did successfully leave after checking out. At the same time, there were other attempts, particularly in Hungary in 1956, that ended much less successfully and were crushed by Soviet military intervention.

Consider the instances when troops were used in Eastern Europe to preserve orthodox communist regimes. Just a few months after Stalin died in June 1953, there was a large-scale uprising in East Germany (not just in East Berlin, as is often said: mass demonstrations against the communist regime occurred in more than 600 cities). The tone, almost from the beginning, was profoundly anti-Soviet as well as anti-communist. The East German regime proved wholly incapable of dealing with the uprising and was on the verge of collapse, so Soviet troops were deployed in very large numbers: nineteen divisions, numbering some 390,000 soldiers. It was done with relatively little bloodshed, considering the scale: there were only about 40 casualties, which is a surprisingly small number if you bear in mind that the two countries involved had been ferociously at war with each other only eight years earlier.

Much larger was the revolution that occurred in Hungary, starting on October 23, 1956, and then continuing with four days of fighting after the massive Soviet intervention on November 4. The counterinsurgency operation in this case was extremely violent. About 2,500 Hungarians were killed, which, considering how brief the period of fighting was, is a very large number. About 760 Soviet troops were also killed, which provides a sense of the intensity of the resistance on the part of the Hungarian revolutionaries. In this case the Hotel California policy was strictly enforced.

Then there was the Prague Spring of 1968, a sweeping program of liberalization in Czechoslovakia led by communists, but ones who actually thought that communist parties should be popular and not simply rest on coercion. The Prague Spring lasted for eight months but was brought to a crushing end in August 1968 by an invasion carried out by the Soviet

Union along with the participation of other Warsaw Pact countries, including Hungary, Bulgaria, and Poland. Ostensibly an East German unit also took part, although in reality it never joined in, because of an intervention by Gomułka, the Polish leader, as well as some of the pro-Soviet Czechoslovak leaders, who indicated that the introduction of East German combat troops onto Czechoslovak soil would be a grave mistake in light of memories from the war. In the end, the East Germans did not actually take part, although the East German regime insisted until 1989 that they had—making this an example of a case in which a regime boasted about an atrocity that it had not actually carried out.

For more than a decade after the Soviet-led invasion of Czechoslovakia, the Soviet bloc seemed relatively stable, despite crises in Poland in 1970 and 1976. But the façade of stability came to an abrupt end in mid-1980 when a severe and prolonged crisis began in Poland, a crisis that soon posed enormous complications for the integrity of the bloc. The formation of Solidarity, an independent and popularly based trade union that soon rivaled the Polish Communist Party for political power, threatened to undermine Poland's role in the bloc. Soviet leaders reacted with unremitting hostility toward Solidarity and repeatedly urged Polish leaders to impose martial law, a step that was finally taken in December 1981.

The Soviet Union's emphasis on an "internal solution" to the Polish crisis was by no means a departure from its responses to previous crises in the Soviet bloc. In both Hungary and Poland in 1956 and in Czechoslovakia in 1968, Soviet leaders had applied pressure short of direct military intervention and sought to work out an internal solution that would preclude the need for an invasion. In each case, Soviet officials viewed military action as a last-ditch option, to be used only if all other alternatives failed. An internal solution proved feasible in Poland in 1956; but attempts to reassert Soviet control from within proved futile in Hungary in 1956 and Czechoslovakia in 1968. During the 1980–81 Polish crisis, Soviet officials devised plans for a full-scale invasion, but these plans were to be implemented only if the Polish authorities failed to restore order on their own. Only in a worst-case scenario, in which the martial law operation had collapsed and civil war had erupted in Poland, does it seem at all likely that the Soviet Union would have shifted toward an "external" option.

The successful imposition of martial law in Poland by General Wojciech Jaruzelski in December 1981 upheld the integrity of the Soviet bloc at relatively low cost and ensured that Soviet leaders did not have to face the dilemma of invading Poland. The surprisingly smooth implementation of martial law in Poland also helped prevent any further disruption in the bloc during the final year of Brezhnev's rule and the next two and a half years under Yuri Andropov and Konstantin Chernenko. During an earlier period of uncertainty and leadership transition in the Soviet Union and Eastern Europe (1953–56), numerous crises had arisen within the bloc; but no such upheavals occurred in 1982–85. This unusual placidity cannot be attributed to any single factor, but the martial law crackdown of December 1981 and the invasions of 1956 and 1968 probably constitute a large part of the explanation. After Stalin's death in 1953, the limits of what could be changed in Eastern Europe were still unknown, but by the early to mid-1980s the Soviet Union had evinced its willingness to use "extreme measures" to prevent "deviations from socialism." Thus, by the time Mikhail Gorbachev assumed the top post in

Moscow in March 1985, the Soviet bloc seemed destined to remain within the narrow bounds of orthodox communism as interpreted in Moscow.

Although Gorbachev initially carried out few changes in the Soviet bloc, he began shifting course within a few years of taking office, as he steadily loosened Soviet ties with eastern Europe. The wide-ranging political reforms he was promoting in the Soviet Union generated pressure within eastern Europe for the adoption of similar reforms. Faced with the prospect of acute social discontent, the Hungarian and Polish governments embarked on sweeping reform programs that were at least as ambitious as what Gorbachev was pursuing. By early 1989 it had become clear that the Soviet Union was willing to countenance radical changes in eastern Europe that cumulatively amounted to a repudiation of orthodox communism.

In adopting this approach, Gorbachev did not intend to precipitate the breakup of the Soviet bloc. On the contrary, he was hoping to strengthen the bloc and reshape it in a way that would no longer require heavy-handed coercion. But in the end his policies, far from invigorating the bloc, resulted in its demise. In early June 1989, elections were held in Poland that led, within three months, to the emergence of a non-communist government led by Solidarity. Political changes of similar magnitude were underway at this time in Hungary. Although the four other Warsaw Pact countries—East Germany, Bulgaria, Czechoslovakia, and Romania— tried to fend off the pressures for sweeping change, their resistance proved futile in the final few months of 1989, when they were engulfed by political turmoil. The orthodox communist rulers in these four countries were forced from power, and non-communist governments took over. In 1990, free elections were held in all the East European countries, consolidating the newly democratic political systems that took shape after the communist regimes collapsed.

By that point, events had moved so far and so fast in eastern Europe, and the Soviet Union's influence had declined so precipitously, that the fate of the whole continent eluded Soviet control. The very notion of a "Soviet bloc" lost its meaning once Gorbachev permitted and even facilitated the end of communist rule in Eastern Europe. This outcome may seem inevitable in retrospect, but it was definitely not so at the time. If Gorbachev had been determined to preserve the Soviet bloc in its traditional form, as his predecessors were, he undoubtedly could have succeeded. The Soviet Union in the late 1980s still had more than enough military strength to prop up the communist regimes in eastern Europe and to cope with the bloodshed that would have resulted. Gorbachev's acceptance of the peaceful disintegration of the bloc stemmed from a conscious choice on his part, a choice bound up with his domestic priorities and his desire to do away with the legacies of the Stalinist era that had blighted the Soviet economy. Any Soviet leader who was truly intent on overcoming Stalinism at home had to be willing to implement drastic changes in relations with eastern Europe. Far-reaching political liberalization and greater openness within the Soviet Union would have been incompatible with, and eventually undermined by, a policy in eastern Europe that required military intervention on behalf of hardline communist regimes. The fundamental reorientation of Soviet domestic goals under Gorbachev therefore necessitated the adoption of a radically new policy vis-à-vis eastern Europe that led, in short order, to the dissolution of the Soviet bloc.

HE Emanuelis Zingeris

The realities of my family experience were rather strange. I am one generation removed from the Holocaust; my mother was captive in a Nazi concentration camp. I spent my academic life in the archives, trying to study what happened to the Yiddish culture and heritage that had existed in Lithuania during the interwar period, in our "Weimar" time. There were success stories from 1918 until 1940, not only in Czechoslovakia but also in five countries that said goodbye to Bolshevik Russia when the Russian Empire collapsed and became independent members of the League of Nations in Geneva to boot: Finland, Poland, and the Baltic states. Observe that Ukraine and Georgia, which did not become members of the League of Nations, became captives of the Bolsheviks once more after two years of independence.

During the period of Soviet occupation, this prewar period appeared to be a sort of alternative reality. We felt captive every day, at risk of "becoming Soviet." But I remember that even in my middle school we resisted the pressure not to have a Christmas tree. Soviet realities were never accepted in the Baltics. We kept hold of our local memories, and our memories of the armed struggle against the Soviet Union that continued in the woods all the way up until 1965.

Inside this Soviet hell, where everything was upside down—religion was anti-moral; progress was anti-progress—it was extremely important for us to be able to think that one day we would come out of the cave of Soviet reality. So, in 1988 and 1989, our movements were actually related to the prewar stories, as well as to the Mitteleuropean experience of Charter 77 in Czechoslovakia and Solidarity in Poland. And the speed of our integration into the European Union and NATO was based on our history of successful prewar statehood, our twenty-two years of freedom. That history was also central to how we understood the situation of our friends in Ukraine and Georgia, with reference to their ambitions to become members of our European Union and NATO communities.

As to the question of how we coped with the fact that Vilnius was under Polish rule during the twenty years between the First and Second World Wars, I would say that this was compensated for by our anti-communist solidarity, and by the fact that our relations with Poland were based on our feelings of brotherhood toward Poland's Solidarity. In the Vilnius region we have Polish TV, Polish relatives, Polish contacts in the academy and literature. We were in close contact with Poland.

The Soviets made a mistake thinking that our academicians would be very weak opponents. Mr. Vytautas Landsbergis was a pianist, but he was also a chess player. We had experience ironizing about the Soviet Union, but we also were able to think very quickly about how to declare independence during its period of weakness.

We received massive support from Russian democrats, and on July 28, 1991 we signed our agreement with Russia. It included a recognition on the part of Mr. Yeltsin of the Molotov-Ribbentrop Pact and of the illegal occupation of the Baltic countries. But one day later, on July 29, Soviet troops attacked our border officers in Lithuania and killed our guards. I remember a huge demonstration for Baltic independence on Manezhnaya Square in Moscow, and Sergei Kovalev and other friends telling me, "Emanuelis, let's build democracy together." My answer was, "Okay. How about we build democracy separately?" Yeltsin had declared the Communist Party forbidden, and we had the idea that they would not rebuild the party structure.

You can imagine that during the seventeen months from March 11, 1990, when Lithuania declared independence, to August 20, 1991, when Estonia did, we in the Baltic countries were under immense pressure, trying to knock on every door from Iceland to Copenhagen, asking them to recognize us. We didn't want to be recognized just out of Moscow's mercy, but to be recognized by our Western friends. Five countries— Iceland, Denmark, Slovenia, Croatia, and the Russian Federation, actually—recognized Baltic independence. It mostly came after the Soviet attacks against the TV tower in Vilnius and the bloodshed there when thousands of people came to defend the parliament.

That's the history of Baltic independence. How do I feel now? I absolutely, purely feel like I'm the last person on the Western side of Checkpoint Charlie, at the very last outpost of the West. That's why I want a massive Western and NATO presence in the Baltics.

In the center of Vilnius, we established a huge plaza named after Sumner Welles, who issued the declaration that the United States would never recognize the occupation of the Baltic states. In Kaunas, during the interwar period, we had "W" painted on the walls in honor of Woodrow Wilson and his support of national self-determination. Our next step will be to establish a plaza in memory of Wilson in Vilnius. That is our way to show our appreciation for the United States and its clear policies against the abandonment of the Captive Nations. Today, that approach must be applied to policy toward Ukraine.

Discussion

Audience: Two short questions for Professor Friedman. Didn't the Muslim army generals have something to do with communism being thwarted in Indonesia? They had been educated at our War College. And when you referred to Western scholars who took a benign view of Indonesian communism, did you mean George Kahin and Ruth McVey? You didn't mean Justus van der Kroef, did you?

Jeremy Friedman: Regarding the scholars I was referring to, it's not just Ruth McVey. There's actually a whole group: Donald Hindley, Rex Mortimer, and lots of other people. Justus van der Kroef is probably a bit in-the-weeds for this kind of discussion. As far as generals, it's pretty interesting. A lot of the officers in Indonesia, especially air force and naval officers, were trained in the Soviet Union; some were also trained by the United States. One of the interesting moments that I've found in my research is that, because the Indonesian Communist Party had tried to distance itself from the Soviet Communist Party, in June of 1964, Anastas Mikoyan, the titular head of the Soviet government, came to meet the Indonesian communist leaders and threatened them by telling them, "Look, we trained the officers of your military, and if you guys don't behave"—if the Indonesian communists didn't behave—"the Indonesian bourgeoisie and military are going to have a change of heart, and it will not be to the benefit of the Indonesian Communist Party." The Soviet Communist Party leader was trying to keep the Indonesians in line by threatening them with the Indonesian bourgeoisie and the military! That shows you exactly how this franchise model operated and how they tried to keep people in line.

Martin Palouš: At the end of the 1990s, one of the first post-Cold War rounds of NATO expansion was already a done deal, due to the efforts of President Bill Clinton and his administration. I had students from the Baltic countries who were all writing their papers arguing for NATO membership of the Baltic states, and I was stupid enough to tell them, "You need to be realistic; that will be no easy thing." President George W. Bush must be recognized here as the one who through the "Vilnius Ten" made the 2004 wave of enlargement happen. I find that continuity in the US foreign policy toward the region quite interesting, and I found a certain amount of relief in these current times of confusion hearing what Vice President Pence recently had to say when he was travelling in the region. Do you have any predictions about what the United States policy in this area is going to be going forward?

Mark Kramer: Both sides of my family were originally from Latvia, and my father's family was deported to the Gulag, so the status of the Baltic states has always been something that I have cared about deeply. With regard to the current situation, the Baltic states, as you know, were invited to join NATO at the Prague Summit in November 2002 and became members in 2004. They enjoy full protection under the Article Five guarantee.[86] I think anything that raises doubts about the solidity of the United States' willingness to fulfill that guarantee is extremely damaging, and I have been dismayed that there have been comments over the last year or so that do raise doubts about it. I think that that already has done a certain amount of damage. I, nonetheless, am quite convinced that Russian

---

[86] Article Five of the North Atlantic Treaty enshrines the principle of collective defense: "The Parties agree that an armed attack against one or more of them in Europe or North America shall be considered an attack against them all."

leaders do take Article Five commitments seriously and even now would be very hesitant about undertaking direct aggression in the Baltic states, which would in fact require a fulfillment of that article. The graver concern I have is about efforts to try to destabilize the situation in the Baltic states. Twenty years ago, that would have been a much more salient concern because, particularly in Estonia and Latvia, where there are large ethnic Russian minorities, there were a significant number of people who had lived under Soviet communism and wanted to return to something like it. Nowadays, two generations have passed. I visited Estonia three times this year, and I was refreshed to learn that even among ethnic Russians now there is an acceptance that Estonia should be an independent country. The ground is less fertile for destabilization than it was twenty years ago.

Emanuelis Zingeris: Mr. Landsbergis and I were the authors of the law on citizenship, which essentially said, "Citizenship for everyone." In the 1990s, everyone received Lithuanian citizenship, with no consideration given to ethnicity or anything. Probably even Russian officers received Lithuanian passports or else left Lithuania after selling their apartments. It was an option for everyone: we understood that we should be as open as possible and create liberal democracy as quickly as possible and create tolerance for the sake of our country, understanding what had happened during the Holocaust. It was done with great scrupulosity, in order to fight against Russia's propaganda machinery, since they usually use every opportunity to call others fascist—the Ukrainians, Balts, and Poles among them. Even our president, Valdas Adamkus, who was actually from Chicago, was called a fascist. Actually, he was a great guy and directly elected—I admire him especially for his visit to Tbilisi along with President Kaczyński of Poland in August 2008, during the bombings and the war defending Georgia. Our integration speed was extremely high. We worried about our friends and allies in Ukraine and Georgia during the 1990s and the 2000s. At the NATO summit in Bucharest, we argued that Ukraine should be put on the path to NATO membership lest it be attacked by Russia. We warned the world, including you Americans, about the Russian danger; everyone thought it was just Baltic paranoia. Thank God you are now bipartisan in seeing that Russia really does pose a danger, and you now have a more common-sense view about the dangers totalitarian regimes pose even here in your country, especially after the last election.

Lindita Komani: Albania, as Mr. Kramer rightly stated, came out of Russian captivity but went into another captivity, that of China. We had ten years or more of direct Chinese influence, and then after that we were totally isolated and fought our way out of communism at the very tail end of communism's fall in Europe. From an international point of view, what do you think were the most important actions that led to the fall of communism in Albania? We have our own perspective, with our own heroes, but it would be interesting to know who, on the international level, enabled this.

Mark Kramer: First, let me state that being outside the Soviet bloc did not by any means guarantee a lessening of repression. Some of the worst atrocities in China, which have been very ably documented by Frank Dikötter, occurred when China was on the verge of leaving the Soviet bloc, or after it had already left. Albania under Enver Hoxha was one of the worst, most tyrannical of the communist regimes—that was true when it was part of the Soviet bloc, and it was true when it left the Soviet bloc. Hoxha aligned Albania for a little more than a decade with China, at the height of some of Mao's worst excesses. But eventually Albania staked out its own, particular, rather strange form of communism, which until the end remained extremely oppressive. I would argue that external influences were overwhelmingly important in bringing about the fall of communism in Albania in 1991. Nothing internal would by itself have led to the end of communism there, but since, externally, communism was falling apart everywhere, it made it much easier for those who wanted to challenge the regime to press it.

Audience: Dr. Haynes, was the 1948 presidential campaign of Henry Wallace funded by Moscow?

John Earl Haynes: There are several points to keep in mind. The decision to create the Progressive Party was essentially made by the American Communist Party. It proceeded to use its allies in the left wing of the Congress of Industrial Organizations and in various Democratic Party bodies and liberal organizations around the country to establish an organizational framework, Progressive Citizens of America, which morphed into the Progressive Party in 1948. If there was any Soviet funding for that effort, it was quite small. Between 1941 and 1947, there was a significant period during which no senior American communist leader was able to visit Moscow to consult on policies with Soviet officials or the International Department. The International Department's priorities immediately after the war were simply turned elsewhere. The American party was pretty low on its list of priorities. One of the things the official sent by the American party wanted to ask when he was in Moscow was the following: They knew they had to oppose Truman's Cold War policies. But should they do it by trying to stop Truman's renomination by the

Democratic Party and promoting a Henry Wallace campaign within the Democratic Party? Or should they pull out and establish an independent third party? There were American communist leaders on both sides of that argument, and they wanted Moscow to resolve it. Rather to the American party's frustration, International Department officials essentially said, "Well, you know, there's an argument for both sides and we don't really have any good advice." That returned the argument to the United States. Because close communications had not been reestablished with Moscow after the war, some of the American Communist Party leaders became sort of like our Cold War Kremlinologists, reading *Pravda* and trying to interpret what they should do based on what Moscow was doing elsewhere. The argument was finally resolved with the creation of the third party. I think that this was actually the result of a misinterpretation on American communist leaders' part. When the Cominform was formed, American communists took it as a sign that they should take more dramatic and extreme measures to oppose Truman's policies and pulled their allies out of the liberal movement to establish an independent third party. Soviet funding for the American party was reestablished in the late 1940s and '50s, but at this point, 1947–48, it had not yet been reestablished. The American party did this really with its own resources. I might add that the decision to create the Progressive Party and to back the Wallace candidacy really broke the back of the American Communist Party. They had anticipated that the Wallace movement would do well: that although Wallace probably wouldn't get elected president, he would do well enough to block Truman's reelection, and perhaps even establish the Progressive Party as the dominant party on the liberal left. In fact, the Progressive Party and Wallace did extremely poorly in the 1948 election, and, further, the

Communists found that once they had pulled out of the Democratic Party and failed with the Progressive Party, getting back in was a lot harder. What's more, they lost their institutional position in the CIO; CIO leaders were adamant that Truman's reelection was necessary for the political protection of the labor movement. The Taft-Hartley Act had been passed by the Republican-controlled Congress;[87] Truman had vetoed it. Then Congress overrode the veto and it became law. The CIO leadership was convinced that if Republicans won the presidency in 1948, Taft-Hartley would be only the beginning of what would be done to the labor movement. They were adamant that Truman had to be president.

Peter Robinson: To my kids and my students today, the idea that there was a Communist Party USA seems ridiculous. They look back and think that anyone involved must have been a crank. And yet we know that Whittaker Chambers, no fool, wrote in *Witness* that when he broke with the party, he did so in the conviction that he was leaving the winning side to join the losing side. Looking back on a lifetime of scholarship on communist activity in this country, what was the moment when the Communist Party USA posed the greatest danger? Did they ever stand a chance, or were they always deluded fools and cranks?

John Earl Haynes: Well, I think they were more than losers, fools, and cranks. They were effective in the Popular Front period in the late 1930s and again during World War II, when they readopted the Popular Front or the National Front policy. But they could only really work when they were moving in mainstream politics and essentially hiding their own identity

---

[87] The Labor Management Relations Act of 1947, known as the Taft-Hartley Act, restricted the activities of labor unions.

and manipulating their friends and allies. Whenever they emerged in their own right, as they did during the 1920s and '30s, during the Nazi-Soviet Pact period and after the Progressive Party debacle, when they were clearly identified on their own, then they generally collapsed. Communists were particularly strong in New York City, and in the American Labor Party and the Democratic Party in Wisconsin, Minnesota, Oregon, and the state of Washington, and in a few other cities, including Detroit and Chicago. But with the exception of the Independent American Labor Party in New York, under New York's rather strange electoral system, they were never a dominant force in any of the state Democratic Parties, and the 1948 Progressive Party campaign really broke them. In the aftermath, they were driven out of the Democratic Party and out of the left wing of the CIO. There were some communists who returned to mainstream politics in the Vietnam War era, but not in large numbers. The American party was then, as it is today, an extremely small movement. It lost its Soviet funding after 1989. In a sense, the chief financial support for the American Communist Party today is actually the United States government through Social Security payments to its members, most of whom are well over Social Security age.

Bounchanh Senthavong: During the first half of the twentieth century, almost all of the Third World was hungering for independence. At the time, the ideology of communism resonated with that desire. Laos was a French protectorate for almost one hundred years, so communism was attractive there as well. Today, Laos is still dominated by communism. But it is a small country, unable to shake off the system or defend itself from the ideology. I would like the international community to take a bigger role in forcing the Laotian regime to guarantee human rights and improve the situation in the country.

Jeremy Friedman: Because Lenin claimed that imperialism was the highest stage of capitalism, many communists began to claim that imperialism was a *necessary* stage of capitalism, a part of capitalism; to be anti-capitalist was to be anti-imperialist. But there is no necessary connection there. There's a relationship between capitalism and imperialism; there's also a relationship between science and imperialism, technology and imperialism, racism and imperialism. All sorts of things are connected to imperialism, none of which are necessarily integral to it. The United States also had an anti-imperialist policy, although it did not follow it consistently. There were failures in the wake of the Versailles Treaty and World War II. Ho Chi Minh petitioned Wilson at the time of the Versailles Treaty; Wilson wasn't responsive. The United States tried to be anti-imperialist in the wake of World War II and found itself at the mercy of many of its European allies. So we couldn't push for independence in Vietnam and Algeria because that would hurt the French; we couldn't push for independence in Indonesia because that would hurt the Dutch; we couldn't push for independence in Angola because that would hurt the Portuguese. Many compromises were made. It was really the failure of the United States to stick to its anti-imperialist principles at key moments that created an opening for the notion that communism was intimately tied to the independence of the developing world, which has led to the situation where Laos and Vietnam are still communist countries today. I think that if the United States manages to stick to those principles, it will be a better defender of small countries around the world, as you describe.

Mark Kramer: Actually, the continued existence of communism in Laos is not the exception; it conforms to a pattern. Cuba and the Asian communist regimes, with the exception of Mongolia, which was a Soviet-dominated communist system, all survive. Those regimes came to power in large part on their own and so were more entrenched and more difficult to get rid of.

Audience: I'd like to ask the panelists what they see as the difference between the successful communist coup in Czechoslovakia in 1948 and the failed attempts in Austria, Malaysia, and Greece.

Mark Kramer: Almost nowhere in eastern Europe were the communists able to come to power on their own. They came to power solely because of the influence of Soviet forces. However, there was one exception: Czechoslovakia. The *coup d'état* carried out by the communists in February 1948 was supported by the Soviet Union, but the Czech communists and pro-communist intellectuals had done a great deal to bring it on. Some of that might be explained by the fact that many Czechs—in Slovakia, the situation was very different—entertained what I think was a somewhat delusional sentiment that the Soviet Union had supported the independence of Czechoslovakia in 1938–39, whereas the evil Western countries Britain and France had turned against and betrayed them. It is true, certainly, that the Soviet counteroffensive into eastern Europe in the final year and a half of the war resulted in the demolition of the Wehrmacht, including in Czechoslovakia. So in some sense, those sentiments were understandable, but it is still striking, when one goes back, that many Czech intellectuals were bringing on and even welcoming the regime that ultimately destroyed them.

Jeremy Friedman: In August of 1948, a few months after the coup in Czechoslovakia, the Indonesian Communist Party leader Musso, who had been an exile in Moscow for twelve years, was returned by the Soviets to Indonesia and took over the Indonesian Communist Party. He intended to implement what was called his "Gottwald plan," which was to do in Indonesia exactly what had been done by Klement Gottwald in Czechoslovakia. That was the plan: infiltrate the government, form a coalition, and then simply use their military force to take over the government peacefully. And this happened prematurely in September 1948, and the reason it failed is because Sukarno, the Indonesian nationalist leader, got on the radio and said in a clear speech to the people, "It is either me or Musso. You have to choose." The Indonesian people chose Sukarno. Every country's different. It's very complicated to talk about individual countries' situations, but the fact that there was a strong, popular, nationalist leader who was nevertheless not communist and was willing to hold on to power is what stopped the Gottwald plan in Indonesia.

Truth Without Ideology:
Accounting Communism's Crimes

Dr. Murray Bessette

When the Victims of Communism Memorial Foundation was authorized by Congress in 1993, it was tasked with educating this generation and future generations about the ideology, history, and legacy of communism; with commemorating the more than one hundred million victims of communism; and with working toward the freedom of those still suffering under totalitarian systems. Broadly speaking, *Reflections on a Ravaged Century* works through these interconnected elements of the Foundation's mission.

The previous panels have focused on the connection between communist ideology and the history that resulted from communist practice, with respect to politics, economics, civil society, and foreign affairs. Today's conversations will focus, rather, on the difficulties confronted in uncovering the truth about this history, in memorializing its victims, and in obtaining justice within both communist and post communist systems. The relationship among Truth, Memory, and Justice is like that which exists among life, liberty, and the pursuit of happiness: the latter presuppose and are founded upon those that precede them. Without Memory, there is no Justice; without Truth, there is no Memory.

This relationship, moreover, can also be seen in the personification of blind Lady Justice, who holds both the sword of truth and the scales of memory.

Cutting to the who, what, where, when, and why of communist crimes with respect to both their victims and their perpetrators is a necessary preliminary to an account that correctly memorializes by weighing the contributing factors of each event, rather than mythologizes through forgetting what one would rather not recognize. The temptation to mythologize the past, to elide its worst episodes, is ever present. We see it today in Russia—where Putin rehabilitates even the likes of Stalin—and in China—where the Tiananmen Square massacre is treated as if it never happened.

Truth and reconciliation are twined, because forgiveness is possible only on the basis of memory, not forgetting. Properly ascribing responsibility entails recognizing that in some instances, lines will be blurry, and that rather than painting a picture in black and white, we will often be using various shades of gray. Ultimately, for a post communist society to be reconciled to its communist past requires that justice be done to that past, and this in turn entails recognizing something particularly pernicious about the evil of communism. Because communism would twist the entire world into an unnatural shape, the communist himself is also a victim of his totalitarian efforts: he bends his psyche to ends that are inconsistent with human nature and thereby deeply wounds his soul.

The final overcoming of communism through memorialization and reconciliation is dependent upon knowledge of the truth about the ideology, history, and legacy of this most deadly ideology. Knowledge of this fact is not unique to us. Communists in power understand and have always understood this fact. They fear Justice. They fear how she will weigh them in her Memory. They fear the Truth that will cut through their Potemkin illusions and false hopes and thereby free the minds of those they would hold captive. It is for this reason that communists in power fear truth above all and why living in truth poses a radical challenge to the continuance of their rule.

Dr. Frank Dikötter

The themes of this conference are truth, memory, and justice, but as a historian who has worked on China for a third of a century, I have had to deal with untruth, amnesia, and injustice on a staggering scale. It began, for me, the moment I went to university. I studied Russian, and there was no lack of Sovietologists critical of the Soviet Union, including Robert Conquest, Martin Malia, Richard Pipes, and Alain Besançon. I also studied Chinese, but where were the sinologists critical of the Chinese Communist Party? I was fortunate in that I picked up a book on the Cultural Revolution written in 1971 by Simon Leys. His name was an alias for Pierre Ryckmans, and although he was by vocation an expert on nineteenth-century Chinese art, he wrote searingly about the horrors of Maoism. His work was met with relentless hostility in Europe from both public intellectuals and professional sinologists, many of them convinced that China, somehow, was "different."

The world has changed enormously since 1971, but while there may be far less injustice in the People's Republic today, neither truth nor memory have been allowed to flourish. China imposes a state of enforced amnesia about its own past. And beyond its own borders, there are still plenty of true believers, fellow travelers, and other apologists in the China field, despite all the new evidence that has come to light. A history of untruth, injustice, and amnesia, in other words, should look at both history and historiography—at the politics of horror on one hand and the politics of apologia on the other. I will look at the first in some detail, more briefly at the second.

The Chinese Communist Party, to this day, refers to its victory in 1949 as a "liberation." The term brings to mind jubilant crowds taking to the streets to celebrate freedom, but in China the story of liberation and the revolution that followed is not one of peace, liberty, and justice. It is first and foremost a history of calculated terror and systematic violence.

For decades we have been told that the new regime's first act was "land reform," as peasants were finally given a share of the land they craved. But land distribution was not about the land, it was about breaking up local power structures and forcing a majority of villagers to eliminate their own leaders. Work teams sent by the Communist Party were given quotas of people who had to be denounced, humiliated, beaten, dispossessed, and then killed by the villagers, who were assembled by the militias in collective denunciation meetings. No one was allowed to stand on the sidelines; any who did risked being denounced in turn. A large enough quantity of blood had to be shed to make a return to the past impossible. The assets of the victims were distributed to the perpetrators, always along class lines, creating a pact sealed in blood between the poor and the party.

Liu Shaoqi, the second-in-command, reported from Hebei that some victims had been buried alive, tied up and dismembered, shot, or throttled to death. Some children were slaughtered as "little landlords." Close to two million victims, many of them hardly any better off than their neighbors, were liquidated, many millions more stigmatized for life as exploiters and class enemies.

Less than a year after liberation came a Great Terror, designed to eliminate all enemies of the new regime. Mao handed down a killing quota of one per thousand, but in many parts of the country, two or three times as many were executed, often on the flimsiest of pretexts. Entire villages were razed. Schoolchildren as young as six were accused of spying for the enemy and tortured to death. Sometimes cadres simply picked a few prisoners at random and had them shot to meet their quota. In a beautifully compiled report addressed to Chairman Mao, while ensconced in the Shaanxi Provincial Archives, Minister of Public Security Luo Ruiqing proudly counted 301,800 killings in less than a year for a mere six provinces. By the end of 1951, close to two million people had been murdered, sometimes during public rallies in stadiums, but more often than not, away from the public eye, in forests, ravines, beside rivers— alone or in batches.

Even without the benefit of hindsight, the atrocities committed in the early years of the regime were evident from a variety of sources, not the least of which were reports published by the party itself as well as material smuggled across the border into Hong Kong. In 1955, Richard Walker published a book entitled *China under Communism: The First Five Years*.[88] He provided an account of the terror that has been amply vindicated by the recent archival evidence, but he was hounded out of the field by the dean of Chinese studies in the United States, Professor John King Fairbank at Harvard University, a historian who did more than

---

[88] Richard Walker, *China under Communism: The First Five Years* (New Haven: Yale University Press, 1955).

anyone else to make sure that the People's Republic received good press. It is difficult to think of a Sovietologist who would have been forced out of his profession in the United States because of an evidence-driven approach to Stalinism. Richard Walker's pioneering work continues to be denounced for its supposed "ideological bias" to this day, one recent example being a book ambiguously entitled *Dilemmas of Victory*.[89] The authors are historians who cover the first five years of the People's Republic, like Richard Walker, yet they manage to reduce both land reform and the Great Terror to fewer than five pages. Apparently, one should not dwell too much on the errors of the past. The equivalent in Sovietology would be a book on the early Bolshevik years stripped of both the Red Terror and War Communism, but with plenty on rural midwives and factory workers.

In 1958, people in the countryside were herded into giant collectives called People's Communes. By turning every villager into a foot soldier in one giant army, to be deployed day and night to transform the economy, the Chairman thought that he could catapult his country into the future. But the Great Leap Forward was a disastrous experiment, as tens of millions of people were worked, beaten, and starved to death. The archives document in striking detail how food was used as a weapon by local party cadres against people who were too young, too old, too sick, or too weak to contribute to the regime through their labour. People did not starve to death, they *were starved* to death. Detailed verbatim reports on leadership meetings also illustrate that Mao knew very well what was

---

[89] Jeremy Brown and Paul G. Pickowicz, eds., *Dilemmas of Victory: The Early Years of the People's Republic of China* (Cambridge, MA: Harvard University Press, 2010).

happening in the countryside yet pressed ahead with collectivization nonetheless.

For decades the Great Famine was barely mentioned, although, again, there was plenty of evidence available at the time. Thousands of refugees crossed the border into Hong Kong, but their testimonials were discarded by sinologists as "tainted." When in 1976 Ivan and Miriam London published an article entitled "The Three Black Flags" illustrating much of the horror of the famine on the basis of interviews collected in Hong Kong with the help of László Ladány, a Hungarian Jesuit, it was very much ignored within sinological circles. As late as 2009, the only two book-length studies of the Great Leap Forward were authored by journalists, namely *Hungry Ghosts*,[90] a pioneering book written in 1996 by Jasper Becker, and more than a decade later, the two-volume *Tombstone*,[91] published in 2008 in Chinese by the journalist Yang Jisheng. Where were the sinologists?

After the catastrophe of the Great Famine, Mao must have wondered who would become China's "Khrushchev," the man who had denounced Stalin after his death and started de-Stalinization. Most of all, how would the Chairman be able to spot him, since even Stalin had failed to identify his nemesis? Mao's answer was the Cultural Revolution. In a campaign that would remain unique in the annals of communism, Mao became the only leader to unleash ordinary people against the very instrument that had propelled him to power, namely, the party itself. Once

---

[90] Jasper Becker, *Hungry Ghosts: Mao's Secret Famine* (New York: The Free Press, 1996).
[91] Yang Jisheng, *Tombstone: The Great Chinese Famine, 1958–1962* (New York: Farrar, Straus and Giroux, 2012).

the military had done its job, Mao used it to purge the people in turn. Anyone but the most blinkered ideologist could have seen the madness and destruction of the Cultural Revolution at the time. Simon Leys, posted in Hong Kong, saw bodies tied together floating down the Pearl River to Victoria Harbour. Every day the newspapers in Hong Kong gave eyewitness accounts.

When the first account of a Red Guard entitled *The Revenge of Heaven* was published by Ivan and Miriam London in 1972, it, too, was dismissed as mere sensationalism.[92] Scenes of rape and murder by its author Ken Ling seemed exaggerated to the trained eyes of the professional sinologist, but what jarred most were scenes of starving villagers begging for food in Shandong province. "From time to time we saw corpses by the tracks," Ken Ling wrote. But the received wisdom was that after "shortages" during the Great Leap Forward, the People's Republic had once and forever solved the problem of hunger. Yet detailed, meticulously compiled evidence from the Shandong Provincial Archives illustrates that fourteen million people in that province *alone* went hungry in 1967, some of them forced to sell their own children.

One of the discoveries I made when working on the history of the Cultural Revolution a few years ago is that a good many of its "experts" *actually believe* that they are studying the Revolution. Last year the *Los Angeles Review of Books* published a piece in which five scholars marked the fiftieth birthday of the Cultural Revolution. Their concern was not so much to point out what went wrong and what that entailed for so many millions of people, but what could be *salvaged*—a concern that appears to

---

[92] Ken Ling, *The Revenge of Heaven* (New York: Ballantine, 1972).

be all the more urgent, since even the Chinese Communist Party condemns this one episode of its own history.

Another discovery is that these experts are all younger than I am. For many years I thought that Maoists, like Stalinists, were a dying breed, but it turns out that they renew themselves very successfully. There is at least one defender of Mao in every sinological department in every major university. As the distinguished philosopher John Gray pointed out in a recent review of a collection of some of the Maoists' essays on the *Little Red Book*, "Reading the essays brought together here, you would hardly realise that Mao was responsible for one of the biggest human catastrophes in recorded history."[93]

Mao died in 1976, and soon enough Deng Xiaoping was extolled instead, portrayed as the great architect of "economic reforms." These reforms, in fact, had been forced on the party by millions upon millions of villagers who had used the chaos of the Cultural Revolution to reconnect with the past, opening black markets, sharing collective assets, dividing the land among themselves, and operating underground factories. They effectively outmaneuvered the one-party state and destroyed the planned economy from below. If there was a great architect of economic reform, it was the people. But the party used economic growth to rebuild itself, determined to maintain a monopoly on power.

For a decade or two a measure of debate was allowed about the Cultural Revolution, as a flurry of memoir literature appeared in the 1980s. Even the archives opened from 1998 to 2012, an era historians like myself

---

[93] John Gray, "How the West Embraced Chairman Mao's Little Red Book," *The New Statesman*, May 14, 2014.

will look back upon as a golden age. During this golden age many local historians, both amateurs and professionals, could be seen in the archives, busy trying to make sense of the past. Even then, however, there were strict limits, as the party did not allow any public debate to take place about Mao's Great Famine. The filmmaker Hu Jie made a short documentary some ten years ago about villagers who erected a memorial arch to remember those who had died during the Great Leap Forward. Within days the police destroyed the monument. For good measure they also arrested some of the village leaders.

The wall has come up again. Xi Jinping issued a clear warning the moment he came to power in 2012: any attempt to look critically at any one episode of the history of the Chinese Communist Party is tantamount to committing the crime of "historical nihilism." In concrete terms, this means that professional historians are regularly warned by the security services not to publish anything controversial, the penalty being loss of employment. Websites dedicated to oral history have been taken down; the few private museums that existed on the Cultural Revolution have closed their doors. Even in Hong Kong, there are efforts to impose a state of official amnesia. Controversial books have vanished from the shelves— all the more since five publishers went missing in 2015, only to reappear weeks later on state television to confess to their crimes. Two of the most informative magazines that for forty years provided a platform for historians who cherish freedom of speech have ceased to operate. But never mind Hong Kong: the People's Republic now exerts pressure on publishers and even on universities abroad to make them conform to the party's version of its own past. In Australia it is enough that a university lecturer refer to Taiwan as an independent country to be pressured into apologizing to students from China. Farewell Truth, Memory, Justice; welcome back, George Orwell.

HE Dr. Vytautas Landsbergis

The greatest victim of communism was the human soul, human spirituality. Humanity was replaced by bestiality. We cannot celebrate a disaster lasting one hundred years, but we should learn from what happened. The Bolsheviks were populists who promised freedom, justice, peace, and benefits for everybody, excluding their enemies, but developed a regime of terror, state slavery, and war. The Revolution was immediately exported by means of war—aggression and disaster were not intended to be confined to Russia alone. That ongoing process of revolution and desired world governance has not ended yet. The basic thing to understand in contemporary European history is that the totalitarian regime of the Bolsheviks became an example, an inspiration for other fascist ideologies and dictatorships.

What about their ideology inspired so many and did so much damage? Bolshevism took root in the rationalism of the eighteenth and nineteenth centuries. The understanding of the nature of human dualism, *anima et ratio*, was reduced to favor *ratio* while *anima* was increasingly treated as marginal. Talk of the human heart and brotherhood were dismissed as poetry and outdated Christian religion. The concept of history became mystified, its rules discovered by Marx and company, taking on the features of a deity or a supernatural force of predestination. Those beliefs had long-lasting effects on culture and politics throughout the world; but this anniversary accords an opportunity to reflect on their results over one hundred years in Russia.

Why Russia? Because for now, Russia is the number-one danger and threat for the entire human world. To say this is not demonization, but realism. The human world is getting more and more dehumanized and, unfortunately, Russia plays, perhaps unconsciously, a big role in that evil process. The illnesses of the world are now concentrated and best expressed in Russia, and the illnesses of Russia itself are inherited from its past.

Consider some aspects of Russia's mentality. It is obsessed by largeness of territory. After all its successful (for a time) land conquests and their partial colonization, Russia is large indeed. If your mentality is primarily territorial, this fact may cause you to suffer a sort of delirium or mania of grandeur and to strive to be ever larger. The tsars' foreign policy aimed at expanding their realm "until all seas." The vastness of one's country—it looks fine on a map—seems to symbolize its importance. As a consequence, the diminishing of this sacred territory becomes immensely painful, "a tragedy for mankind." This builds up a completely mistaken system of values and action. The size of your dominions compensates for failures in all other senses. Such a Russia is worth living for, dying for, and killing for—so claims the top ideologist of Putin's Kremlin, Alexander Dugin.

The current Russian state and its leadership are on a fundamentally wrong path. To a great extent, the trend stems from theoretical and practical communism. Communism, during the Soviet Union, was a near-mystical belief that overrode all other understandings of world affairs as wrong—and not only wrong but also hostile to "the people" (the new class *nomenklatura*, that is) and thus counterrevolutionary. The best medicine for "contras" was to eliminate them — if you had sufficient force. As Chairman Mao said, "Whoever has the gun rules the village." Those who dare to resist simply drop out of the game—and out of life. That was the basis of the Red Terror, introduced by Lenin and perfected by Stalin.

Here we should correct the commonly used term "crimes of communism." It was not an abstract idea or teaching that was responsible for crimes, but concrete persons, organized structures, and entire states. Political and economic opponents, including the working and productive peasantry, were expropriated and eliminated "as a class." That social racism remains largely uninvestigated. The most extreme means, like the artificial famine known as the Holodomor, were implemented by fanatical Bolsheviks to break and crush the Ukrainian countryside. Millions died of starvation, left without food under the merciless observance of their rulers, the perpetrators. In their view of history, what they were doing was correct. To a normal human understanding, it had nothing in common with humanity, but with bestiality. Some, especially communist thinkers, claim that the destruction of private and family farming helped Stalin to build Soviet industry, especially military industry, and thus win the war. But Bolshevik communism destroyed Russia more than any war. More than half a century after the war, the population of Russia still suffers from poverty. The only difference in the government's explanations is that previously capitalist encirclement was guilty; today, it is the Americans and NATO.

On its expansionist path, post-communist—or neofascist—Russia is isolating itself, turning itself into a larger version of North Korea. "We will beat them, we will win"—this mantra governs the Kremlin's strategic mind. "Don't forget that we have a bomb," Mr. Putin repeats. Russia feels itself to be besieged. The idea of Russia as a fortress surrounded by enemies has two deeply rooted sources. The first is the vision of the tsars; the second is the vision of Lenin and his followers, who aimed to strengthen the Soviet Union through permanent revolution (Trotsky) and permanent enlargement (cf. Stalin's oath at Lenin's coffin). It was to be a process that continued until the Red Empire and its satellites governed the entire world. Against that vision, friendly suggestions that Russia should prefer the wellbeing of its people to the "liberation" of the rest were destined to fail.

Take the "problem" of pride and respect. When someone expects deference, the absence of appeasement feels like a terrible abuse. I experienced this during the last Soviet years. When in a political dialogue you disagreed in even the most polite manner with an alleged boss, speaking as an equal and looking into his eyes, you seemed provocative and annoying. Respect your master! This explains why the "disobedience" of Ukraine has been punished so severely. Only Yeltsin was different. Boris Yeltsin was a unique leader of Russia who wanted to make it a normal, internationally cooperative, and welfare-building state. It did not happen, unfortunately.

The recent situation has become not better but worse. They must fear us; if they don't fear us, we are disrespected. The greatest failure of the West toward the end of Cold War was that there was no peace treaty, no request to recognize the crimes and to punish the communist criminals, no request to change the former inhuman mentality and behavior. Lithuania officially pursued an idea of purification—the tribunal for communist crimes—but no one wanted to listen or consider this. The

Budapest Accords became the best example that a paper, even signed, is nothing.

What is the current situation? Western democracies are opposing the Empire of the Lie and are losing. They don't dare to say "Stop lying" or to confront our current situation of global war. Even bleeding Ukraine was avoiding clarity too long. Some say that anything is better than war; anti-democratic, anti-Western hard and soft tyrants don't think so. War is on the table for them. The weak Westerners and *Putinverstehers* seem to fail to understand that Russia prefers their capitulation, not cooperation. Is it better to sink into a cloaca of lies and slander than to die on a battlefield in the name of dignity and liberty? That is the question that must now be considered.

Dr. Andrei Illarionov

The subtitle of this panel, "Accounting Communism's Crimes," is highly appropriate, because communism and crimes are inseparable. What is most striking is the sheer size, scale, and scope of the crimes committed by the communists of the last century, and especially that all those crimes happened not in one country, or a few countries, but in each country and on each territory that had been captured, occupied, and ruled by communists. Those crimes are not the result of mistakes, accidents, or the psychopathy or paranoia of one ruler or a few leaders. They happened everywhere, without exception, from Russia to all its conquered countries and territories, from Ukraine to Cuba, from Finland during the Finnish Civil War to Angola, from Yugoslavia to North Korea and Cambodia. It is a result of the systemic application of mass coercion, violence, terror, and murder, regardless of any factor or resistance, real or non-existent.

Why crimes on such a scale? First of all, because of ideology. Communism is a pure ideology of terror and terrorism. Let me cite the father of communism, Karl Marx: "There is only one way in which the murderous death agonies of the old society and the bloody birth throes of the new society can be shortened, simplified, and concentrated, and that way is revolutionary terror." That's from an article in *Neue Rheinische Zeitung* in November 1848.[94] In the same newspaper one year later: "We have no compassion; we ask no compassion from you. When our time comes, we shall not make excuses for our terror."[95] Vladimir Lenin: "No revolutionary government can avoid executions of landlords and capitalists." Yakov Sverdlov, the head of the All-Russian Central Executive Committee: "We need to apply mass terror." Grigory Zinoviev, head of the Comintern: "We must carry along with us 90 million out of the 100 million of Soviet Russia's population. As for the rest, we have nothing to say to them. They must be annihilated."

Why was terror necessary? Because communists had a very clear aim for their new society: the creation of a new social homogeneity, a classless society, without any of the wrong classes, social groups, or ethnic communities. Again Marx: "The mode of production of material life determines the social, political, and intellectual life process. It is not the consciousness of man that determines their being, but on the contrary their

---

[94] Karl Marx, "The Victory of the Counter-Revolution in Vienna," *Neue Rheinische Zeitung,* November 6, 1848, trans. the Marx-Engels Institute, https://www.marxists.org/archive/marx/works/1848/11/06.htm.

[95] Karl Marx, "Suppression of the *Neue Rheinische Zeitung,*" *Neue Rheinische Zeitung,* May 18, 1849, trans. the Marx-Engels Institute, https://www.marxists.org/archive/marx/works/1849/05/19c.htm.

social being that determines their consciousness."[96] Therefore these social formations, the closing chapter that forms prehistoric society, it being social structure, must be destroyed, and then its makers must be eliminated: thence the liquidation of classes, not absolute categories, but literally liquidation of each and every member belonging to the so-called wrong classes, social group, ethnic communities.

What were the methods for this terror? There were many, all that had been accumulated by humanity: confiscation of property, deportation, arrest, hostage-taking, confinement to camps, torture, execution, extrajudicial killings, and so on. What was the chief instrument of these crimes? Secret police organizations, from the Cheka to the OGPU to the NKVD to the KGB and the FSB. There is no communist party or communist country without secret police. Secret police and communism are inseparable.

Historians are still debating the categorization of the crimes and terror in Russian history. I would name at least four waves of mass terror, all aimed at so-called enemies of people—social strata considered to be incompatible with a classless communist society, thus deserving liquidation. During the first wave, the Red Terror of 1917–1922, the victims of communism were members of the imperial family, the aristocracy and nobility; members of the government of the Russian Empire: governors and governors general of *guberniyas*, members of both chambers of the parliament (State Council and State Duma), generals, admirals, officers of the imperial army and fleet, Polish officers and

---

[96] Karl Marx, *A Contribution to the Critique of Political Economy* (Moscow: Progress Publishers, 1997), accessed at https://www.marxists.org/archive/marx/works/1859/critique-pol-economy/preface.htm.

gendarmes; members of all non-communist parties, including leftist parties; public figures, societal leaders, journalists, professors; religious leaders, bishops, priests, monks; academics, scientists, persons of culture, the arts, the cinema; and business people and entrepreneurs.

During the second wave, successful and wealthy peasants, the so-called *kulaks*, joined the enemies of the people, alongside bourgeois specialists, historians, and even communist officials.

During the third wave of terror, the so-called Great Terror, the enemies of the people included many members of non-communist parties; the former imperial army and imperial government; leaders and priests; professors, teachers, academicians, scientists, and statisticians; communist officials; officials of the Soviet government; Soviet generals and officers; officials who refused to come back to the USSR from abroad; many ethnic groups within the USSR: Germans, Poles, Romanians, Ukrainians, Belarusians, Estonians, Latvians, Lithuanians, Finns, Bulgarians, Greeks, Iranians, Afghans, Koreans, Bulgars, Karachays, Kalmyks, Chechens, Ingush, Crimean Tatars, Turks and Meskhetians, Yakuts, Kazakhs, "Harbinians" (ethnic Russians from Harbin); members of foreign communist parties; international volunteers during the Civil War in Spain; the participants in the Uyghur uprising on the territory of China; and monks from Tuva.

During the fourth wave: Jews, doctors, biologists, economists. If Stalin had not died, the terror would have continued.

How many people have been killed in the former Soviet Union? We have only estimates. Some basic numbers: 2.5 million killed due to the communist-organized Civil War; at least three million murdered in four waves of terror; 1.6 million murdered or starved to death in the Gulag; one million executed by the Soviet government during the Second World War—that doesn't include those who died in the war for other reasons, although the war itself can be attributed to communists to a very high extent; at least eight million total killed for political reasons; twenty million dead of starvation; eight million who were deported, emigrated, or escaped from the territory of the Soviet Union. The total human losses amount to at least 36 million people, or about 24 percent of the Soviet population in 1922.

These mass secret-police-executed terror campaigns have occurred in all territories conquered by communists, including eastern Poland, Estonia, Latvia, Lithuania, Bessarabia, Bukovina, and, after the Second World War, in Poland, Czechoslovakia, Hungary, Romania, Yugoslavia, Mongolia, Albania, China, Korea, Vietnam, and Cuba. The victim groups were largely the same: members of government and parliament; government officials; generals and officers of the army and the police; members of all non-communist parties; religious leaders and priests; professors and teachers; academics and scientists; public figures; persons of culture, the arts, and the cinema; intellectuals; and businesspeople. Think of the massacre at Hue in South Vietnam during the Tet Offensive, when the North Vietnamese Army took the old capital of Vietnam, Hue, for four weeks from January 31 to February 28, 1968. When the city was liberated eight weeks later, it was found that more than 4,000 people had been deliberately killed. Who were they? All non-communist political party members, civil servants, religious leaders, schoolteachers, American civilians, and other foreigners.

When in October 2008 I visited the liberated territories of Georgia that had been occupied by Russian troops during the short aggression, I found that terror had been applied against the families of government officials, police officers, priests, and, strikingly, schoolteachers. Same pattern, same machine, same organization.

What kind of lessons can we learn from these one hundred years of communism? Unfortunately, the ideology of terror, violence, and coercion has not died. The practice of striving for a monopoly on political power has not died. The secret police, the organization that is the chief instrument for committing all those crimes, is still alive in many countries. So as long as this ideology, this practice, and those organizations, especially the secret police, are still alive, we cannot think that that combination is dead.

Dr. Harvey Klehr

In the moral calculus of blame for the crimes of communism, the largest share must, of course, be reserved for those who created and led the regimes that engaged in mass murder almost from their origins. The Lenins, Maos, Stalins, Hos, Kims, and their compatriots deliberately and with malice aforethought concocted plans to fundamentally transform the societies they ruled and concluded that for reasons of security and success they had to eliminate large numbers of their fellow citizens whose class background, religion, ideology, or some other trait represented an obstacle or a threat. The communist parties they led called upon hundreds of party members, motivated by idealism, fanaticism, and in many cases, careerism and brutality, to willingly persecute millions of people—people guilty of no crime but deemed unworthy material for the beautiful society that was to be constructed.

Previous speakers at this conference have eloquently and at length catalogued the crimes of communism; I will not repeat them. But many of the enablers of communism also deserve condemnation and a historical reckoning. Fortunately for a sizable percentage of them, they live in Western Europe and the United States, where they were able to spew their lies with impunity. Thus, they survived physically, but they also sold their souls. They devoted their lives to propagandizing on behalf of repressive regimes and retelling the lies manufactured by them. And since the collapse of many communist regimes in the late 1980s and early 1990s, some of them have persisted in denying the crimes of communism, making them the equivalent of Holocaust deniers. In the United States, where the Communist Party never enrolled more than 100,000 members, the communist virus infected significant numbers of intellectuals and creative artists. Men and women to this day admired as paragons of moral commitment and truth-telling and honored for their contributions to American cultural life defended mass murderers, slandered the oppressed, and pretended to be victims when they were called to account. From Lillian Hellman to Arthur Miller to Theodore Dreiser and Paul Robeson, they lent their talents and their names to propaganda designed to buttress communism. In an era in which Americans have had to confront difficult questions about public monuments to slaveholders who waged war on the United States, it seems appropriate that we reconsider public acclaim for people who supported the destruction of their own country, glorified tyrants, and figuratively spat upon their victims.

Paul Robeson, the celebrated athlete, actor, and singer, honored by a commemorative stamp a few years ago by the United States Postal Service, sacrificed his career to the cause of communism. Although often presented as a victim of irrational anti-communism, he could stand as a paradigm for the moral failings of communist loyalists. His own son, himself a longtime communist, has told the story of his father's singing tour of the Soviet Union in 1951: He asked to meet his old friend, Itzik Feffer, rumored to have been purged because of his wartime membership in the Jewish Anti-Fascist Committee. Feffer had in fact been arrested and horribly tortured and was destined to be murdered. He was cleaned up and brought to Robeson's dressing room. Aware that it was bugged, Feffer drew his finger across his throat, indicating that he was a dead man. Did Robeson come to the defense of his old friend? No, he added a Yiddish song to his performance that night and on his return to the United States stayed silent about Itzik Feffer. He remained silent until the day he died. At a time when his own public voice might have saved his friend, he betrayed him.

Then there are the Jewish communists who denied or apologized for the anti-Semitic Stalinist campaigns of the late 1940s and early 1950s against "rootless cosmopolitans." Some of them knew the writers and artists who either disappeared or were publicly denounced, just as they knew Victor Alter or Henryk Erlich, Jewish Bund leaders in Poland, arrested and killed by the Soviet Union as Nazi spies. That did not stop these people from condemning, not those who killed Alter and Erlich and the Yiddish writers, but those who protested against their murder. Nor does it now prevent apologists for dictatorial regimes from parroting the Soviet-invented slander equating Israel with Nazi Germany and resurrecting anti-Semitism under the guise of anti-Zionism.

Most Western communist intellectuals have been less complicit enablers. While the Popular Front period during the late 1930s was the highpoint of such activity, defending totalitarianism from the safe perch of free societies enjoyed a comeback in the 1970s and 1980s. Intellectuals and professors as varied as Fredric Jameson and Theodore Von Laue defended Stalin, despite his cruelties, or perhaps *because* of them. Von Laue wrote in the 1970s about how Soviet totalitarianism was "a remarkable human achievement despite its flaws" since it enabled Stalin to build a modern society and since the large number of uneducated peasants he destroyed were an obstacle that had to be surmounted. From his perch at Clark University in Massachusetts, presumably with no uneducated peasants in sight, Von Laue had no need to consider the human costs of communism.

While most American communists and their defenders did little more than contribute to the lies and public support for tyrannical and cruel regimes and denied assistance and succor to those it persecuted, a not insignificant number of Americans did more. They actively worked on behalf of the Soviet Union and betrayed their own nation. As a result of material coming out of Russian and American Cold War archives since the collapse of communism, we now can identify more than 350 Americans who worked for Soviet intelligence agencies, primarily the GRU, Soviet military intelligence, and the NKVD, more popularly known by the name of its successor, the KGB, from the 1930s to the early 1950s. We can identify 350; there are another 150 for whom we have code names but, as yet, no identification. Technically, none of these people were traitors, since the United States was never at war with the Soviet Union. But they were supplying vital information, much of which wound up doing incalculable harm to American interests. During World War II, some of them provided information that enabled the Soviet Union to build an atomic bomb two to three years before it would have been able to with its own resources. We now know that Stalin's approval of the North Korean invasion of the South was predicated on Soviet possession of an atomic bomb. It is at least arguable that atomic espionage by Americans enabled the USSR to develop an atomic weapon while Stalin was still alive. Historical what-ifs are always exercises in futurology, but let me offer one: Can the four million casualties, including 40,000 dead Americans, of the Korean War plausibly be blamed on those Americans who aided and abetted Soviet intelligence? This sorry record has failed to prevent many Americans—far too many—from trying to honor apologists for tyranny and continuing to do so years after their complicity was proven by records from Russian archives. Bard College has an Alger Hiss chair commemorating a man who worked for Soviet intelligence for more than a decade and lied about it for nearly half a century.

It's one of the ironies of history that the current holder of that chair is my good friend and editor, Jonathan Brent, who is taking part in this conference. As an editor at Yale University Press, he created the immensely valuable Annals of Communism series, which has done so much to expose communism's crimes. But it is remarkable in itself that an important American university has an Alger Hiss chair. I look forward to the establishment of a Benedict Arnold chair soon. New York University has a website devoted to the innocence of Hiss. New York City, currently earnestly debating tearing down statues of General Grant and Christopher

Columbus, passed a resolution honoring Ethel Rosenberg, who aided and abetted her husband's atomic espionage. Other American cities, including Seattle and San Francisco, have honored communist activists with resolutions and statues.

Leading American academics have praised communists as avatars of democracy and freedom. Eric Foner, holder of a distinguished chair at Columbia University and the former president of both the Organization of American Historians and the American Historical Association, wrote a book, published in 1998, that lavished praise on the Communist Party of the United States for its unparalleled contributions to the advance of American freedom. Less than a decade before that, as the Soviet Union was entering its death spiral, he had complained about the efforts of Soviet reformers to document the Gulag. He denounced "the obsessive need to fill in the blank pages of the Soviet system." Think of it—a historian objecting to filling in the blank pages of history. Foner also urged Gorbachev to deal with calls for Latvian, Estonia, and Lithuanian independence "just as Lincoln treated Southern secession."

Relatively few of these enablers of communism have apologized for their years, in many cases decades, of apologetics. Noam Chomsky has refused to own up to his denials of the Cambodian genocide. *The New York Times* has refused to repudiate the Pulitzer Prize awarded to Walter Duranty, who shamelessly lied about the Ukrainian genocide. While our self-proclaimed "paper of record" continues to denounce the excesses of the McCarthy era, it has been far less zealous in coming to terms with the now overwhelming evidence about the complicity of hundreds of American citizens with the KGB and the GRU. That record should never be forgotten or forgiven.

Discussion

Flagg Taylor: I happened to read an article earlier this week entitled "When Susan Sontag Told the Truth about Communism," and it referred to her speech at a rally for the Polish Solidarity trade union in New York in 1982. I had never heard about it before—it was a remarkable story about how she had repudiated some of her previous beliefs. Dr. Klehr, I wonder if you know of other examples of leftist public intellectuals who had similar moments in which they repudiated their previous beliefs.

Harvey Klehr: Sontag's speech really was a shock to that crowd—in addition to her calling communism "left-wing fascism," it was perhaps even more shocking that she said that Americans could have learned more about communism from reading *Reader's Digest* than *The Nation*. That hurt very badly. Other than Sontag, nobody immediately comes to mind. A lot of people went silent. There was Whittaker Chambers, a long time ago, and David Horowitz well before the collapse of the Soviet Union. The response of many people on the American left to the collapse of the Soviet Union was, "We've been burdened by the albatross of the Soviet Union, which really didn't go about establishing communism the *right* way; now that that bad example is gone, perhaps we can get back to the *ideals* of communism, unencumbered by the Soviet Union." I think for a lot of American leftists it was just a terrible embarrassment; they didn't want to talk about it, and, quite frankly, they were rather happy that in the West not that much was made of the collapse of communism. We never came to terms with it in the way we came to terms with the collapse of fascism, which was ended with war crimes trials. I don't know whether that would have been a good thing or a bad thing, but we didn't have that anywhere with communism, so I think that for many people in the West, the crimes of communism simply slowly receded. It never stuck in their consciousness. If you are around university students now, you know that they don't have a clue about communism—not only its crimes but its history altogether. When you tell them that communist regimes were responsible for more murders than Nazi regimes, they look at you like you're mad.

Emanuelis Zingeris: Dr. Dikötter, can you compare the Chinese internal resistance to communist ideology with that in Russia? Dr. Illarionov, I read recently that Ukraine dismantled 2,380 monuments of Felix Dzerzhinsky, Vladimir Lenin, and other war criminals. Do you think it would be appropriate to erect a statue of Fanny Kaplan, the left-wing activist from Kiev, jailed for eleven years before the Revolution, who attempted to assassinate Vladimir Lenin for the reason that he dissolved the Constituent Assembly and replaced it with the Soviets?

Frank Dikötter: It seems to me that all these one-party states are very much the same. They change over time, no doubt, but they are the same in that people learn their lessons very quickly. You don't speak out; you stay quiet. People become great actors: they know when to jump up and denounce a neighbor or family member and when to go back to business as usual. So resistance becomes very indirect. You don't oppose power. You do things on the sly, quietly. If you're a worker, you stop working; if you're a farmer, you eat some of the grain before it reaches the grain inspector, *etc.* It seems to me the biggest hero in the case of the People's Republic is one who has been overlooked to this day. We talk about Deng Xiaoping as the architect of economic reform. He's applauded at home and abroad by many apologists. But the truth is that ordinary people in the countryside, villagers who had been starved during the Great Famine, used the chaos of the Cultural Revolution from 1966 to 1976 to claim back some very basic freedoms. They opened black markets, they operated underground factories, they traded. They pretty much undermined the entire command economy from below. They forced the regime to allow them to have very basic economic freedoms. That's the origin of economic reforms. The true reformers are the people, not Deng Xiaoping. There are, of course, dissidents, like Wei Jingsheng and others. Deng Xiaoping was forced to lead the regime toward basic economic freedoms. But on the other hand, of course, by doing that, ordinary people allowed the regime to continue to thrive because they produced economic growth, and Deng Xiaoping used economic growth to consolidate the power of the party and maintain a monopoly of power. In that sense, the Cultural Revolution is the origin of the China we know today.

Andrei Illarionov: There was a very serious resistance to communism, including military resistance, in almost every country. In Russia, as we know, there was a civil war in which millions of people fought against communism and millions perished. Uprisings and armed revolts against communism continued non-stop for 40 years, from 1917 until the mid-1950s. There was further warfare during and after the Second World War, when groups like the Polish Home Army and Baltic countries' partisans fought against Soviet occupation. There were civil wars in Russia, Finland, Yugoslavia, China, Vietnam, Laos, and Cambodia, and resistance movements in each occupied country. In no country were people ready to give up. In response to your question, I would suggest something slightly different, inspired by a decision the Parliament of the Republic of

Lithuania made on August 24, 1991. In that resolution, the Lithuanian Parliament called for the organization of a criminal tribunal for communism and suggested that it could occur in Vilnius. I fully support this idea. An alternate tribunal could be held at some moment in the future in Sevastopol for those responsible for the occupation and annexation of Crimea and for instigating and starting the war in Donbas. But the main tribunal should be held in Moscow, sooner or later. The biggest mistake of the victors in the Cold War, compared to the victors in the Second World War, was that they did not have anything comparable to the Nuremberg tribunal.

Memory Without Myth:
History, Warts and All

Prof. Paul du Quenoy

One of the questions I'm most frequently asked by students is why we know so much about the Holocaust and the history of Nazi Germany, but comparatively so little about the crimes of communism, the Gulag, and the sad history of the Soviet Union. The easiest answer that I've been able to come up with is that the histories are actually quite different. Nazi Germany suffered total defeat in World War II. Victorious allies occupied the country, liberated the concentration camps, brought the perpetrators to justice, freed the survivors, exposed the documentation, invited the international media in to photograph and document the horrors that had happened, and created a public culture that encourages the memorialization of this event. These actions were taken with the purpose that the Nazi regime, its fascist ideology, and the crimes it perpetrated be seen as a betrayal of the most basic principles of humanity and should never again be allowed.

In the case of the Soviet Union, none of this ever happened. The Gulag was never liberated. Not one perpetrator in the Soviet case was ever brought to justice. Many of the victims—those who survived—were often left to live shattered lives rebuilt in the shadow of a state and society ruled by the same government and ideology that had sent them to the Gulag in the first place and could easily have done so again if it so wanted.

Memorializing the events before 1991 was simply impossible. The documentation remains secret and still has yet to be fully revealed. Exploring this even in a freer, post-Soviet Russia is extremely difficult. The leadership of the country still largely comes out of the Soviet Communist Party, out of the security organs that perpetrated much of the violence, and, as a result of that, we know much less about the Gulag than we do about the Holocaust. I hope our panelists will be able to give us a broader perspective on how the history of communism is remembered in post-Soviet Russia today and what the problems and challenges faced in this context are.

Dr. Jonathan Brent

I want to begin by referring back to what Professor Paul Hollander said about belief structures. Belief structures and memory are closely tied together. In fact, one could say there is no memory without belief. I want also to talk a little bit about how the connection of memory to belief is related to what Dr. Landsbergis was saying earlier this morning about the destruction of the soul. Soul is a very big word—small but big—and I don't use it lightly. What I think Dr. Landsbergis was referring to is the destruction of some inner principle of being human: what it is that makes us human. And one of the most important things that makes us human is precisely our memory and its ability to reinforce and to be reinforced by our beliefs.

We can talk about the Katyn massacre, we can talk about the liquidation of the kulaks as a class, we can talk about the Great Terror and all of these hideous crimes—these cruelties that were meted out largely to innocent people. We know that millions of people died in the Gulag. But characterizing the leadership of the Bolshevik regime as a *mafioso* group, which we sometimes hear, does not help us understand what actually happened. This was not a set of crimes that was committed by bad people, by evil people, although they certainly did evil things. These were crimes that were, in some sense, committed by a much larger structure that involved ideology, a total belief system. But it also involved something else that we have to talk about: *the complicity of ordinary people*. We have to talk about society, and the way that society was terrorized and the way that society enabled evil. We have to talk about the children who denounced their parents. We have to talk about the wives who denounced their husbands. We have to talk about the workers who denounced their bosses. We have to talk about the insane cruelty of people who would denounce their neighbors because they had a few grains of wheat more than they did. This too we have to talk about. Because part of the problem of memory in Russia today is that it isn't so easy to identify everyone who was guilty when so much of the society was complicit in this.

Let's be clear about one thing: denunciations were rarely, if ever, the actual causes of arrests or imprisonments. Rather, they were, for the most part, pretexts. Isaac Babel, the great Russian writer, was denounced by numerous people years before he was arrested, and, when he was arrested, it was not for the reasons for which he had been denounced. Doctors in the Doctors' Plot were denounced long before they were arrested. The denunciations were never the precipitating factor. When Anna Akhmatova was asked "Why was so-and-so arrested?", she famously responded, "Why are you asking me why so-and-so was arrested? So-and-so was arrested for nothing! So-and-so was just arrested."

And yet there were reasons. One of the reasons, as Bukharin outlines in his letter to Stalin that he wrote in December 1937, was to create a society of total distrust, a society in which people were always looking at each other suspiciously, always thinking about saving themselves before they themselves were denounced by their neighbors. This is a society that is fundamentally destabilized. It is fundamentally, therefore, an illiberal society in which there is no longer a social contract.

After he was released from jail in 1953, Vladimir Vinogradov, one of the doctors of the Doctors' Plot, was interrogated by Beria. Beria didn't want to put him in jail again; he just wanted to know what it was that Vinogradov said: "What did the doctors actually do during the Doctors' Plot?" Vinogradov fell silent. The interrogator asked him, "Why have you fallen silent? Answer the question." Vinogradov said, "I am speechless. I have no words left. I cannot answer these questions anymore." Why? Because he had been so completely compromised by the system. He had denounced, he had recanted, he had lied, he had told the truth. He could no longer remember what the truth actually was. And this state of not knowing the truth is the state in which you cannot any longer remember anything clearly, and in which in some fundamental, deep way, a way that is disastrous for human civilization, the truth no longer exists. This was, to my mind, the great civilizational criminal act of the Soviet system. It destroyed the possibility of telling the truth.

Perhaps the most interesting literary depiction of this is the short novel *Sofia Petrovna* by Lydia Chukovskaya.[97] She wrote it in 1939, but it was not published in the Soviet Union until the late 1980s under Gorbachev. The mother in the novel, Sofia Petrovna, has been defending and defending her son while still believing in the greatness of Stalin and the Soviet system. Finally, she gets a letter from her son, and the letter says, "Mother, please come and help me. I confessed to everything. They beat me terribly. I need you." And these words from him to her, "I have confessed to everything," it seems, in the framework of the novel, make her lose her mind. She takes the letter and burns it and stamps on it. That act of burning and stamping on the letter is precisely what Anna Akhmatova writes about in *Requiem*, where she says when she looks in the mirror: "Must smash my memories to bits / Must turn my heart to stone all through."[98]

In closing, I want to talk about a very strange thing that happened in 1957 when *Doctor Zhivago* was being published. The Central Committee organized a commission to read the novel and put Dmitry Polikarpov in charge. He concluded that it was a brilliant novel, but that, unfortunately, it was anti-Soviet. It valorized and encouraged bourgeois egoism. A couple of months later he was sent to the countryside to find out what intellectuals were talking and thinking about. His report to the Soviet leadership said, "These damned intellectuals! They don't care about the grain harvest. They don't care about Sputnik! They don't care about our advances in technology! They don't care about how well the Soviet

---

[97] Lydia Chukovskaya, *The Deserted House*, trans. Aline B. Werth (London: Barrie and Rockliff, 1967).

[98] Anna Akhmatova, *The Word That Causes Death's Defeat: Poems of Memory*, ed. Nancy K. Anderson (New Haven: Yale University Press, 2004), 159.

Union is fulfilling its goals! All that these damned intellectuals care about are the crimes of Stalin that Khrushchev spoke about in the 1956 speech." He concludes, "Comrades, it is obvious to me that our society is undergoing a deep and profound *perestroika*," and he uses the word *perestroika* in 1957. And then he says, "It is our job to manage this process. It won't be easy, and it won't be quick." When he says that, he is sending a signal, a signal that could only have been sent at this point in time: That these writers are not to be shot. This process is not to be stopped. This process is to continue and develop and they are going to be part of it.

It is a tiny ray of hope, and despite the fact that in American academia today there is so much criticism of American liberal democracy and downplaying of the history of communism, I believe there is also much hope that our children will see the light. This matter of education is not just an ornament; it is of the most dire importance in rebuilding American life today.

David Satter

I'll begin with a reference to the Soviet ideology, Marxism-Leninism, an arcane and repellent concept that was held up as a substitute for the entire religious heritage of the West. I mention this because people in the Soviet Union did not think of themselves as evildoers. They didn't think of what they were doing as aggression and destruction. On the contrary, they were in the process of building a new world, and they wanted the blessings of that new world not only for themselves but for everyone else as well. Anything that conflicted with this image of a perfect society—without class conflict, without war, in which everyone had a job and everyone was prosperous—was simply repressed. That includes the entire history of the violent process through which that society was created.

But that history was always there, beneath the surface. In the years of the Soviet Union, from 1976 to 1982, I was a correspondent in Moscow. The true terrible story was mentioned in rumors, in whispers, in facts that couldn't be confirmed, information that someone had about a meeting somewhere where someone, for example, met Raoul Wallenberg. Many of those reports in the end were not verified. Others were: for example, that there had been a massacre in Novocherkassk of workers who protested a rise in the cost of food products.

Information was hard to come by. It was for that reason that the dissident movement was based on information: on collecting truthful facts about the country's history. It was also, paradoxically, the motivation for the release of the first truthful information in the USSR about the crimes of the Stalin period. Anyone in the leadership who wanted to get rid of his opponents—and the outstanding example was Khrushchev, who desperately wanted to get rid of Beria and his henchmen—had one available weapon: they could reveal a little bit of the truth about what had happened, about all the atrocities, and then blame their political opponents while carefully masking their own crimes. That is, in fact, the story of the 1956 Secret Speech, and the 1961 speech by Khrushchev at the 22nd Party Congress, which went even further.

It is also the story of *perestroika*. When Gorbachev set about reforming this totalitarian structure, ostensibly to make it more efficient and more capable of surviving in the long run, he had to rely on free information, because only free information could force his political opponents to change the country. Gorbachev was not capable of changing anything alone. He had to motivate and command the Communist Party apparatus, which was totally opposed to any change, to carry out his will. The only way to do that was to energize the population by providing them with information. But what happened during the years of *perestroika* was that the population turned to history. These were the most damning facts of all. The Memorial Society, which began in the mid-1980s, expanded to become the largest, and in many ways the most influential, organization in the country. It wasn't registered, in part out of fear that it could be the basis of a powerful political opposition.

It turned out that despite the hopes of the totalitarian regime, as Hannah Arendt said, "the holes of oblivion do not exist."[99] There was always someone that remembered something. The location of a mass execution, the place where people were buried, the tortures and confessions. These stories came out and appeared in the Soviet press, and it absolutely revolutionized the consciousness of the country because it was no longer possible to imagine that "we in the Soviet Union are doing only good and we want only good things for the world, but the world won't let us live in peace." Suddenly it became clear that this heroic tale that had been inculcated by official propaganda was in fact concealing a bloody fabric of atrocities, and that even the people who had grown up in the country during the time when these crimes had occurred had only vague notions of what had happened, both because people were afraid to talk about it and because it was simply difficult and painful to believe.

---

[99] Hannah Arendt, *Eichmann in Jerusalem: A Report on the Banality of Evil* (New York: Viking, 1963), 212.

There was one incident I recall about the *perestroika* use of history. There was a letter to *Moskovskaya Pravda,* which is an evening newspaper in Russia, from someone who recalled his mathematics teacher in St. Petersburg (then Leningrad). He said that the teacher had been very strict, and that he hadn't been sure if he would become his favorite teacher, but that the teacher had been very conscientious. But one day he disappeared, and another teacher took his place. The former student never knew what happened to him. And now, reading the lists of the shooting victims of the Great Terror that began to be published in the Soviet press, he found his name. And he said, "Now I know what happened to him, after so many years."

But again, there was a problem with attempting to undertake a controlled release of history without a change in underlying values. History began to be seen by everyone as a political weapon. At one point, it had inspired people because it was used as a weapon against the communist regime. But once the regime fell, the millions of people who had been active in the effort to resurrect the country's true history melted away, and there was only a small number of activists left from the Memorial Society. And the promises to create monuments to those who had died melted away as well. All over the country, in one locality after another, at the sites of executions, or just in the center of towns, those promises had literally been carved in stone: there were plinths and pedestals on which were written, "On this site there will be a monument to the victims of Stalinist terror." They're still there, but no monuments were ever constructed. Society's interests shifted to other subjects, and the moral importance of resurrecting history, once there was no longer a political motive, was lost. In 1996, the Mask of Sorrow, a monument by

Ernst Neizvestny commemorating the victims of the Kolyma slave labor camp, was unveiled in Magadan, but that coincided with the 1996 presidential election in which Yeltsin was anxious to demonize the communists.

What does not exist, and what needs to exist in Russia today, is an awareness of the critical importance of the country's psychology. The dead must be honored, the history must be commemorated, the facts must be resurrected, independent of any political motive. That, unfortunately, has not happened, because the whole communist experience, including the dominance of Marxism-Leninism, was only possible because the heritage of the West, which values the life and the importance of the individual, was destroyed. That can be resurrected only by a reaffirmation of the importance of the individual, the first step toward which is a commemoration of those who were so mercilessly destroyed. Until Russia faces that challenge, is willing and able to live by the values of the West— including the importance of individual human life—and is able to commemorate those nameless millions who were destroyed, the country will not be able to emerge from the cycle of destructive dictatorship and contempt for human life in which it is still caught.

Elena Zhemkova

The influence of the Soviet legacy is huge. First of all, it is fear— the mystical fear that freezes a single person in front of the state mechanism, a machine that is capable of everything. It is not necessary to arrest people. You just need to arrest a few, and fear will be present for the many. Second of all, people are not united: there is total distrust toward each and every one. Even family ties have been weakened and destroyed.

Third, there is xenophobia: the rejection of everything that seems to be alien or does not comply with the standard. Xenophobia is a conformist reiteration of the resentment of anything that is foreign. Finally, there is the dual mentality and dual thinking that is always used as a survival mechanism and results in cynical behavior and the loss of any values in society.

This is the legacy that still oppresses Russia today. Much scientific and academic research has been done on the topic of the Terror, including in Russia. And yet, the myth of Stalin remains strong, and the topic of Stalin remains vivid. In many senses, Russia continues to be a country with an unpredictable past. Why? And why is our work processing and remembering the past so difficult? Thirty years ago, during the influx of information about the Stalin regime's crimes, it seemed easier. But why is it so hard now? First of all, because it is difficult to distinguish the evildoer from the good. A common person, a simple person, really does need to be able to make this distinction, because for him or her to decide what to do and what role to fill, it's important to identify with one of the two sides, preferably with the good side. In the worst-case scenario, you can identify with evil, which is what happened in Germany during the Nazi era.

So, practically, this is why people in my country perceive what happened as a natural cataclysm, as some kind of natural catastrophic phenomenon. They empathize and sympathize with the victims, but they do not identify the perpetrators. What is important to emphasize is that unlike in Nazi Germany—where the Nazis were killing people who "didn't belong": Jews, Poles, "others"—we in Russia were killing our own. This is incomprehensible to an average Russian today. They cannot understand. Therefore, for the new generation that was born and raised in the 1990s and the 2000s, has no experience of the Soviet past, and has received no information about it, this era now becomes a renaissance, a golden era. And naturally, the figure of Stalin resurfaces. Not Stalin the mass murderer and organizer of terror, but Stalin the perfect organizer, innovator, and victorious leader in the war. This, of course, is not the real Stalin; this is the myth of Stalin.

We do realize that to properly comprehend the past, and in order to find a way out of those blind alleys, we have to identify with our civil consciousness. Not guilt—we're not to blame in anything. We have to identify with the civil and civic responsibility that each and every person accepts for themselves. That means that if a person identifies with civil society of any form today, they ought to say, "I'm responsible for what my group has been doing, yesterday, today, and tomorrow." This civic responsibility demands and requires everyday efforts from everyone. The question arises: have we done enough?

In a year, we'll launch a database on our website featuring three million victims of repression—not just anonymous millions, but three million with real names and real biographies. But how few three million is compared to the many, many more millions we've talked about! There are lots of books, lots of exhibits: for example, the list of Katyn victims' names. This is all crucially important and, nonetheless, there are still people in Russia today who claim that the Germans were to blame for the deaths at Katyn.

A week ago, there was an action conducted in Moscow to demand the names of these victims. More than five thousand people showed up for the rally. Anyone could partake. We just told them, "Look, if you want to partake in the rally and if you want to commemorate their memories, come

on over. We'll provide you with the materials; you can read up on them."
We did get the state permits for the rally; we didn't want it to be
unsanctioned or unauthorized. People started lining up for the event at
10:00 a.m. and they were still in line until 10:00 p.m. And believe me, on
the 29th of October, Moscow weather is not pretty. Some people were
actually standing in line for four hours just to read one single biography.
But five thousand people in attendance isn't a lot for the city of Moscow,
where we have 13 million people.

We have truly done a lot. We're not embarrassed or ashamed. As
my grandma used to say, "When you arrive in paradise and they ask you
for your achievements, don't be embarrassed to give them a report about
what you have done." But we still don't have the feeling of victory. Does
that mean that we shouldn't have done what we've done? Of course not!
We must all remember that the key to solving this tragedy of history is to
remember the biography of each and every person. We need to continue
down that path; the road we have to travel is going to be a long one.

Dr. Lee Edwards

Rarely in history has a political movement and its leaders
promised more and produced less than communism. With its dictators—
from Lenin and Stalin, to Mao and Castro, to Pol Pot and Kim Jong-un—
truly, truly Bolshevism was the god that failed. As we mark the 100th
anniversary of the communist seizure of power in Russia, what have we
learned about the "–ism" responsible for the deaths of more than one
hundred million victims? As a start, here are seven of the most common
myths about communism.

Myth #1: Communism has never failed because it's never been tried.

This is absolutely absurd. The reality is communism, in many different forms, has been tried in nearly forty different countries since the Bolshevik Revolution. It's been tried in large industrial countries like the Soviet Union and in small agricultural countries like Cuba and Laos. And, everywhere it's been tried, communism failed abysmally, as proven by the stubborn resistance of dissidents in every communist country and the bravery of freedom fighters in Hungary in 1956 and in Czechoslovakia in 1968, of Solidarity in Poland in 1980, and of course of the Chinese people in Tiananmen Square in China in 1989.

Communism has failed for 100 years because it rests on two false assumptions: one, private property is merely a modern phenomenon that can be easily eliminated; and two, human nature is infinitely malleable and can be readily refashioned.

Myth #2: Karl Marx, the founder of communism, was one of the great thinkers and prophets of the nineteenth century.

Reality: Marx and his close colleague Friedrich Engels developed a doctrine of so-called "scientific socialism," which stated that an egalitarian society without private property not only should happen, but, by reason of economic evolution, must happen. Assuring the proletariat they had nothing to lose but their chains, Marx closed his manifesto with a famous call to arms: "Workers of the world, unite." Relying on his doctrine of scientific socialism, Marx's followers pursued the goal of a global revolution, confident in the eventual liberation of man. But Marx did not foresee the emergence of a prosperous and burgeoning middle class founded on the existence of private property. Marxism, wrote Richard Pipes, was dogma masquerading as science.

Myth #3: The Russian people enthusiastically supported the Bolshevik Revolution of 1917.

Communism did not come to Russia through a popular uprising but was imposed from above by a small militant minority hiding behind democratic slogans such as "All power to the Soviets." In fact, industrial workers constituted only 2 percent of Russia's population, and only 5.3 percent of workers belonged to the Bolshevik Party. The communists' chosen course of action was to rule through a dictatorship, and it was a dictatorship not *of* the proletariat but *over* the proletariat and all other classes. And that dictatorship continued for some seven decades in the Soviet Union and continues today in many countries, including China.

Myth #4: The communists delivered on their promises to give the Russian people bread, land, and peace.

In reality, the communists in 1917 initiated a bloody civil war in Russia and conflicts in Europe as part of their goal to communize the world. The Molotov-Ribbentrop Non-Aggression Treaty of August 1939 allowed Hitler to concentrate his armed forces in Western Europe and Stalin to invade Poland and occupy the tiny Baltic states of Estonia, Latvia, and Lithuania.

And that's not all. In the closing months of World War II, the Red Army advanced on a thousand-mile front taking Warsaw, pushing into Germany, and moving in to Hungary and Czechoslovakia. Soon an iron curtain descended, turning the countries of Eastern and Central Europe into Soviet satellites. During the forty-six-year Cold War that ensued,

Russia and its East European collaborators, joined by China, North Korea, Cuba, North Vietnam, and Cambodia, among others, conducted a steady campaign of agitation, propaganda, and often armed conflict in pursuit of the Marxist-Leninist goal of a communist world.

Despite their promises, communists failed to deliver the goods, literally. From the birth of the Soviet Union there was strict rationing of food, clothes, and living space, leading to large families living in tiny apartments with scant electricity and little running water. Exceptions, of course, were always made for the *nomenklatura*, who led a privileged and cosseted life. As for land, well, one of the first acts of every communist regime is to seize all the land and set up giant communes that routinely lead to widespread famine, like Ukraine in the 1930s and China in the late 1950s and '60s. Estimates are that as many as 40 million Chinese died in the so-called Great Leap Forward of Mao Zedong.

Myth #5: Stalin was the great dictator who initiated a reign of terror to retain the communist hold on power.

Well, that's true, but only part of the truth. The reality is that Lenin, a fanatical Marxist, first established a ruthless despotism, while Stalin extended and perfected it. Lenin defined dictatorship as "power that is limited by nothing, by no laws, that is restricted by absolutely no rules, and rests directly on coercion." He was prepared to resort to unlimited terror to destroy his opponents and cow the rest of the population. Lenin abolished all legal institutions, turning the application of justice over to "revolutionary tribunals" headed by reliable party members and to the new secret police, the Cheka, the predecessor to the infamous KGB. And it was

Lenin who instituted the system of forced labor camps, the Gulag, to which millions of political and other prisoners were sent in the decades to come.

Following in Lenin's footsteps, Stalin ruled absolutely and with an iron fist. Here are three examples of his blood-stained rule: the Holodomor of 1932–1933, the forced famine in Ukraine that took the lives of at least seven million Ukrainians who had been herded into giant collective farms; the Great Terror of 1936–1938 was a campaign of show trials and executions that took nearly one million lives, including every possible political opponent of Stalin; and we should not forget to mention the Katyn Forest massacre of 1940 whereby some 22,000 Polish leaders—military officers, civil servants, land owners, intellectuals, priests, and policemen—who would have resisted Stalin's tyranny, were murdered.

When someone alluded to the ever-growing number of victims, Stalin is alleged to have remarked: "Death solves all problems. No man, no problem."

Myth #6: There are no more communist countries.

The reality is that five communist regimes retain their power through the suppression of human rights and the denial of the most elementary political rights. They are China, Cuba, Laos, North Korea, and Vietnam.

The so-called "People's Republic" of China is the most prominent example of our misunderstanding. Despite the many skyscrapers and the ubiquitous Starbucks stores—and I've had a chance to visit both Beijing and Shanghai and see them with my own eyes—China is not a capitalist society but a captive nation ruled by a communist party 90 million members strong that lives by the old Marxist slogan "Political power grows out of the barrel of a gun." The Party and the People's Liberation Army are one and the same.

Economic liberalization has not produced political liberalization, although some Western experts keep predicting it will. How long do we have to wait till the promises of Deng Xiaoping are realized? In fact, if you talk to Chinese dissidents, they will tell you they still cannot mention publicly the Tiananmen Square massacre of 1989 without being placed under house arrest or in jail or threatened with severe penalties. China qualifies as a totalitarian society when judged by whether it allows free speech, a free press, the rule of law, religious liberty, an independent judiciary, and free and open political elections. Its so-called "Chinese capitalist system" prohibits a majority interest in any of its corporations and enterprises by foreign interests.

Myth #7: Nazism was responsible for more deaths than communists.

Now, if any one of us is asked "How many Jews died in the Holocaust?" I'm confident our quick response would be six million. We have learned that correct answer in our schools and universities, through the books and articles we have read, the movies and TV programs we have watched, the conversations with families and friends and colleagues, and there is a continuing campaign to remind us of the Holocaust and to proclaim "never again"—and rightly so, rightly so. The Holocaust carried out by the Nazis, their deliberate attempt at genocide, was the greatest crime and evil of the twentieth century.

Now, if we are asked how many victims of communism there have been, many of us would hesitate. We would respond with a variety of answers of five million, twenty million, fifty million. Few would provide the right answer: at least 100 million men, women, and children—more than all the deaths of all the major wars of the twentieth century. It's a difficult number to comprehend, to get our mind around, even perhaps to accept. Surely, we say to ourselves, there couldn't have been that many.

But we can be certain of saying at least 100 million victims because of the painstaking research of the editors of *The Black Book of Communism*, published by the Harvard University Press. Moreover, the editors of that study were six French intellectuals, all former Marxists. They certainly couldn't be wrong when talking about communism, right? And it was published by Harvard University, so therefore *veritas*, right? It must be true. And it is.

Each and every communist regime has prevailed by way of the pistol to the back of the head and a death sentence to a forced labor camp. There is no exception, whether in China under Mao Zedong, or North Korea under Kim Il-sung; or Vietnam under Ho Chi Minh, or Cuba under Fidel Castro, or Cambodia under Pol Pot, or Ethiopia under Mengistu Haile, or Soviet Russia under Stalin. According to Stéphane Courtois, the editor-in-chief of the *Black Book*, the leading mass murderer is Pol Pot of Cambodia, who in three and a half years engaged in the most atrocious slaughter—of about one-fourth of the country's population.

Since *The Black Book of Communism* was published in America in 1999, new research about Maoist China and Stalinist Russia has come to light that increases the number of victims in China by at least 10 million, and in Russia by a similar number. China's experience under Mao was unprecedented as to the sheer number of people who lost their lives—as many as 70 million Chinese. As for the Soviet Union of Lenin and Stalin,

Courtois says "the blood turns cold at its venture into planned logical and politically correct mass slaughter."

We must ask ourselves: At what price, communism? At what price, this utopian ideal that appeals to so many young people, apparently? We shouldn't limit ourselves to sheer numbers, as shocking as they are. The Chinese philosopher Lin Yutang listed the little terrors that prevailed in China: making children of twelve years of age subject to capital punishment, sending women to work in underground coal mines, harassing workers during their lunchtime with threats of prison if they're late in returning to work. There were the costs in terror. One Soviet defector wrote about Soviet life, "We lived in a world swarming with invisible eyes and ears." There were the costs in thought control. The content of everything in print and broadcasts was limited to authorized truths. After visiting Stalinist Russia, the leftist French writer and Nobel Laureate André Gide said, "I doubt that in any country of the world, even Hitler's Germany, is thought less free, more bowed down, more terrorized." There were the costs to the world. There was no crisis anywhere in the world from Southeast Asia to the Caribbean, from Africa to the Middle East, in which the ideological ambitions of Moscow, driven by Marxist-Leninist thought, were not involved throughout the twentieth century. This was, and is, the reality of communism: a pseudo-religion posing as a pseudo-science enforced by political tyranny.

In summation, one of the wisest men of the past century, a man who lived under both Nazism and communism, grasped the main errors of Marxism better than anyone. The man I'm referring to is Pope John Paul II—we Catholics call him Saint John Paul II. Here's what he thought. One, Marxism denies man's personal autonomy: "Socialism considers the individual person as simply an element, a molecule within this social organism." Two, Marxism denies the right to personal property: "Man loses the possibility of personal initiative and becomes steadily dependent on a social machine." Three, Marxism denies law and replaces it with force; its view that the end justifies any means inevitably leads to terrorism and war. Four, Marxism denies freedom. It detaches human freedom from obedience to the truth, and from the duty to respect the rights of others.

This is the reality of communism: A god that failed, a science that never was, a political system that ought to sit abandoned and bereft on the ash heap of history.

Discussion

Paul du Quenoy: Thank you very much. And congratulations to you Elena on what we would all consider a success, even if it's a partial one, even if the numbers are not what you had hoped for. The work that you and Memorial Society are doing is wonderful and important, and we all hope that it will continue and meet with greater successes in the years to come. To pose a question to the panelists, a concept that you all seemed to get at during your talks but didn't quite name is what is commonly called "atomization": the dissolution of societies into individuals who either lack trust in each other, as Jonathan was saying, or don't relate to each other at all, as David was expanding upon, or who willingly forget the past and its crimes, as Elena was discussing. How can we diagnose the problem and proceed with a corrective measure? What can we, as journalists, scholars, or venture capitalists, possibly do to reverse that?

Jonathan Brent: I have to constantly emphasize to my students that the USSR did not begin with the Great Terror. It began with slow measures. It began with often tentative approaches to small problems. But eventually, by the mid- to late 1920s, they had removed all institutions of civil society that were not Bolshevik, including publishing houses and cultural and scientific institutions. The Church was also suppressed. There was no quadrant of society where an individual could go for an alternative view of anything. All of society was restructured to emphasize and reinforce the message coming from the top. This had a devastating effect on people's ability to think critically. So, if you ask what we can do, what we must do, we must strengthen the institutions of civil society in this country. We have to strengthen the institutions of discourse, of plurality of voices. We have to ensure that our young people can find different areas in which their ideas and aspirations can be developed that do not necessarily reinforce a line coming from the top. Frankly, we are threatened, partially, in a paradoxical way, because of the proliferation of different forms of media today, by the destruction of that plurality of authentic voices that all these different media are supposed to represent.

Paul du Quenoy: I very much agree. In the Revolution itself, it was the opposition media that was the first thing to be taken over, within a few hours of the seizure of government in Petrograd in 1917. The next thing they went after were theaters. Theaters were nationalized within a few weeks—before banks. The Soviet government controlled all the institutions of expression, of culture, several months before they took over the things communists usually want to take over, namely private business, industrial enterprises, and banking institutions. These were left for later decrees. Controlling the media in that way was extremely important to them.

David Satter: The USSR made it a policy to abolish all independent structures and then reorganize people under the Communist Party. If you wanted to have a chess club, it had to be organized by the party, it had to have a party organization that was in charge and answered for the ideological fidelity of the chess club. If it was a large collective, it had a First Department that was linked to the KGB; if it was small there might have just been some informers. It led to the complete atomization of society because no one could be sure that any conversation would not be reported on. People were arrested and sentenced for anti-Soviet propaganda because of careless conversations they had on trains with strangers. So everyone was very careful. Conversation was restricted to the kitchens of people's apartments, and even there were found informers. The effect of this was, of course, to deaden any initiative. Here is an example of the ultimate result of this process in post-Soviet Russia. In Nizhny Tagil, a town in the far north in Siberia where they make tanks, a criminal gang began operating, tempting girls to come to meetings and then forcing them into prostitution. Those who resisted were killed. Over time, the bodies of 30 to 40 young girls who had disappeared in the town were buried in a forest outside the town. It was only a miracle, a lead developed in an unrelated investigation, that led to the discovery of the ring and the arrest of the perpetrators. But the terrible fate of the girls was not what was most striking to me. What was more striking was the reaction of the people in Nizhny Tagil. There were no commemorations, no candles, no indication on the part of anyone that anything unusual had happened. When the issue was raised with people, they treated it as an event as unavoidable as the weather! The girls who had been in captivity but were rescued refused to cooperate with the police and provide vital information that might have protected other girls in the future. That's the end result of the atomization of society and the feeling of powerlessness that was inculcated by a regime that dominated everything and arrogated all decision-making power to itself and destroyed the moral conscience in people. It is only by reviving moral qualities in post-Soviet Russia that the country has a future.

Elena Zhemkova: I think it is important to remind people that the picture is much more complex than what it seems at first sight. People tend to think that the violation of human rights did not happen at the beginning of the Soviet Union's history, that it was just something incidental that took place much later on. It's crucial to show them that the destruction of the rule of law happened at the very beginning of the Revolution.

Paul du Quenoy: In that respect, of course, the famous example is Lenin's speech to the Komsomol in 1918, in which he explains the communist understanding of morality. He said that morality is completely subordinated to the class struggle: *We don't subscribe to any nonsense about universal moral values. For us, anything that advances the cause of the Revolution is good.* Hitler, of course, adopted the same principle but said that whatever the master race did was good. The rejection of universal values and the attempt to substitute something manmade in their place is the source of all the horrors that took place in the twentieth century.

Jonathan Brent: I'd like to refer to something Elena mentioned earlier: the difficulty of distinguishing the guilty from the innocent. When I started working on my book on the Doctors' Plot, Vladimir Pavlovich Naumov, the Russian historian with whom I was working, asked me, "Do you know something about the Doctors' Plot?" I said, "It was Stalin's plot against the Jewish doctors, who were innocent." "Not exactly," he said. I said, "You mean they were guilty? That Jewish doctors really did murder Kremlin leaders?" He said again, "Not exactly. In this world that you're about to enter, nobody is guilty, and nobody is innocent." This is the world that Shakespeare invokes in *Macbeth*: "Nothing is, but what is not." That's part of why Vinogradov was left speechless. There are no words to describe that situation.

Paul du Quenoy: If I can go back to Elena's original comment, I think this is a glaring flaw in the academic teaching of Russian history in the Western world. We ignore the fact that this begins with Lenin during the revolutionary period and even beforehand, if you examine the intellectual history of the Bolshevik Party. Instead, what you're bound to encounter in a university classroom is a story about a fundamentally good Lenin whose good intentions were subverted by a bad Stalin. If they had only stayed on course or followed a different sort of leader, everything would have been just fine, and it would have been much more like some kind of Social Democratic country in Scandinavia rather than some horrible Soviet Union that we're here to talk about. The idea of reintroducing civil society institutions into post-Soviet Russia is a very good one. The practicalities of it under Putin are quite difficult, as people have mentioned. But what is the official view of this? How is the government itself participating in the memorialization projects? Does it promote its own particular history? As the husband of a woman from a Russian émigré family that ended up in the United States, I can tell you that there is a very pervasive effort on the part of the Russian government through their consular officials and diplomats to promote the vision that there is one "Russian World." Wherever you are in the world, you can be part of this "great Russian project." In order to do this, you have to accept, as the title of this panel says, "the history of Russia, warts and all"—that we've had great tragedies, but we've also had great triumphs. That can lead to some very unpleasant situations indeed. I want to ask the panelists today what they think of this problem, and how or whether the Russian government is addressing it.

David Satter: Regarding the "Russian World," there have been various attempts to fill the vacuum that was created when the Russian people lost an ideology. You can say a lot of negative things about Marxism-Leninism, but it structured the way they thought. It's strange to acknowledge it, but it even provided some positive values. Its core values were completely nihilistic, but it stressed the need to cooperate, to be generous with people, to provide for people. To a certain extent, Russian society assimilated that idea as long as the communists were in power. Once the communists lost power and their place was taken by criminals, which is what happened after the fall of the USSR, people fell into an ideological despair. They lost one set of values which somehow guided them, and nothing was provided to take their place. The importance of this vacuum was recognized by the post-Soviet Russian government, which made various attempts to create some kind of substitute, since you can't inspire people simply with the practice of unlimited stealing. Even though the Russian constitution said that there should never be a state ideology, Yeltsin convened a group to formulate one. Luckily, they couldn't think of anything. At another point, people around President Putin decided to establish a kind of philosophy in support of the Russian World. *Russian World* is never really defined, but it really denotes support for the Putin regime. That's the real motivating and animating factor in Russia today, which is simply the desire to guarantee against all possible challenges to the small group of criminals who are in charge of the country. The real alternative, to establish a society based on law, is going to require two steps. First is a serious understanding of the country's history, which most Russians are also confused about. That includes both the atrocities of the communist period and those of the postcommunist period, which are building up every year, the most recent example being the murder of Boris Nemstov, the opposition leader. On the basis of an understanding of the truth, it would then be possible to reconvene a constituent assembly—to replace the assembly that was abolished by force in January 1918—capable of creating a real constitution for Russia, which among other things would embody a separation of powers and would allow those parts of the country that want to secede to go their own way, creating conditions for a democratic way of life in the part of the country that remained.

Paul du Quenoy: For the time being, we see the opposite of that. There is only one Russia, and that is under Vladimir Putin, and if you disagree with that, you're not part of the Russian community.

David Satter: Well, that's the interpretation that they've tried to inculcate, and to some extent they've had success because of the lack of an adequate answer from the West.

Paul du Quenoy: I'm the chairman of the Russian Ball here in Washington, D.C.—an émigré organization founded by White Russians who ended up in Washington, working, in many cases, for the US government during the Cold War. Because 2016 was the 25th anniversary of 1991, our theme for the ball that year was celebrating the 25th anniversary of the fall of the Soviet Union. As chairman I received an angry letter from the now infamous Ambassador Sergey Kislyak saying, "How dare you insult the glory and power of the USSR! How do you think this will be a good thing for Russia?" to which I responded, "Well, Mr. Ambassador, we're celebrating the great cry of freedom that happened in 1991, and we're quite happy to exclude you and the embassy from it if that's something you don't feel you can support." I'm happy to say that's the last time I ever talked to him. I'd like to ask one further question, perhaps a counterintuitive one: Do we see legacies of the USSR in any way in the West, for example in our media, our educational institutions, and our institutions of free thought?

Jonathan Brent: If you don't mind, I'd like to answer this with an anecdote about the publication of the Annals of Communism series at Yale University. First of all, the National Endowment for the Humanities would not fund it. Secondly, when Harvey Klehr and John Haynes's *The Secret World of American Communism* was about to be published, we received a letter from one of the most eminent American historians at Harvard, who said, "What is new in this book is not original, and what is original in this book is not new." *The New York Times* refused to review the book. Yale University Press was delighted that we probably would not publish the book, because, as one person on staff said, "Why do you need to dredge all this up again?" I persevered against this professor at Harvard and several others, and eventually I got my way. We were going to publish the book. But I realized that if the *New York Times* had already said they weren't going to review it, and several other outlets had refused as well, how could I justify this extremely expensive project I had concocted? My great friend Sam Lipman told me to talk to Hilton Kramer, who told me to hold a press conference. I said, "You're out of your mind! Who's going to come to this press conference?" They said, "Don't worry about it!" We held a press conference, but there were three people in the audience. I thought to myself, "I'm sunk. Not only is nothing going to happen, but my whole reputation is out the window." But one of the people was from *The Wall Street Journal*, one was from the Associated Press, and one was from United Press International. The next day this book was in headlines all over the world. This effectively silenced the critics. However, when I brought the book to my committee on the Spanish Civil War, which proved on the basis of highly secret GRU documents that the Comintern and Stalin were prepared to sell out the Spanish Republic, a member of the history department at Yale said that she was going to sue me personally over this book because I was slandering the honor and the memory of progressive movements in the United States. We had to convene a special meeting of administrators at Yale to prevent this lawsuit from going forward. When I brought a book on children in the Gulags to the committee—there had been no previous book on the fate of children during the Stalinist period— one member of the English department said, "Why do we need another book on children? Children have been abused from the beginning of time. What is special about this?" More than two million children died in Soviet orphanages and in the Gulag. Many were even shot! Another professor, a very famous guy on the Left, a political scientist, whose book I'm sure many of you have read, said that "we have to be very, very careful that we don't indulge in commie-bashing. I advise you to turn this book down."

At that meeting, another man from the Yale history department, a Cuban who was born in Cuba during the revolution, who was separated from his parents, who were killed in the camps, did something unprecedented in the history of Yale University Press: He actually stood up and said, "I am sorry, I do not normally speak this way. But I have only one word for what I have heard: bullshit." This silenced the board. They didn't pass the book, but I accepted their silence as approval, and we published the book anyway. This is how deep the resentment against exposing this history is in a lot of academia. It's very dangerous.

David Satter: A lot of people have a deep career investment in false interpretations. Oftentimes, this is just as effective as fear and intimidation. People who have been saying things based on false assumptions for a long time are extremely resistant to reevaluating what they've conveyed to others. This was really a problem during the Soviet era because of the extraordinary talent for manipulation that the Soviets demonstrated. They controlled visas, they controlled access, they could expel correspondents, and, in this way, they could shape the way in which people wrote and reported. Oftentimes journalists and scholars would make a mental compromise to tell only part of the truth so that they could get a visa, without ever conveying to the reader, who assumed they were getting the whole truth, that they had made that compromise. The Soviets were also adept at facilitating people's careers, not only in academia but in government. It was very common for someone to advertise themselves as a Soviet specialist on the basis of their high-level contacts. *Time* magazine, during the time I was in Russia, was absolutely averse to having any contact with dissidents or unofficial sources of information, because they were waiting for their one interview with Brezhnev, which would come once every two years, during which Brezhnev would mechanically repeat the contents of *Pravda* and the magazine would report on what his tie looked like! That was not restricted to *Time* at all. It was an entire syndrome. There was a journalist by the name of Victor Louis, who was a KGB agent and prided himself on his high-level information, who circulated among Western correspondents. I once met him at a cocktail party, just after he had written an article saying that the Soviet Union had invaded Afghanistan because, after years of being pushed around by the West, with the West encircling the USSR with their bases and carrying out all kinds of aggressions against it, the USSR had finally stood up for itself by strengthening its strategic position and invading Afghanistan. About five minutes after Louis had made these statements in my presence, the Voice of America was reporting back that the *New York Times* was reporting that the real reason for the invasion of Afghanistan was not that the USSR was expansionist, but that because, for the first time, the Soviet leaders felt they were standing up for the security of the Soviet Union. And he said to me, "You know, American correspondents are always stealing my best ideas."

Nadezhda Kutepova: We've talked about the victims and about our own responsibility: Are we to blame or not? But we have not talked about the perpetrators, the people responsible for the murders and executions. Of course, those were concrete people with concrete names and concrete titles and positions in the state hierarchy, and we know that those executioners ended up quite comfortably at the end of their careers. That sends an indecisive and rather confusing message to people. I do know that the Memorial Society has published a list of the names of those people directly involved in the NKVD's repression and terror, and that anyone who wants to can check the list on the internet to see if one of his ancestors appears on it. But I have also read reports that people can appeal for the removal of their ancestors' or relatives' names from that list. How do you treat that list, and how do you react to those relatives' appeals? We do not want those criminals to be on the "goody two-shoes" list.

Elena Zhemkova: That is correct. We did publish a database with 38,000 biographies, not the names, to be exact, and we have kept adding to this database. This is quite a normal process because we cannot give half-truths. By the way, not all the evildoers ended up cushioned at the end of their careers. There are examples of really devastating outcomes as well. All the information in the database is completely available and open to the public, and it's open-source based. So not only will we not delete parts of our list, it cannot be deleted. Regarding your question about positive examples, I'd like to point to our biography of the victims of Katyn, which is a voluminous book, and fully illustrated. We searched high and low so that we could put a face to the story of each one of the victims. We published it in a large number of volumes because it was very important for us to provide the copies not only to libraries in Russia but also to libraries elsewhere. The book was published with Russian money, privately donated. It wasn't one rich donor: it was lots and lots of people who donated whatever they could. I'm very proud of the pages at the end of the book enumerating those donors. That was very important. I'm proud that not one of those several hundred donors told me that they'd give me the money anonymously.

Audience: Does the reluctance to report the truth about Bolshevik history reflect a willingness to repeat those errors? More broadly, does it reflect a lack of absolute morality?

Paul du Quenoy: Speaking as an academic, absolutely. We have campus protests here in the United States where they chant, "The revolution will not uphold the Constitution."

Jonathan Brent: This is a big question. I think that the reluctance on the part of American academics, first of all to study, and then to report on, and then to discuss truthfully all that we've been discussing in this conference, has to do with the generational divide. The conflict with the Soviet Union was seen as a Cold War conflict, and over a long period of time a new kind of history, "social history," largely based on Marxist models, was being taught in universities. I think that the reluctance on the part of most American academics is not necessarily based in a desire to whitewash the Soviet Union as much as it is based on a desire to attack America and Western liberalism and to destroy the models of Western society. That's what, in my view, we have to pay the most attention to.

Justice Waits for Russia:
Can the Russian People Be Free?

Andrew Nagorski

"Can Russians be free?" is not a simple question. It's a question every journalist, diplomat, and academic who's gone to Russia for decades, perhaps even for centuries, has talked about. I remember, when I was going there for the first time in the early '80s, my reading list went back to *Journey for Our Time* by the Marquis de Custine,[100] the French aristocrat who traveled to Russia in the early nineteenth century and wrote extensively about the despotism of that time—in fact, he even coined a phrase about Russia that I heard Elena Zhemkova mention in a previous panel, about how fear replaces thought. That idea keeps coming up. My reading list also included *Russia under the Old Regime* by the historian Richard Pipes,[101] who made it sound like Russia had always lived with tyranny, with no restraints on state institutions and state leaders. On the other hand, I remember that when I met Pipes when he was part of the Reagan administration, he favored doing something different, on the

---

[100] *Journey for Our Time: The Journals of the Marquis de Custine,* ed. and trans. Phyllis Penn Kohler (London: Phoenix Press, 2001).
[101] Richard Pipes, *Russia under the Old Regime,* 2nd ed. (London: Penguin, 1995).

premise that there were Russians who will welcome change, will want to change, and need support.

There were also the visionaries, people like Andrei Amalrik, who wrote *Will the Soviet Union Survive until 1984?* I remember Solzhenitsyn writing in *Foreign Affairs* in 1980 a rebuttal to the view that Russians cannot live with freedom and making the case that the idea that Russia has lived only with tyranny was a misunderstanding of history, particularly of the late tsarist era, when many institutions and individuals spoke out and began to operate in a far freer context.[102]

Then there were the periods under Gorbachev and Yeltsin, when at least for a little while, you could ask, "When will Russia become a normal, boring country?" It didn't sound like a stupid question; it seemed like a real possibility. Right now that seems very far away, but that is the question that we're faced with on this panel.

Dr. Mark Galeotti

Always mistrust national generalizations. It's easy for people to say that Russians need authoritarianism, or at least are doomed to it, whether for reasons of faith or history, geography or bad luck. But let us not forget so many past such assertions: that Germans were irredeemably militaristic, that Italians would never challenge the mafia. These easy stereotypes often say more about ourselves. They are also frequently music to the ears of the authoritarians, the exploiters, the conservatives, and the ideologues, because they carry with them the message that there can be no

---

[102] Aleksandr Solzhenitsyn, "Misconceptions about Russia Are a Threat to America," *Foreign Affairs* 58, no. 4 (Spring 1980): 797–834.

real change, so there should be no real hope. And, of course, there is always room for both.

This is true even in the most unpromising and miserable of circumstances. I've just finished writing a book on the evolution of Russian organized crime, and, as part of the research for it, I spent several months reading every Gulag memoir I could lay my hands on. It was, I will admit, not the most lighthearted time in my life. Nonetheless, it is humbling how often hope could survive even the crushing weight of slave labor and institutionalized barbarity. I was especially struck by the wave of strikes and protests that rocked the camp system even before Stalin's death, and certainly after. Despite the frankly inevitable suppression that would follow, and the equally inevitable savagery with which that would be administered—when the Steplag camp revolt of 1954 was put down, tanks rolled over prisoners barricading the gates—nonetheless, people were willing, time and again, literally to put their lives on the line. And, in a way, they won. This was the death knell of the mass labor camp system; by 1960, the Gulag population was just one-fifth of what it had been in 1953. Of course, that did not happen simply because of the justice of the strikers' cause, even less because of any humanitarian impulses on the part of the regime. We can hardly forget that of all people it was Lavrentiy Beria, Stalin's last and most inhuman secret police chief, who was the first Politburo advocate for scaling down the camp system.

Rather, it was because at the very time when the protests, strikes, and brutal internecine conflict within the underworld were combining to make the Gulag system ungovernable, so too a cynical and pragmatic elite were coming to question its value. Slave labor—unhappy, unproductive, and unskilled—was no longer what the Soviet economy needed. The gulags were restive, and no one wanted to manage and guard these seething mills of misery and murder in the distant east and north. It was time for a change, so change happened, and, while this was still a carceral society, the Gulag archipelago shrank to a relative atoll, thanks to the serendipitous combination of fearless resistance from below and cynical and self-interested pragmatism from above.

By training and inclination, I am a historian, so I am allowed the indulgence of thinking in the long term. I don't see positive change as happening tomorrow or next year, but I am unfashionably optimistic about Russia, not least because I see stirrings from above and below. We know about the daily-tested but never-quenched passions for freedom and justice felt by so many ordinary Russians, and others can talk about them with greater insight and personal experience. Let me instead talk about the elite. They have in the main done very well because of Putin, but we should never put too much faith in the power of gratitude in kleptocratic politics. And that is who they are, kleptocrats who loved the early Putin years, years of economic growth and unfettered theft, clad in a flimsy mantle of nationalist rhetoric. Those were the days—their days. But now they find themselves serving a different Putin, one who seems increasingly to believe his own grandiose rhetoric about civilizational threats from the West, who seems increasingly to believe his own mythology. Like so many authoritarians, Putin has become a caricature of himself, and he has carefully removed from his inner circle any who would challenge his prejudices and his apparent commitment to building his historical legacy by "making Russia great again."

Russia is still a kleptocracy, but sanctions and economic slowdown are biting. More to the point, the price of empire is becoming ever clearer. The cost of subsidizing the "invisible oblast" of the Donbas is eating into an overstretched regional support budget. A shrinking pie is being claimed disproportionately by the Rotenberg brothers and others of Putin's personal friends and cronies, leaving that much less for everyone else. Even the old glorious hypocrisy, of being able to steal freely in Russia and hide and spend it freely in the West, is ever more constrained.

For most of the elite, these are worrying times. They are not exactly going hungry, and Moscow—the only city which truly counts in their geography—is still a vibrant, cosmopolitan, fun city for them. But in recent trips to Russia, I have been struck by an underlying unease, even disillusion, rooted in a sense that they are now stuck with a Putin whose goals are not theirs, and who is prepared to sacrifice their interests in the name of his nationalist crusade.

It is not the first time that Russia's elite have felt like this. In 1915, Vasili Maklakov, the tsarist-era jurist and Constitutional Democrat, brother to the Interior Minister, wrote an article in which he elaborated the parable of the "mad chauffeur." Russia was like the passengers in a car with no brakes, negotiating steep, winding mountain roads, when they realize that the driver has gone mad. Do they try and struggle for the steering wheel, and risk sending the car plunging off the precipice, or do they sit tight and just hope to make it to the safe lowlands?

That was two years before 1917, but I do not see a new revolution in a couple of years. It took the cataclysmic shock that was the First Word War and the astonishing complacency and stupidity of a Nicholas I to bring down tsarism, even though the system was in terminal decline. However, I sense a widening gap between an elite that is primarily interested in itself and a tsar—and his closest allies—who, while protecting their own quality of life, are willing to see rich and poor Russians alike suffer in the name of chasing a vain dream of global prominence.

One thing Putin does understand is power, and he has created a system in which interlocking and mutually suspicious power agencies watch and check each other. He is unlikely to fall to an assassin's bullet or a political coup. But he is getting older, and by all accounts is increasingly disconnected from much of the detail of governance and bored by its rituals. Maybe he will find a successor he thinks he can trust; maybe mortality will take the choice from him.

In any case, some day he will leave power and, whomever he anoints, I think we will see the elite ensure that what follows Putinism is something much less ideological, much less confrontational with the West. It will not be democracy as we know it, and it will still very definitely be a kleptocracy, but it will not be what Russians have now. To me, Putin is the last toxic gasp of both *Homo sovieticus* and also that bewildered and angry resentment at the world with which all post-imperial societies have to grapple as they ask not just *how* did we lose the power and status we once had, but also *who* took it from us? These two ingredients have mixed to make an especially dangerous and unpleasant brew, a zero-sum nationalism that believes Russia is elevated if other nations and communities are diminished.

The elite as a whole may mouth the spiteful platitudes of the new order, that the United States is committed to shattering the Russian Federation, that Europe is a union of the degenerate and the debased. Yet they have certainly not been putting their money where their mouths are: total Russian financial wealth held abroad is greater than that held by the entire population in Russia itself, and about three times the state's net foreign reserves. They are still looking for ways to move not just their money but their families to the West, to buy homes, to gain citizenship. On a crude level, they want iPhones and BMWs, holidays in Italy and the south of France, children with degrees from Oxford and Harvard—not YotaPhones, Lada Grantas, Crimean dachas, and MGU diplomas.

The reassertion of non-ideological kleptocracy will, however, be a difficult and contentious transition, and will open up new opportunities for pressure from below. Having stolen so much, their priority will be fixing property rights, which will also allow the emergence of a genuinely free market, and also an alliance with a re-emerging urban middle class. If they are smart, they will realize that democratization is likely to protect them and allow them to hand the boring work of government to a new generation of political leaders. History teaches us that while political transitions are always unpredictable and ultimately uncontrollable, what devours old elites is not democracy and rule of law but rather their absence. Besides, a new regime eager to mend bridges with the West—sadly, we still love kleptocrats—will not feel the need to treat stirrings from society with the brutish savagery or airy dismissal that might be their instinct.

In any case, on whom would they rely for repression? One of the lessons of 1917 was that soldiers and police are people, too, and not immune from the subterranean processes reshaping and liberating new expectations about the relationship with power. Unlike most Western scholars, I have spent the last twenty years, when I can, talking to police and other security officers, not just the senior figures but ordinary men and women on the beat, and it is striking— the gradual change that has taken place even here.

Compared with the 1980s, compared with the 1990s, today's cops are more liberal, more honest, more willing to question the status quo. Please note the "more": I would hardly be willing to say that, overall, we could call them truly liberal, wholly honest, or outspokenly radical. But the younger officers I speak to are certainly aware of the corruption all around them, and censorious about it (even as they often take small-scale kickbacks themselves). They are often contemptuous of the regime they defend, sometimes brutally so. (One of my more surreal experiences has been drinking with OMON riot police—a special purpose unit in the Federal Police—who had been involved in the arrests of communist diehard Sergei Udaltsov, and hearing them extol him for his willingness to take on the state.)

But these are the riot-armored "cosmonauts" the regime deploys to silence protests and disperse vigils. And some day they may not follow orders. An elite that feels it can neither respect nor replace its tsar; power structures that increasingly feel disconnected from the very system they are meant to protect; a population that may be mesmerized by the mythology of the tsar but is ever more unhappy with what his policies mean for their day-to-day lives—these can sometimes be the ingredients for bloody revolution. But they can also be the conditions for more measured change. Putinism is not Stalinism, but just as that combination of an elite that comes to realize that the status quo is neither sustainable nor useful, and a population willing to continue to push for change was able to end the era of "high Gulagism," then so too someday I am sure it will bring reform, democracy, and justice to Russia.

Paul A. Goble

No people, regardless of its history, culture, or current situation cannot become free, and no people again regardless of those things cannot lose its freedom. The mistake is to assume that the transition to freedom or unfreedom is something that can be made in a single leap and to ignore that history, culture, and geography play key roles in whether a country is moving in one direction or the other.

Americans by nature are traditionally optimists, inclined to believe that people can easily forget the past or ignore geography and focus on the future. They are thus among the readiest to proclaim victory where one hasn't been achieved, especially if they believe that they played a role in that development or see benefits for themselves in making such judgments. Thus, all too quickly in 1991, Americans proclaimed victory after the Soviet system collapsed and the USSR came apart, confident that people who were now calling themselves democrats and free market capitalists were just that, and not the authoritarian communists prepared to violate all the rules of the game they had been playing only days or weeks before.

Russia today is not free. It is not a democracy. And it is a criminal economy rather than a genuinely rule-governed one. There are many people who refuse to admit just how dire things are, because that would force a recognition that we and the peoples of Russia did not achieve as much as we have always wanted to take credit for. And thus, we have fallen into two related traps: either we have concluded that there is no hope for change, or we have decided that we can identify a single individual or small group who can turn Russia around on a dime, or, perhaps better a kopek.

Both of those positions are wrong. Russia can change. It has changed a great deal but not always in good ways. And change won't come in an instant. It will take hard work over decades not days—and, importantly, the cooperative efforts of the peoples of Russia, their neighbors, and the broader international community. Pessimism is understandable, but it is not permissible. The peoples of Russia deserve better, and so do we.

If the peoples of Russia are to make this transition successfully, and if we are to be of any use, we need to recognize the difficulties ahead. I would like to focus on three that seem to me to be among the most important. First of all, everyone must recognize that Russia is still an imperial state held together by force. Second, everyone must realize that the Russian nation is far from consolidated as a single whole and thus is not in a position to be an arena for free and competitive elections. And third, and most profoundly, the residents of Russia, ethnic Russians and most non-Russians as well, remain "Soviet people" at a deep structural level. Unless they are able to escape from that, Russia will not be a democracy. It must be our task to help those among the peoples of Russia who are pursuing that goal by being very clear about each of these three points.

Russia remains an empire in terminal decline. Portions of it fell off in 1917. Other larger portions did so in 1991. And many more will unless and until the Russian political system can make living inside the borders of that country more attractive than going it alone. At least 25 percent of the population is non-Russian, and there are nearly two dozen republics, many of which want more power and would go their own ways if they could. So far, the Putin regime seems to be working to convince them that they are right. All this has been highlighted by the recent developments following the declaration of independence by Catalonia, including Madrid's effort to find a way to provide enough autonomy to the Catalans that they will be quite prepared to remain in a united federal Spain.

One Russian commentator, Igor Yakovenko,[103] says that, unlike many in Moscow, the Spanish government recognized quickly that its attempt to hold in Catalonia by force was costing it both support within that region and across the European Union and so decided on a more cautious approach. But Moscow has adopted a different approach. The Russian state in its various guises has "at all times sought to preserve the unity of the country with the help of force. A century ago, this was one of the factors of the collapse of the empire which then was assembled again by force of arms. And then it fell apart again 26 years ago." Yakovenko continues: "Today, there is not a single positive cause why Siberia and the North Caucasus, the Far East and the Volga region should carry out Moscow's commands and more generally even remain in the borders of a single country while not having any rights to decide independently the problems of their development. The single cause which keeps Russia in its current borders is repression directed against any centrifugal forces." And "by its placing a taboo on the theme of federalism, the Kremlin has created conditions for the disintegration of the country." The last reassembly of

---

[103] Igor Yakovenko, "Rossiya v zerkale Katalonii" [Russia as a reflection of Catalonia], Posle Imperii [After Empire] (blog), October 30, 2017, http://afterempire.info/2017/10/30/catalan-mirror/.

the empire by force lasted about seventy years; this time "it will last far less long."

Russians should be learning from the Spanish government's response to the Catalonian events. But polls show that "more than a third of our fellow citizens don't know where Catalonia is located: 26 percent honestly admit they don't know, five percent put it in Italy, and one percent" put it in a whole range of other countries, including the United States and the former Yugoslavia.

Moreover, according to the Russian Public Opinion Research Center (VTsIOM) survey, two out of five Russians say that Catalonia's relations with Spain are "not important for Russia," although slightly more say that it is. Sixty-eight percent say Moscow should remain neutral, 14 percent say it should back Catalonia, and 5 percent support Madrid's position. Russians also appear to be ignorant about the enormous number of regionalist movements and parties "in all countries of Europe." Some support these groups if they weaken Russia's opponents, but most oppose any movement that calls into question existing borders anywhere lest that spread to Russia itself.

According to Yakovenko, "in Russia, the problem of the striving of regions for independence is resolved simply" and forcefully. First, the Kremlin transformed the Federation Council by eliminating elections to it. Then it banned the creation of regional parties. Most recently, it has imposed criminal sanctions against any calls for separatism, something Moscow defines ever more broadly. "The very idea of federalism in the Russian *Federation* (!)," Yakovenko says, "has been declared a crime and is completely officially defined as a form of extremism." Indeed, "any measures with the word 'federalism' and related terms are taboo in the Russian Federation" of today.

A year ago, the Supreme Court of the Russian Federation issued an explanation of Article 280 that clearly extended extremism to include separatism and federalism. "That is," Yakovenko says, "a Plenum of the Supreme Court specifically stressed that in order to be imprisoned for two or three years it is totally unnecessary to call for any specific action ... [or] for the use of force." It is now sufficient, he continues, "to pronounce the words about the federalization of the region ... or its statehood." Those things are now crimes in Putin's Russia. "The idea of federalism, the striving of people living in a region to take their fate into their own hands, this on the one hand is a constituent part of the idea of freedom, the main value of the Western world and on the other a manifestation of that very growth of diversity which is the only thing that can oppose social entropy, stagnation, and decline."

Thus, Yakovenko says, "to preserve the unity of a country in conditions of freedom is possible only by having given the regions such a level of sovereignty and autonomy that people living there will feel comfortable and the benefits from living within a single state will significantly exceed the potential benefits of leaving it." The United States for more than two centuries has been a model of this, and Spain now, having recognized the error of using force against Catalonia earlier, is as well. But this is a model Russia hasn't followed. Unless it does, it won't survive in its current borders for long however much force it employs.

Most people outside of Russia and a large majority inside haven't paid much attention to a debate that has been going on within the expert and policy communities in Moscow, an effort to define the Russian nation, a nation that is not fully consolidated and whose basis is still up for grabs. Vitaly Ivanov, a former minister for culture and nationality affairs in Chuvashia, says that current efforts to promote a "civic Russian nation" (*rossiiskaya natsiya*) are just like those in Soviet times to promote a "Soviet nation" (*sovetskaya natsiya*) and potentially even more dangerous. Its advocates "are trying to convince us that 'a civic Russian nation' is not an ethnonym but rather a poly-ethnonym, but we understand all too well that with time, its ethnic meaning may eclipse such a poly-ethnonym entirely."[104] That is, Ivanov continues, the civic Russian nation will replace national self-consciousness, something that "for representatives of the indigenous peoples of the Russian Federation is simply unacceptable." They "will resist this trend" and insist that it be rejected as an insult to their dignity. Other experts agree. Damir Iskhakov, a leader of the World Congress of Tatars, says that under the current constitution, citizens of the Russian Federation have come to accept the idea of "nations in a nation" as an aspect of the idea of a "multi-national civic Russian people." But everyone must remember that a "federative state can exist only if the rights of numerically small peoples will be observed." Unfortunately, Iskhakov says, this is far from the case in Russia today. He notes that ethnic Russian national organizations are also opposed to this new term, viewing it as an attack on their identity as well.

Mikhail Shcheglov, the head of the Society of Russian Culture of Tatarstan, agrees. He says that the very idea of a civic Russian nation replacing ethnic identities is "fundamentally wrong." Neither ethnic Russians nor non-Russians will ever accept it. In Shcheglov's view, some

---

[104] Ilnar Garifulin, "Slovar dlya 'rossiskai natzii'" [Dictionary for a "Russian Nation"], *Ideal Real*, May 8, 2017, https://www.idelreal.org/a/28469649.html.

unknown forces in the depths of the Kremlin pushed Russian ethnographers to advance this idea for unknown reasons. It gained the backing of some Russian journalists. And Vladimir Putin was confronted with a kind of *fait accompli*: He had no option but to agree with it, although clearly he should see that it is not in his interests either. The main problem, Shcheglov says, is that Russia today doesn't have a clearly defined nationality policy and all the talk of "a civic Russian nation" is getting in the way of its elaboration.

Drawing on these observations, one observer in Tatarstan says that those behind the civic Russian nation have put the cart before the horse in that they have slyly introduced on the territory of Russia "the absolutely alien" idea of "the nation-state" not directly but rather via the idea of a "civic Russian nation." "As is well-known," he continues, "the concept of an ethnic nation always and invariably presupposes the construction around it of a nation-state," a state that, however much some might deny it, would be based on "a single ethnos which would serve as its real foundation and symbol." In the case of the Russian Federation, Ilnar Garifullin says, "it isn't hard to guess which ethnic group" would occupy that status if the current borders are maintained. Nor is it implausible that, as a result, "the remaining indigenous peoples which have their own national autonomies in the form of republics ... would inevitably lose their political status."

But there is an even more fundamental problem with the civic Russian nation idea, he suggests, and it is this: "Political nations have been built around some common idea which is capable of unifying various ethnic groups with at times varying interests into something monolithic." The Communist Party of the Soviet Union (CPSU) tried to build a "Soviet nation" around the idea of the construction of a communist society, but, as history showed, that effort collapsed. And, at the present time, "the sense of being attached to one country (*i.e.*, of being a citizen of Russia) cannot by itself be a unifying idea." That is "a simple fact" which no one can dispute. And that makes the arguments of those pushing for a civic Russian nation based on "historical-cultural values" problematic. What could these be for peoples of "absolutely different confessions, languages, and ethnicities" that would tie them together in one country rather than simply make them part of "all the peoples populating the planet?"

The biggest hurdle Russia must overcome to become free and democratic is this: despite all the external changes over the last twenty-five years, Russians and many non-Russians living among them remain "Soviet people," Aleksandr Asmolov, a psychologist at Moscow State University says, not in terms of the specific ideological program pushed by the communist regime but rather according to three deep structures that informed that program, ensured its widespread acceptance, and guarantee its continuing vitality.

Asmolov argues that these three deep structures—a "cult of the center," which gave rise to the cult of personality; a world defined as one of permanent crisis and conflict; and "a flight from freedom" and decision-making—still define the residents of that country to this day.[105] "At various times" over the Soviet period, he continues, "these three characteristics took different and specifically concrete forms. But the

---

[105] Denis Yermakov, "Sovetskii chelovek okozalsya na redkost moshnoi konstruktzii" [The Soviet person turned out to be an unusually powerful construct], *Profil*, October 31, 2017, http://www.profile.ru/obsch/item/121081-sovetskij-chelovek-okozalsya-na-redkost-moshchnoj-konstruktsiej.

mechanism of the system, the mechanism of the selection of the people who formed it always was in operation"—and very much continues to operate now.

"The Soviet system in large measure became the heir of Russian imperialism," the psychologist says. "If one rephrases the formula of Viktor Chernomyrdin—whatever party we create, it will all the same turn into the CPSU—whatever state we make, it will always be 'a tsarist empire' in its despotic dimension." That sets Russia apart from many other countries, Asmolov argues. "If you like, we have historically imperial totalitarianism." And it hasn't ended yet. Indeed, "when people say that the USSR may return, I view such statements with irony because there can be another form of archaic development. But it can be even more horrible, with greater eruptions of 'the Black Hundreds' spirit, because such a matrix exists alongside one when the world became more diverse." That is especially possible, he says, because "today there are completely different mass technologies of manipulation which were not available to the Soviet leadership." Among them is "the technology of television-promoted hatred."

This Soviet man didn't disappear when Soviet power weakened and died. There was a brief period when it appeared he might, but it did not last long. External censorship disappeared for a time, but "thanks to the Soviet system there existed a superego which controlled and reproduced all the very same stereotypes." "The Soviet man turned out to be an extraordinarily strong construction," Asmolov says.

No one should have been surprised when Yuri Levada reported that polls show that "as soon as our man was freed, he began to throw himself backwards not even to yesterday's world but to that of the day before that. He became a traditionalist, he began to show himself as a pre-Petrine and not simply a pre-Soviet man." The pollster's work showed that "the desire for a stable world when the stereotypes of the Soviet man are working does not free him from the fear of an open door but frees him only from taking his own decisions. Such a man is afraid and defends himself against any choice." The situation is no longer totalitarian, but it is authoritarian in much the same way.

"We live in a time when we are encountering three key challenges: the challenge of indeterminacy, the challenge of complexity, and the challenge of diversity—and in this era … even a small signal can change the movement of the entire system." Thus, there is hope for change and the end of the Soviet man. But as of now, it is only a hope. "If earlier there was an ideology and the communist ideal with rhetoric about 'freedom, equality, and brotherhood' were on the throne, now in order that there be a permanent crisis, on the throne in the system has turned out to be security," Asmolov says. But one thing is very clear: "[T]he current de-ideologized system is less stable in comparison with Stalin's" because "no system which stands on the vertical alone can long exist. One way or another, the vertical in a polycultural and diverse system sooner or later will break into pieces." Whether that will be the end of the Soviet man or whether such a man will demand yet another system that conforms to his underlying views remains very much an open question—and it defines the area of struggle now and in the future.

Vladimir Kara-Murza

Russia is a country of symbols. After defeating an attempted *coup d'état* by communist and KGB hardliners in August 1991—when hundreds of thousands of unarmed people went into the streets of Moscow and literally stood in front of the tanks sent by the coup leaders— Muscovites gathered on Lubyanka Square, by the headquarters of the KGB and the monument of its founder, Felix Dzerzhinsky. For decades, the nineteen-foot bronze statue of the man who had established the system of terror that claimed the lives of millions stood at one of the main vantage points in the city. The statue of Dzerzhinsky hanging in a noose as it was lifted from its pedestal by a crane remains one of the most enduring images of Russia's democratic revolution.

If anyone told the crowds gathered on Lubyanka that evening that, just eight years later, an officer from the organization they had just defeated would become president of Russia, few would have believed it. Vladimir Putin began with symbols, too. In one of his first acts in office— over vehement protests from Russia's cultural intelligentsia, his own predecessor Boris Yeltsin (who had put him in the Kremlin), and the liberal opposition in Parliament—Putin reinstated the music of the Stalin-era Soviet national anthem as the national anthem of the Russian Federation. As noted already, Russia is a country of symbols. The message was unmistakable.

There were many reasons for what, in 1991, would have seemed such an unlikely course of events. The principal mistakes were made early on, and they were made by Russia's own democratic leaders who were unable—or unwilling—to go through with the full-fledged process of decommunization that was undertaken in other countries of eastern and central Europe, and that would have made it impossible for the old system to make a comeback. The Soviet regime remained half-condemned. Some of the Soviet archives were opened—but not fully, and not for long. The repressive nature of the former regime was officially recognized both by Russia's Parliament and by its Constitutional Court—but no lustrations followed against former communist officials or KGB operatives. As prominent Russian dissident Vladimir Bukovsky warned in 1991—responding to the oft-used warning of the opponents of lustrations about a "witch hunt"—"If we don't hunt the witches, the witches will come back to hunt us." Indeed, they did. Genuine economic difficulties in the Russia of the 1990s—some caused by the legacy of Soviet rule, some by global circumstances, some by mismanagement from Russia's own government—contributed to the preparation of fertile ground for *revanche*. There were mistakes on the part of Western leaders, too: unlike its neighbors in eastern and central Europe, Russia was never really offered the path of full European and Euro-Atlantic integration that served as such a powerful impetus for reform in other post-communist states.

All of these reasons are valid; they have all contributed to the outcome, with varying degrees of importance; and they should be studied and analyzed to avoid a repeat of the same mistakes the next time Russia embarks on a democratic transition. But there is one "reason" sometimes offered as explanation that, in my view, lacks validity. It is that tired stereotype that Russians are somehow uniquely "unsuited" to freedom, democracy, and the rule of law, that after short experiments with these notions at the beginning and at the end of the twentieth century they just returned to their "natural" way of living under a "strong hand."

This stereotype is superficial. It is insulting. But, most importantly, it is not true. As a matter of historical fact (rather than stereotype), every time the Russian people could actually *choose*—in a more or less free election—between dictatorship and democracy, they always chose democracy. In 1906, when the first parliamentary election in Russia ever was won by the pro-reform Constitutional Democratic Party, the supporters of tsarist autocracy failed to win a single seat. In 1917, Bolshevik usurpers lost the Constituent Assembly election to the SRs, leftist proponents of a democratic republic. (The Bolsheviks proceeded to shut down the Assembly by force and disperse the demonstrations in its support.) In 1991, pro-democracy leader Boris Yeltsin defeated the Communist Party candidate in Russia's presidential election 57 percent to 17 percent.

At the risk of stating the obvious, Vladimir Putin's regime is not the result of a democratic choice by Russian citizens. It has come to power by a backstage deal of the elites and is holding onto it by artificially eliminating any competition. It is not difficult to "win" if your opponents are not on the ballot. Since at least 2008, meaningful opposition has been barred from national elections in Russia. This will be the case again in the upcoming presidential vote in March 2018. Two prominent opposition leaders had been planning to run against Putin. One is former Deputy Prime Minister Boris Nemtsov; the other is anticorruption campaigner Alexei Navalny. The former will not be running, because he was killed on a bridge in front of the Kremlin in 2015, the latter because he has been disenfranchised by the authorities with a politically motivated court conviction. When real opposition is actually present on the ballot, it scores significant results, as with Navalny's 27 percent second-place finish in the Moscow mayoral vote in 2013, Nemtsov's election to the Yaroslavl Regional Duma the same year, and the election of nearly 300 democratic opposition lawmakers in Moscow's 2017 municipal elections. And these successes came despite the handicaps of the electoral process in today's

Russia, such as a lack of access to the media; the lack of a level playing field; and, in many cases, the lack of an honest counting of the votes.

To state the obvious once again, a government with "86 percent support"—which is what official pollsters claim for Putin—would not need to rig elections, censor the media, or harass and imprison its opponents. This is the behavior of a regime that is insecure and uncertain. And, looking at the protests that have started in Russia in 2017, it has reason to be. In the spring and summer of this year, tens of thousands of Russians—mostly young Russians—went to the streets across the country to voice their protest at the pervasive government corruption and at the political conditions that have allowed it: a lack of transparency; a lack of accountability; a lack of the rule of law; and the sheer arrogance and impunity of the small group of people that has been in power for nearly two decades. In fact, a significant number of Russians who went out to protest against Putin have never lived under anything except his regime. They are university and high school students, young professionals, those in their late teens and early twenties. They are the people who grew up (and were, in many cases, born) under Vladimir Putin. And they are increasingly saying "Enough." The protests took place in more than 200 towns and cities, from Vladivostok to Kaliningrad. The peaceful protesters were met with threats, police batons, and mass arrests. But they came back. And they will come back again. The best guarantee of a democracy—any democracy—is the citizens who maintain it. This emerging movement for transparency and the rule of law in Russia is the best guarantee that our country will one day take its rightful place among free nations—and the best repudiation of that tired (and false) stereotype that Russians are somehow uniquely "unsuited" to living in a free society.

Discussion

Audience: How do you see the fact that some of the Central and Eastern European countries that managed to convert themselves to democracies and join the EU are now drifting a little bit, namely Hungary, Slovakia, Poland, and perhaps Austria? How do you see that compared to Russia, where you ended up with Putin? Whereas the other ones ... some of them actually got over it. Some of them outlawed the communist parties, but they converted. And, somehow, they managed to do it.

Vladimir Kara-Murza: I think there are two main factors for that difference between what happened in Russia and what happened in other postcommunist countries in central and eastern Europe, one domestic, one external. The domestic one, which we talked about a little bit, was the lack of a real decommunization process like the ones that happened in other central and eastern European countries. It's inconceivable that a former officer of the Stasi could become a German chancellor today. Yet in Russia, a former Soviet KGB officer came to power. That was a major mistake of the democratic leadership in the Russia of the early '90s, Yeltsin's leadership. There were some small steps taken in 1991 and 1992, but it was never finished. If you look at the 1991 law on the rehabilitations of the victims of communism that was passed by the Russian Parliament, it not only condemned the repressive nature of the regime but actually, in theory, introduced the need of criminal responsibility for the people who perpetrated those repressions. This was never followed up. And, in 1992, the constitutional court of Russia *did* declare that the communist regime engaged in repressions against millions, but this was never followed up on. There were never lustrations. The external factor is less important, but it should not be overlooked. Unlike other countries in central and eastern Europe, Russia was never offered the prospect of fully rejoining the European family. Václav Havel called the entire reform process "our return to Europe" to signal that institutional integration was coupled with domestic reforms. We never had that. On the 26th of December 1991, the day after the red flag came down from the Kremlin, there was a meeting of NATO ambassadors in Brussels. At that meeting, the ambassador of Russia, who the day before was the ambassador of the USSR, passed a letter from President Yeltsin to Manfred Wörner, the Secretary General of NATO. That letter said, "We are today raising the question of Russian membership of the NATO." He never even received a response. This is true also of European integration. Last time I looked at a map, Russia was a European country. There shouldn't be any obstacles, providing the Copenhagen Criteria are met, to our joining the EU. We never had the offer. For Poland, the Czech Republic, the Baltic states, and Hungary, it was a powerful motivation for reform. We never had that. There will come a day, sooner or later, when Russia again starts down a path of democratic transition. And we should definitely learn from the mistakes that Yeltsin's government made. But I think it's important for the outside world, particularly for Europe, to stand ready to welcome a future democratic Russia into its own ranks. It's been almost 30 years since that famous speech by George H. W. Bush in West Germany about a "Europe, whole and free." Well, the two largest nations in Europe are Russia and Ukraine, and they're still not fully in. You can't be whole and free without the two largest nations. I think it's important to remember that.

Audience: Several times over the last few days, we've heard panelists say that everybody was guilty. I am of Polish birth, I'm a US citizen, and I also happen to be a daughter and granddaughter of political prisoners, from gulags through Gestapo to just garden-variety communist prisons. I actually have a problem with this phrase, not because I want to draw a line between people I hold dear and strangers, but because you will never have a reckoning if you blur the line between perpetrators and the rest of us, most of whom are cowards who look on and hope that our number won't come up. This isn't really about wanting to become a perpetrator but hoping to survive. I think most people just want to survive. I'm wondering, and this is something for you to ponder and hopefully to address, whether there isn't a direct correlation between saying "We are all to blame" and not ever having a lustration or reckoning. There wasn't one anywhere except for Germany—this was the only country that had any cleanup. It's not that everybody else did except for Russia; no country did. There was *never* a day of reckoning. All of the ex-communists, the higher they were, the richer they now are. They now own property, shares; they made out like bandits from stock exchanges in their countries. What is the correlation between "We're all guilty" and not having a reckoning?

Mark Galeotti: Obviously, "everyone is guilty" is at once true and unhelpful. It's true that everyone has some kind of responsibility in these systems, but it's also unhelpful precisely because it lumps perpetrators and bystanders together. Am I guilty if I do not go out of my way to look for trouble in the name of good? This becomes a philosophical discussion because there are no neat answers. I absolutely agree that there is a need for some sort of justice. Justice is absolutely fundamental. Justice is not the same as vengeance. Justice can actually recognize that people do things that are morally wrong or morally imperfect and not therefore also treat them the same as the executioner or the secret police officer or whatever. We need to have some degree of clarity about the whole spectrum. But the key thing is that that cannot be created in advance. It has to come from discussion. One of the themes that has come up in this conference quite often is the need to discuss these things. We can't have a scheme that says, well, if you have more than sixty guilt points you'll be put on trial, and if you have fewer you're fine, and this is what each misdemeanor is worth in points. We have to be able to talk these things through. From that will come some sort of social conception about who did what, but also an acceptance that we are ultimately all essentially fallible human beings, but that does not mean that it's all fine.

Vladimir Kara-Murza: I made a film twenty years ago about the Soviet dissident movement, and one of the people I interviewed for this film was Natalya Gorbanevskaya. She was one of seven people who, in August 1968, came out on Red Square in Moscow to protest against the Soviet invasion of Czechoslovakia. They paid such people with years in prisons, in labor camps, or, what was worst of all, in psychiatric hospitals, which is what happened to her. I asked her why, if she knew what the consequences would be, she did this. I'll never forget what she told me. She said, "For me going out to that demonstration was a selfish act." I asked her what she meant, and she said, "I wanted to have a clean conscience." That's a very important motivation, not just for those Soviet-era dissidents, but for a lot of us in the Russian democratic movement today. It was certainly the strongest motivation for my friend Boris Nemtsov, who was a leader of the Russian opposition. He felt that if he watched what was happening, what Putin was doing, and did nothing, he was complicit. And he did not want to be complicit. This is a motivation for a lot of us, so I guess we are all selfish, as Gorbanevskaya said.

Emanuelis Zingeris: Just yesterday, Ukrainian authorities reported that they removed 2,380 communist-era statues from their country. Still, it's not only Mr. Zyuganov who continues celebrating communist propaganda. While it's true that Mr. Putin didn't celebrate the centenary of that terrible coup a few days ago, the current Russian government seems to embrace the remnants and symbols of the communist regime. There are thousands of sculptures and symbols of one of the most murderous regimes in the world in every village of Russia. That's more than an aesthetic problem. Vladimir, a very small but existential question: How can we stop the killings of Russian democratic leaders in Russia? What should we do in the West to show that we care? How can we work together to stop the murder of the best of the Russian people?

Vladimir Kara-Murza: The statue of Dzerzhinsky went down in 1991, as did Sverdlov and Kalinin and the memorial plaque of Andropov. But the others stayed. Lenin stayed. And the streets were renamed in Moscow but not anywhere else. I'm actually shocked, as I go around different cities in the Russian provinces, how many of the toponyms are holdovers from Soviet times: Dzerzhinsky Street, Uritsky Street, Red Army Street. And that emphasizes how unfinished the job is. In fact, one of the very first things Mr. Putin did even before he became president was that he brought back and reinstalled the plaque of Yuri Andropov on Lubyanka Square, as if to show exactly what he was going to be doing. It took Ukraine 26 years after the fall of the USSR to get rid of the Soviet statues, so I guess we'll have to wait for the time to come, but we will have to do it. I happen to think symbols are very important and you can't build a future when you have your streets named after Soviet executioners. The assassination of Boris Nemtsov was, of course, the highest profile political assassination in modern Russia: the leader of the opposition shot by five bullets in the back on a bridge 200 yards from the Kremlin. Two and a half years on, there is complete impunity for those who ordered and organized this highest-profile political assassination in modern Russia. The immediate perpetrators have been sentenced, but that's it. There is a clear glass ceiling, as to both in the investigation and trial in terms of anything higher up than immediate perpetrators. Five men have been convicted, and all of them have been linked to Ramzan Kadyrov, Vladimir Putin's viceroy in Chechnya. And yet Kadyrov has never been formally questioned, not even once. Neither has Adam Delimkhanov, his right-hand man. Neither has General Viktor Zolotov, who is considered to be the go-between between Putin and Kadyrov. The lawyers of the families have requested several times, publicly, that these people be questioned, and they have not been. We know from a press report in Russia last year that General Alexander Bastrykin, one of the men closest to Putin and head of the Investigative Committee of the Russian Federation, who has also been designated by the United States as a human rights abuser under the Magnitsky law, has *twice* personally vetoed attempts by lower-level investigators to name another person closer to Kadyrov as an organizer of the crime. And, as a result, the only person who is named as an organizer of the assassination, per the official court documents, is a Chechen driver. So we're supposed to believe that the assassination of the leader of the Russian opposition, on a bridge in front of the Kremlin—probably one of the most highly guarded areas not only in Moscow but in all Europe—was organized by a driver.

The only thing we can hope for under current conditions is some form of international oversight over this whole thing. Thank God, Russia is still a member of the Council of Europe. That's probably the only thing that remains from the achievements of the 1990s. We, as Russian citizens, are protected by the European Convention on Human Rights, and the right to life is a pretty important right in that convention. In the absence of a genuine trial, the only thing we can have is international oversight and international attention on this issue so that the Kremlin cannot sweep this under the carpet. We are grateful to principled politicians in other European countries for keeping this in the public's attention.

Inci Bowman: I would like to point out the post-Soviet space Putin is building in Crimea. The Crimean Tatars, who are in their own homeland, have been imprisoned and have been under a lot of pressure, with many searches for missing, murdered, and kidnapped people going on now. I remember seeing one elderly man with a poster that said, "Putin, our children are not terrorists," because that is how the FSB agents treat them. Why is it that Putin is so afraid of 300,000 Crimean Tatars living in Crimea today?

Mark Galeotti: In some ways, Crimea represents the distilled perfection of High Putinism. It is an illegal territory. It is controlled by what is essentially a criminalized gang given political structure. Sergey Aksyonov was a former gangster who went by the underworld nickname of "Goblin." It is essentially a militarized region, which is, in practice if not in law, treated under martial law. In so many ways what we see in Crimea is the apotheosis of modern Putinism, which makes it all the more important that every form of moral and principled resistance has to be crushed.

Vladimir Kara-Murza: I just want to answer with a quote from Andrei Sakharov, who was Mustafa Dzhemilev's friend. It is an answer to why the Soviet regime, the most developed and strongest machine of oppression in the world, is afraid of a few thousand unarmed resisters. Sakharov said it's not a question of arithmetic but a moral issue, because these people are breaching a psychological barrier of silence. This is very important for authoritarian regimes. I think this goes for the Crimean Tatar movement, for the Soviet dissidents, for the Russian democrats, and for all peaceful resistance movements in authoritarian and totalitarian states.

Andrew Nagorski: That relates to Václav Havel's saying that one honest person can have more impact in a closed society than five million voters in a free society.

Vytautas Landsbergis: Considering that in today's Russian presidential elections, the candidates are selected in advance, like in Stalin's time, wouldn't it be better to speak not of an "election" but of a "selection"?

Vladimir Kara-Murza: I agree completely with President Landsbergis. Every time I write an article about elections in Vladimir Putin's Russia, I always spell the word in quotation marks. The last time we had anything approaching a free and fair and competitive election was more than seventeen years ago. That's not just my judgment. If you look at the official observation reports from the Council of Europe and the OSCE, they have not assessed a single national election in Russia after the year 2000 as free, fair, or democratic, because there is no genuine competition, there's no access to the media, there's no level playing field, and there's not an honest counting of the votes. We know that in 2011, according to estimates by independent observers, about nineteen million votes were stolen in favor of Putin's party. Whether or not to participate is another issue, though. We at Open Russia think that we have to use every strategy, every initiative, every avenue, including this fake and artificial electoral process, which is the reason why we're doing it. You raise an important point about the international attitude. Every time Western leaders call Putin and congratulate him on "winning an election" when they know very well that it was not an election and he didn't win it, I think this is not a very honest practice and this has to stop.

Author Biographies

Dr. Murray Bessette is the Director of Academic Programs at the Victims of Communism Memorial Foundation, where he leads its educational and scholarly activities.

Dr. Jonathan Brent serves on the Academic Council of the Victims of Communism Memorial Foundation, is the director of the *Annals of Communism* series—which he founded in 1992—and CEO and executive director of the YIVO Institute for Jewish Research in New York City.

Dr. Marek Jan Chodakiewicz is the Kościuszko Chair in Polish Studies and professor of History at the Institute of World Politics.

Dr. Frank Dikötter serves on the Academic Council of the Victims of Communism Memorial Foundation and is the author of "The People's Trilogy," a series of books that document the impact of communism on the lives of ordinary people in China on the basis of new archival material.

Amb. Paula J. Dobriansky serves on the Board of Trustees of the Victims of Communism Memorial Foundation and is a Senior Fellow at the Future of Diplomacy Project at Harvard Kennedy School's Belfer Center for Science and International Affairs and Vice Chair of the National Executive Committee, US Water Partnership.

Dr. Lee Edwards is co-founder and Chairman of the Victims of Communism Memorial Foundation, and a Distinguished Fellow in Conservative Thought at the B. Kenneth Simon Center for American Studies at The Heritage Foundation.

Dr. Niall Ferguson is a senior fellow at Stanford University's Hoover Institution and a senior fellow at Harvard University's Center for European Studies.

Dr. Jeremy Friedman is an assistant professor in the Business, Government, and International Economy Unit of Harvard Business School.

Dr. Mark Galeotti is a senior researcher at the Institute of International Relations Prague, where he coordinates the Centre for European Security, and is also the director of the consultancy firm Mayak Intelligence.

Paul A. Goble serves on the Advisory Council of the Victims of Communism Memorial Foundation, is a Truman-Reagan Medal of Freedom Laureate, and a former Special Advisor to the Secretary of State and longtime specialist on ethnic and religious questions in Eurasia.

Dr. Paul R. Gregory serves on the Academic Council of the Victims of Communism Memorial Foundation, is a research fellow at Stanford University's Hoover Institution, holds an endowed professorship in the Department of Economics at the University of Houston, Texas, is a research professor at the German Institute for Economic Research in Berlin, and is emeritus chair of the International Advisory Board of the Kiev School of Economics.

Dr. John Earl Haynes serves on the Academic Council of the Victims of Communism Memorial Foundation and is a prolific author and scholar on the subjects of communism and communist organizations in America.

Dr. Paul Hollander served on the Academic Council of the Victims of Communism Memorial Foundation and was a preeminent American political sociologist and scholar of communism. He passed on April 9, 2019.

Dr. Andrei Illarionov is a senior fellow at the Cato Institute's Center for Global Liberty and Prosperity and one of Russia's most forceful and articulate advocates of an open society and democratic capitalism.

Vladimir Kara-Murza is the coordinator of Open Russia, a platform for civil society and pro-democracy activists launched in 2014 by former political prisoner Mikhail Khodorkovsky.

Dr. Harvey Klehr serves on the Academic Council of the Victims of Communism Memorial Foundation and is a prolific author and scholar on the subjects of communism and communist organizations in America.

Dr. Alan Charles Kors serves on the National Advisory Council of the Victims of Communism Memorial Foundation and is Henry Charles Lea Professor Emeritus of History at the University of Pennsylvania.

Mark Kramer serves on the Academic Council of the Victims of Communism Memorial Foundation and is director of the Cold War Studies program at Harvard University's Davis Center for Russian and Eurasian Studies.

HE Dr. Vytautas Landsbergis is a Lithuanian statesman and scholar and is a Truman-Reagan Medal of Freedom laureate. He serves on the Advisory Council of the Victims of Communism Memorial Foundation.

Dr. A. James McAdams is the William M. Scholl Professor of International Affairs, Professor of History, and Director of the Nanovic Institute for European Studies at the University of Notre Dame.

Andrew Nagorski is an award-winning journalist and chairman of the board of the Polish-American Freedom Foundation.

Amb. Dr. Martin Palouš was the Czech Ambassador to the United States prior to taking office as the Czech Republic's Permanent Representative to the United Nations.

Professor Paul du Quenoy is a Professor of History at the American University of Beirut and Chairman of the Russian Ball of Washington, DC.

Dr. Russell Roberts is the John and Jean De Nault Research Fellow at the Hoover Institution and hosts the podcast *EconTalk*—hour-long conversations with authors, economists, and business leaders.

Peter M. Robinson is a research fellow at Stanford University's Hoover Institution specializing in business and politics, where he edits the *Hoover Digest* and hosts a current affairs television program called *Uncommon Knowledge*.

Joshua Rubenstein has been professionally involved with human rights and international affairs for over forty years as an activist and independent scholar with particular expertise in Russian affairs.

David Satter serves on the Academic Council of the Victims of Communism Memorial Foundation, and as a former Moscow correspondent, is a long-time observer of Russia and the former Soviet Union.

Natan Sharansky is a former Soviet dissident, political prisoner, and lifelong champion of freedom and democracy. He is a Truman-Reagan Medal of Freedom laureate.

Marion Smith is Executive Director of the Victims of Communism Memorial Foundation, Editor of *Dissident*, President of the Common Sense Society, and Chairman of the National Civic Art Society in Washington, DC.

Dr. F. Flagg Taylor, IV serves on the Academic Council of the Victims of Communism Memorial Foundation and is an associate professor of government at Skidmore College.

Marianna Yarovskaya is the director of the film *Women of the Gulag*, which is supported by the National Endowment for the Humanities Bridging Cultures Through Film program.

Elena Zhemkova is the Executive Director of the Russian human rights NGO Memorial Society, a recipient of the Victims of Communism Memorial Foundation's Truman-Reagan Medal of Freedom.

Hon. Emanuelis Zingeris is a Member of the Seimas of the Republic of Lithuania and a signatory of the 1990 Act of the Re-Establishment of the State of Lithuania. He is a Truman-Reagan Medal of Freedom laureate and serves on the Advisory Council of the Victims of Communism Memorial Foundation.

Works Cited

Akmatova, Anna. *The Word That Causes Death's Defeat: Poems of Memory.* Edited by Nancy K. Anderson. New Haven: Yale University Press, 2004.

Amalrik, Andrei. *Will the Soviet Union Survive until 1984?* New York: Harper and Row, 1970.

Arendt, Hannah. *Eichmann in Jerusalem: A Report on the Banality of Evil.* New York: Viking, 1963.

———. *The Origins of Totalitarianism.* New edition. San Diego: Harvest Books, 1994.

Barraclough, Geoffrey. *An Introduction to Contemporary History.* London: C. A. Watts, 1964.

Becker, Jasper. *Hungry Ghosts: Mao's Secret Famine.* New York: The Free Press, 1996.

Browder, Earl. "How Stalin Ruined the American Communist Party." *Harper's Monthly.* March 1960.

———. *Teheran and America: Perspectives and Tasks* (pamphlet). New York: Workers Library Publishers, 1944.

———. "Teheran—History's Greatest Turning Point." *The Communist*, January 1944.

Brown, Jeremy and Paul G. Pickowicz, eds. *Dilemmas of Victory: The Early Years of the People's Republic of China.* Cambridge, MA: Harvard University Press, 2010.

Buchanan, James M., David Gordon, Israel Kirzner, et al. "Readers' Forum: Comments on 'The Tradition of Spontaneous Order' by Norman Barry." *Literature of Liberty* 5, no. 4 (1982): 5–18. Arlington, VA: Institute for Humane Studies.

Chukovskaya, Lydia. *The Deserted House.* Translated by Aline B. Werth. London: Barrie and Rockliff, 1967.

Custine, Astolphe, Marquis de. *Journey for Our Time: The Journals of the Marquis de Custine.* Edited and translated by Phyllis Penn Kohler. London: Phoenix Press, 2001.

Daily Worker. June 23, 1941.

——. April 30, 1946.

Dallin, Alexander and Fridrikh Igorevich Firsov. *Dimitrov and Stalin 1934–1943: Letters from the Soviet Archives.* New Haven: Yale University Press, 2000.

Dimitrov, Georgi. *The Diary of Georgi Dimitrov, 1933–1949.* Edited by Ivo Banac. New Haven: Yale University Press, 2003.

Douglas-Home, Jessica. *Once Upon Another Time: Ventures Behind the Iron Curtain.* Norwich: Michael Russell Publishing, 2000.

Duclos, Jacques. "A propos de la dissolution du P.C.A." *Les Cahiers du Communisme,* Nouvelle Serie, no. 6 (April 1945).

Fukuyama, Francis. "The End of History?" *The National Interest.* Summer 1989.

Garifulin, Ilnar. "Slovar dlya 'rossiskai natzii'" [Dictionary for a "Russian Nation"]. *Ideal Real*, May 8, 2017. Accessed at https://www. idelreal. org/a/28469649.html.

Gray, John. "How the West Embraced Chairman Mao's Little Red Book." *The New Statesman,* May 14, 2014.

Gurian, Waldemar. "Trends in Modern Politics." *The Review of Politics* 2, no. 3 (July 1940).

Havel, Václav. *Open Letters: Selected Writings 1965–1990.* Edited by Paul Wilson. New York: Alfred A. Knopf, 1991.

Hayek, Friedrich. *The Road to Serfdom.* Chicago: The University of Chicago Press, 1944.

―――. *The Fatal Conceit: The Errors of Socialism.* Chicago: The University of Chicago Press, 1988.

Heale, M. J. *American Anticommunism: Combating the Enemy Within, 1830–1970.* Baltimore: Johns Hopkins University Press, 1990.

Hollander, Paul. *From Benito Mussolini to Hugo Chavez: Intellectuals and a Century of Political Hero Worship.* Cambridge: Cambridge University Press, 2017.

―――. *Political Pilgrims: Western Intellectuals in Search of the Good Society.* 4th edition. New Brunswick, NJ: Transaction, 2009.

―――. *Political Will and Personal Belief: The Decline and Fall of Soviet Communism.* New Haven: Yale University Press, 1999.

Jaffe, Philip J. *The Rise and Fall of American Communism.* New York: Horizon Press, 1975.

Jisheng, Yang. *Tombstone: The Great Chinese Famine, 1958–1962.* New York: Farrar, Straus and Giroux, 2012.

Judt, Tony. *When the Facts Change: Essays 1995–2010*. New York: Penguin, 2015.

Keane, John, ed. "Charter 77 Declaration." In *The Power of the Powerless: Citizens against the State in Central-Eastern Europe*. New York: M. E. Sharpe, 1985.

Klehr, Harvey, John Earl Haynes, and Kyrill M. Anderson. *The Soviet World of American Communism*. New Haven: Yale University Press, 1998.

Koestler, Arthur. *Darkness at Noon*. Translated by Daphne Hardy. New York: MacMillan, 1941.

Kołakowski, Leszek. *Main Currents of Marxism*. Translated by P. S. Falla. New York: W. W. Norton & Company, 2005.

Kundera, Milan. "The Tragedy of Central Europe." *The New York Review of Books*, April 26, 1984.

Lenin, Vladimir. *State and Revolution*. Original 1918; Lenin Internet Archive, 1993. Accessed at https://www.marxists.org/archive/lenin/works/ 1917/staterev/.

Ling, Ken. *The Revenge of Heaven*. New York: Ballantine, 1972.

Mark, Eduard. "Revolution by Degrees: Stalin's National-Front Strategy for Europe, 1941–1947." Working Paper No. 31. Washington, DC: Cold War International History Project, Woodrow Wilson International Center for Scholars, 2001.

Marx, Karl. *A Contribution to the Critique of Political Economy*. Moscow: Progress Publishers, 1997. Accessed at https://www.marxists. org/archive/marx/works/1859/critique-pol-economy/preface.htm.

———. "Suppression of the *Neue Rheinische Zeitung*." *Neue Rheinische Zeitung*, May 18, 1849. Translated by the Marx-Engels

Institute. Accessed at https://www.marxists.org/archive/marx/works/1849/05/19c.htm.

———. "The Victory of the Counter-Revolution in Vienna." *Neue Rheinische Zeitung*, November 6, 1848. Translated by the Marx-Engels Institute. Accessed at https://www.marxists.org/archive/marx/works/1848/11/06.htm.

Marx, Karl and Friedrich Engels. *The Communist Manifesto.* Introduction and notes by Gareth Stedman Jones. London: Penguin Classics, 2014.

McAdams, James. *Vanguard of the Revolution: The Global Idea of the Communist Party.* Princeton: Princeton University Press, 2017.

Miłosz, Czesław. *The Captive Mind.* Translated by Jane Zielonko. New York: Knopf, 1953.

Murphy, Raymond E. "Possible Resurrection of Communist International, Resumption of Extreme Leftist Activities, Possible Effect on United States." State Department memorandum. June 2, 1945. In *Foreign Relations of the United States: The Conference of Berlin (The Potsdam Conference)*, vol. 1. Washington, D.C.: Government Printing Office, 1960.

Newell, Waller. *Tyrants: A History of Power, Injustice & Terror.* Cambridge: Cambridge University Press, 2016.

Orwell, George. *Nineteen Eighty-Four.* New York: Everyman's Library, 1992.

Palouš, Martin. "Totalitarianism and Authoritarianism." In *Encyclopedia of Violence, Peace and Conflict,* 2nd edition. Edited by Lester Kurtz. Vol. 3. Oxford: Elsevier, 2008.

Patočka, Jan. *Jan Patočka: Philosophy and Selected Writings.* Edited by Erazim Kohák. Chicago: The University of Chicago Press, 1989.

————. "Kapitoly z současné filosofie." *Sebrané spisy*, vol. 1, Péče od duši 1.

Pipes, Richard. *Russia under the Old Regime*. 2nd edition. London: Penguin, 1995.

Rubenstein, Joshua. *Soviet Dissidents: Their Struggle for Human Rights*. Boston: Beacon Press, 1980.

Rubenstein, Joshua, and Alexander Gribanov, eds. *The KGB File of Andrei Sakharov*. New Haven: Yale University Press, 2005.

Russian State Archive of Socio-Political History (RGASPI).

Ryan, James G. *Earl Browder: The Failure of American Communism*. Tuscaloosa: University of Alabama Press, 1997.

Schlesinger, Jr., Arthur. "Origins of the Cold War." *Foreign Affairs* 46 (October 1967): 22-52.

Schrecker, Ellen. *Many Are the Crimes: McCarthyism in America*. Boston: Little, Brown, 1998.

Service, Robert. *Lenin: A Biography*. Cambridge, MA: The Belknap Press of Harvard University Press, 2000.

Shragin, Boris. *The Challenge of the Spirit*. New York: Alfred A. Knopf, 1978.

Solzhenitsyn, Aleksandr. *The Gulag Archipelago*. 3 vols. New York: Harper and Row, 1974.

————. "Misconceptions about Russia Are a Threat to America." *Foreign Affairs* 58, no. 4 (Spring 1980): 797–834.

Stedman Jones, Gareth. *Karl Marx: Greatness and Illusion*. Cambridge, MA: The Belknap Press of Harvard University Press, 2016.

Turchin, Valentin. *The Inertia of Fear and the Scientific Worldview*. Translated by Guy Daniels. New York: Columbia University Press, 1981.

Walker, Richard. *China under Communism: The First Five Years*. New Haven: Yale University Press, 1955.

Yakovenko, Igor. "Rossiya v zerkale Katalonii" [Russia as a reflection of Catalonia]. *Posle Imperii* [After Empire] (blog), October 30, 2017. Accessed at http://afterempire.info/2017/10/30/catalan-mirror/.

Yermakov, Denis. "Sovetskii chelovek okozalsya na redkost moshnoi konstruktzii" [The Soviet person turned out to be an unusually powerful construct]. *Profil*, October 31, 2017. Accessed at http://www.profile.ru/obsch/item/121081-sovetskij-chelovek-okazalsya-na-redkost-moshchnoj-konstruktsiej.